HOW JESUS BECAME GOD

Also by Bart D. Ehrman

HOW JESUS BECAME GOD

The Exaltation of a Jewish Preacher from Galilee

BART D. EHRMAN

HarperOne
An Imprint of HarperCollinsPublishers

HarperOne

Throughout this book I quote the Bible with some frequency. These quotations are either my own translations or drawn from the New Revised Standard Version.

HOW JESUS BECAME GOD: *The Exaltation of a Jewish Preacher from Galilee.* Copyright © 2014 by Bart D. Ehrman. All rights reserved. Printed in the United States of America. No part of this book may be used or reproduced in any manner whatsoever without written permission except in the case of brief quotations embodied in critical articles and reviews. For information address HarperCollins Publishers, 10 East 53rd Street, New York, NY 10022.

HarperCollins books may be purchased for educational, business, or sales promotional use. For information please e-mail the Special Markets Department at SPsales@harpercollins.com.

HarperCollins website: http://www.harpercollins.com

HarperCollins®, ■®, and HarperOne™ are trademarks of HarperCollins Publishers.

FIRST EDITION

Library of Congress Cataloging-in-Publication Data
Ehrman, Bart D.
    How Jesus became God : the exaltation of a Jewish preacher from Galilee / Bart D. Ehrman.
        pages cm
    ISBN 978–0–06–177818–6
    1. Jesus Christ. 2. Jesus Christ—Historicity. 3. Jesus Christ—Person and offices. I. Title.
    BT304.9.E37   2014
    232—dc23   2013027750

14 15 16 17 18 RRD(H) 10 9 8 7 6 5 4 3 2 1

To Sarah

CONTENTS

ACKNOWLEDGMENTS

I WOULD LIKE TO ACKNOWLEDGE the scholars who have assisted me by reading an earlier draft of this book and providing extensive and helpful comments. If everyone had such insightful and generous friends and colleagues, the world would be a much happier place. My readers have been Maria Doerfler, a remarkable and wide-ranging scholar just now starting to teach church history as an assistant professor at Duke Divinity School; Joel Marcus, professor of New Testament at Duke Divinity School, who for nearly thirty years has generously read my work and consistently spilled lots of red ink all over it; Dale Martin, professor of New Testament at Yale, my oldest friend and colleague in the field, whose critical insights have for very many years helped shape me as a scholar; and Michael Peppard, assistant professor of New Testament at Fordham University, whom I have only recently come to know and who has written a book, which I cite in the course of my study, that had a significant effect on my thinking.

I also thank the entire crew at HarperOne, especially Mark Tauber, publisher; Claudia Boutote, associate publisher; Julie Baker, my talented and energetic publicist; and above all Roger Freet, my perceptive and unusually helpful editor, who has helped make this a better book.

I am dedicating the book to my brilliant and scintillating wife, Sarah Beckwith. I dedicated another book to her years ago, but since I continuously rededicate my life to her, I think it is time to rededicate a book to her. She is the most amazing person I know.

HOW JESUS BECAME GOD

INTRODUCTION

J ESUS WAS A LOWER-CLASS Jewish preacher from the backwaters of rural Galilee who was condemned for illegal activities and crucified for crimes against the state. Yet not long after his death, his followers were claiming that he was a divine being. Eventually they went even further, declaring that he was none other than God, Lord of heaven and earth. And so the question: How did a crucified peasant come to be thought of as the Lord who created all things? How did Jesus become God?

The full irony of this question did not strike me until recently, when I was taking a long walk with one of my closest friends. As we talked, we covered a number of familiar topics: books we had been reading, movies we had seen, philosophical views we were thinking about. Eventually we got around to talking about religion. Unlike me, my friend continues to identify herself as a Christian. At one point, I asked her what she considered to be the core of her beliefs. Her answer gave me pause. She said that, for her, the heart of religion was the idea that in Jesus, God had become a man.

One of the reasons I was taken aback by her response was that this used to be one of my beliefs as well—even though it hasn't been for years. As far back as high school, I had pondered long and hard this "mystery of faith," as found, for example, in John 1:1–2, 14: "In the Beginning was the Word, and the Word was with God, and the Word was God. . . . And the Word became flesh and dwelt among us, and we have beheld his glory, glory as of the only Son from the Father." Even before that, I had openly and wholeheartedly confessed the Christological statements of the Nicene Creed, that Christ was

> *the only Son of God,*
> *eternally begotten of the Father,*
> *God from God, Light from Light,*
> *true God from true God,*
> *begotten, not made,*
> *of one Being with the Father.*
> *Through him all things were made.*
> *For us and for our salvation*
> *he came down from heaven;*
> *by the power of the Holy Spirit*
> *he became incarnate from the Virgin Mary,*
> *and was made man.*

But I had changed over the years, and now in middle age I am no longer a believer. Instead, I am a historian of early Christianity, who for nearly three decades has studied the New Testament and the rise of the Christian religion from a historical perspective. And now my question, in some ways, is the precise opposite of my friend's. As a historian I am no longer obsessed with the theological question of how God became a man, but with the historical question of how a man became God.

The traditional answer to this question, of course, is that Jesus in fact was God, and so of course he taught that he was God and was always believed to be God. But a long stream of historians since the late eighteenth century have maintained that this is not the correct understanding of the historical Jesus, and they have marshaled many and compelling arguments in support of their position. If they are right, we are left with the puzzle: How did it happen? Why did Jesus's early followers start considering him to be God?

In this book I have tried to approach this question in a way that will be useful not only for secular historians of religion like me, but also for believers like my friend who continue to think that Jesus is, in fact, God. As a result, I do not take a stand on the theological question of Jesus's divine status. I am instead interested in the historical development that led to the affirmation that he is God. This historical development certainly transpired in one way or another, and what people personally believe about Christ should not, in theory, affect the conclusions they draw historically.

The idea that Jesus is God is not an invention of modern times, of course. As I will show in my discussion, it was the view of the very earliest Christians soon after Jesus's death. One of our driving questions throughout this study will always be what these Christians *meant* by saying "Jesus is God." As we will see, different Christians meant different things by it. Moreover, to understand this claim in any sense at all will require us to know what people in the ancient world generally meant when they thought that a particular human was a god—or that a god had become a human. This claim was not unique to Christians. Even though Jesus may be the only miracle-working Son of God that we know about in our world, numerous people in antiquity, among both pagans and Jews, were thought to have been both human and divine.

It is important already at this stage to stress a fundamental, historical point about how we imagine the "divine realm." By divine realm, I mean that "world" that is inhabited by superhuman, divine beings—God, or the gods, or other superhuman forces. For most people today, divinity is a black-and-white issue. A being is either God or not God. God is "up there" in the heavenly realm, and we are "down here" in this realm. And there is an unbridgeable chasm between these two realms. With this kind of assumption firmly entrenched in our thinking, it is very hard to imagine how a person could be both God and human at once.

Moreover, when put in these black-and-white terms, it is relatively easy to say, as I used to say before doing the research for this book, that the early Gospels of Matthew, Mark, and Luke—in which Jesus never makes explicit divine claims about himself—portray Jesus as a human but not as God, whereas the Gospel of John—in which Jesus does make such divine claims—does indeed portray him as God. Yet other scholars forcefully disagree with this view and argue that Jesus is portrayed as God even in these earlier Gospels. As a result, there are many debates over what scholars have called a "high Christology," in which Jesus is thought of as a divine being (this is called "high" because Christ originates "up there," with God; the term *Christology* literally means "understanding of Christ") and what they have called a "low Christology," in which Jesus is thought of as a human being ("low" because he originates "down here," with us). Given this perspective, in which way is Jesus portrayed in the Gospels—as God or as human?

What I have come to see is that scholars have such disagreements in part because they typically answer the question of high or low Christology on the basis of the paradigm I have just described—that the divine and human realms are categorically distinct, with a great chasm separating the two. The problem is that most ancient people—whether Christian, Jewish, or pagan—did not have this paradigm. For them, the human realm was not an absolute category separated from the divine realm by an enormous and unbridgeable crevasse. On the contrary, the human and divine were two continuums that could, and did, overlap.

In the ancient world it was possible to believe in a number of ways that a human was divine. Here are two major ways it could happen, as attested in Christian, Jewish, and pagan sources (I will be discussing other ways in the course of the book):

- By adoption or exaltation. A human being (say, a great ruler or warrior or holy person) could be *made* divine by an act of God or a god, by being elevated to a level of divinity that she or he did not previously have.
- By nature or incarnation. A divine being (say, an angel or one of the gods) could become human, either permanently or, more commonly, temporarily.

One of my theses will be that a Christian text such as the Gospel of Mark understands Jesus in the first way, as a human who came to be made divine. The Gospel of John understands him in the second way, as a divine being who became human. Both of them see Jesus as divine, but *in different ways.*

Thus, before discussing the different early Christian views of what it meant to call Jesus God, I set the stage by considering how ancient people understood the intersecting realms of the divine and the human. In Chapter 1 I discuss the views that were widely held in the Greek and Roman worlds outside both Judaism and Christianity. There we will see that indeed a kind of continuum within the divine realm allowed some overlap between divine beings and humans—a matter of no surprise for readers familiar with ancient mythologies in which the gods became (temporarily) human and humans became (permanently) gods.

Somewhat more surprising may be the discussion of Chapter 2, in which I show that analogous understandings existed even within the world of ancient Judaism. This will be of particular importance since Jesus and his earliest followers were thoroughly Jewish in every way. And as it turns out, many ancient Jews, too, believed not only that divine beings (such as angels) could become human, but that human beings could become divine. Some humans were actually called God. This is true not only in documents from outside the Bible, but also—even more surprising—in documents within it.

After I have established the views of both pagans and Jews, we can move in Chapter 3 to consider the life of the historical Jesus. Here my focus is on the question of whether Jesus talked about himself as God. It is a difficult question to answer, in no small measure because of the sources of information at our disposal for knowing anything at all about the life and teachings of Jesus. And so I begin the chapter by discussing the problems that our surviving sources—especially the Gospels of the New Testament—pose for us when we want to know historically what happened during Jesus's ministry. Among other things, I show why the majority of critical scholars for more than a century have argued that Jesus is best understood as an apocalyptic prophet who predicted that the end of the age was soon to arrive, when God would intervene in history and overthrow the forces of evil to bring in his good kingdom. Once the basic tenor of Jesus's public ministry is set, I move to a discussion of the events that led up to his crucifixion at the hands of the Roman governor of Judea, Pontius Pilate. At every point we will be intent on our one leading question for this chapter: How did Jesus understand and describe himself? Did he talk about himself as a divine being? I will argue that he did not.

These first three chapters can be seen as the backdrop to our ultimate concern: how Jesus came to be considered God. The short answer is that it all had to do with his followers' belief that he had been raised from the dead.

A great deal is written today about Jesus's resurrection, both by scholars who are true believers and apologists, who argue that historians can "prove" that Jesus was raised, and by skeptics who don't believe it for a second. It is obviously a fundamental issue for our deliberations. If the early Christians did not believe that Jesus had been raised from the dead, they would not have thought that he was different from any other unfortunate prophet who ended up on the wrong side of the law and was executed for his troubles. But Christians did think Jesus was raised, and, as I argue, that changed everything.

From a historical perspective there is an obvious question: What, actually, can we know about the resurrection? Here we enter into highly controversial topics, some of which I have changed my mind about in the course of doing my research for this book. For years I had thought that whatever else we might think about the stories of Jesus's resurrection, we could be relatively certain that immediately after his death he was given a decent burial by Joseph of Arimathea and that on the third day some of his female followers found his tomb empty. I no longer think that these are relatively certain historical data; on the contrary, I think both views (his burial and his empty tomb) are unlikely. And so, in Chapter 4 I deal with what I think we as historians simply cannot know about the traditions surrounding Jesus's resurrection.

In Chapter 5 I turn to what I think we almost certainly can know. Here I argue that the evidence is unambiguous and compelling: some of Jesus's disciples claimed that they saw him alive after he had died. But how many of his disciples had these "visions" of Jesus? (I leave open the question of whether they had these visions because Jesus really appeared to them or because they were having hallucinations—for reasons I explain in the chapter.) When did they have them? And how did they interpret them?

My overarching contention is that belief in the resurrection—based on visionary experiences—is what initially led the followers of Jesus (all of them? some of them?) to believe that Jesus had been exalted to heaven and made to sit at the right hand of God as his unique Son. These beliefs were the first Christologies—the first understandings that Jesus was a divine being. I explore these "exaltation" views of our earliest surviving sources in Chapter 6.

In Chapter 7 I move to a different set of Christological views that developed later and that maintained that Jesus was not simply a human who had been exalted to the level of divinity, but a preexistent divine being with God before he came to earth as a human. I show the key similarities and differences between this "incarnation" view of Christ (in which he "became flesh"—the literal meaning of the word *incarnation*) with the earlier "exaltation" Christologies. Moreover, I explore key passages that embody understandings of the incarnation in such books as the Gospel of John, the last of the canonical Gospels to be written.

In the following chapters we will see that Christians living after the New Testament was written—into the second, third, and fourth centuries—developed views of Christ even further, with some Christians taking positions that were eventually denounced as "heresies" (or "false") and others asserting views that were accepted as "orthodox" (or "right"). Chapter 8 deals with some of the heretical "dead ends" taken by Christian theologians of the second and third centuries. Some of these thinkers claimed that Jesus was fully human but not divine; others said he was fully divine but not human; yet others said that Jesus Christ was in fact two beings, one divine and the other human, only temporarily united during Jesus's ministry. All of these views came to be declared as "heresies," as did yet other views that were put forward by Christian leaders who, ironically, wanted nothing more than to embrace ideas that were "orthodox."

The debates over the nature of Christ were not resolved by the end of the third century but came to a head in the early fourth century after the conversion of the emperor Constantine to the Christian faith. By then, the vast majority of Christians firmly believed that Jesus was God, but the question remained, "in what sense?" It is in this early fourth-century context that battles were waged in the "Arian controversy," which I explore in Chapter 9. The controversy is named after Arius, an influential Christian teacher of Alexandria, Egypt, who held to a "subordinationist" view of Christ—that is, Jesus was God, but he was a subordinate deity who was not at the same level of glory as God the Father;

moreover, he had not always existed with the Father. The alternative point of view was espoused by Arius's own bishop, Alexander, who maintained that Christ was a being who had always existed with God and that he was, by nature, equal with God. The ultimate denunciation of Arius's view led to the formation of the Nicene Creed, which is still recited in churches today.

Finally, in the epilogue, I deal with the consequences of these particular theological disputes after they were resolved. Once Christians far and wide accepted the view that Jesus had been fully God from eternity, equal with the Father, how did this affect the various disputes Christians had, for example, with the Romans who had earlier persecuted them and whose emperor had been widely believed to be a god? Or with Jews who were now accused not just of killing Christ, but even of killing God? Or with one another as debates over the nature of Christ continued apace, with increasingly greater nuance, for a very long time indeed?

These later debates are intriguing, and highly significant, in their own right. But my strong contention is that they cannot be understood without grasping the history of what went before. And so in our historical sketch we will be particularly interested in the key Christological question of them all: How is it that the followers of Jesus came to understand him as divine in *any* sense of the term? What made them think that Jesus, the crucified preacher from Galilee, was God?

CHAPTER I

Divine Humans in
Ancient Greece and Rome

W<small>HEN</small> I <small>TEACH</small> <small>MY</small> introductory course on the New Testament, I tell my students that it is very difficult to know where to begin our exploration. Is it best to start with our earliest author of the New Testament, the Apostle Paul, who wrote more of the books of the New Testament than any other author? Or is it best to start with the Gospels, which, while written after Paul, discuss the life of Jesus, who lived before Paul wrote his letters? In the end I tell them that probably it is best to begin by telling the story of a highly unusual man who was born in the first century in a remote part of the Roman empire, whose life was described by his later followers as altogether miraculous.[1]

One Remarkable Life

B<small>EFORE</small> <small>HE</small> <small>WAS</small> <small>BORN</small>, his mother had a visitor from heaven who told her that her son would not be a mere mortal but in fact would be divine. His birth was accompanied by unusual divine signs in the heavens. As an adult he left his home to engage on an itinerant preaching ministry. He went from village to town, telling all who would listen that they should not be concerned about their earthly lives and their material goods; they should live for what was spiritual and eternal. He gathered a number of followers around him who became convinced that he was no ordinary human, but that he was the Son of God. And he did miracles to confirm them in their beliefs: he could heal the sick, cast out demons, and raise the dead. At the end of his life he aroused opposition among the ruling authorities of Rome and was put on trial. But they could not kill his soul. He ascended to heaven and continues to live there till this day. To prove that he lived on after leaving this earthly orb, he appeared again to at least one of his doubting followers, who became convinced that in fact he remains with us even now. Later, some of his followers wrote books about him, and we can still read about him today. But very few of you will have ever seen these books. And I imagine most of you do not even know who this great miracle-working Son of God was. I have been referring to a man named Apollonius, who came from the town of Tyana. He was a pagan—that is, a polytheistic worshiper of the many Roman gods—and a renowned philosopher of his day. His followers thought he was immortal. We have a book written about him by his later devotee Philostratus.

Philostratus's book was written in eight volumes in the early third century, possibly around 220 or 230 CE. He had done considerable research for his book, and his stories, he tells us, were largely based on the accounts recorded by an eyewitness and companion of Apollonius himself. Apollonius lived some years after a similar miracle-working Son of God in a different remote part of the empire, Jesus of Nazareth. Later followers of these two divine men saw them as being in competition with one another. This competition was part of a bigger struggle at the time between paganism—the forms of religion supported by the vast majority of everyone who lived in antiquity, who embraced a variety of polytheistic religions—and Christianity, a newcomer on the religious scene, which insisted that there was only one God and that Jesus was his Son. Christian followers of Jesus who knew about Apollonius maintained that he was a charlatan and a fraud; in response, the pagan followers of Apollonius asserted that Jesus was the charlatan and fraud. Both groups could point to the authoritative written accounts of their leader's life to score their debating points.

The Historical and Legendary Apollonius

Scholars have had to investigate the Gospels of the New Testament with a critical eye to determine which stories, and which parts of stories, are historically accurate with respect to the historical Jesus, and which represent later embellishments by his devoted followers. In a similar way, scholars of ancient Roman religion have had to analyze the writings of Philostratus with a keen sense of skepticism in order to weed through the later legendary accretions to uncover what we can say about the historical Apollonius. Generally it is agreed that he was a Pythagorean philosopher— that is, a proponent of the views of the fifth-century BCE Greek philosopher Pythagoras. He lived during the second half of the first century (Jesus lived during the first half). Apollonius traveled through the eastern parts of the Roman empire as a moral and religious preacher. He often lived in temples and was free with his advice to religious and city officials. He had numerous pupils and was well received among many of the Roman elite in the places where he stayed. He was especially concerned that people abandon their rampant materialism and live for what mattered, that is, the affairs of the soul.

For the current study, what is more important than the life of the historical Apollonius is the set of legends that sprang up about him and that were widely believed among people of the time. His great philosophical insights eventually led many people to assume that he could not have been a mere mortal, but that he was himself a god striding the earth. Just over a century after his death, Apollonius was awarded a holy shrine in his home city of Tyana, dedicated by none other than the Roman emperor Cara-calla, who ruled from 198 to 217 CE. We are told that the emperor Alexander Severus (222–235 CE) kept an image of Apollonius among his various household gods. And the emperor Aurelian (270–275 CE), an ardent worshiper of the Sun God, also revered him as divine.

The story of Apollonius's birth, as recounted in Philostra-tus's *Life of Apollonius of Tyana,* is particularly worth our con-sideration. The "annunciation" story is both like and unlike the story earlier found in the Gospel of Luke (1:26–38). When Apollonius's mother was pregnant with him, she had a vision of a divine being, the Egyptian god named Proteus, renowned for his great wisdom. When she asked who her child would be, the god answered, "Myself." The birth was similarly miraculous. The mother was told to go with her servant girls into a field, where she fell asleep on the grass, only to awake to the sound of swans flapping their wings. She prematurely then gave birth. The local people said that a bolt of lightning appeared in the sky at just that moment, and just as it was about to strike the earth, it "hung poised in the air and then disappeared upwards" (*Life of Apollonius* 1.5). The people concluded: "No doubt the gods were giving a signal and an omen of his brilliance, his exaltation above earthly things, his closeness to heaven, and all the Master's other qualities" (1.5). This sign is obviously different from a star that led a group of wise men to a child, but it is in the same celestial ballpark. The local people concluded that Apollonius was, in fact, the Son of Zeus.

At the end of his life Apollonius was brought up on charges

before the emperor Domitian. Among other things, he was accused of receiving the worship that is due only to the gods. Again,
the parallels to the story of Jesus are patent: he too was brought
before officials (in his case, the leaders of the Jews and then the
Roman governor Pilate) and was said to have entertained exalted
views of himself, calling himself the Son of God and the king
of the Jews. In both cases the officials were persuaded that these
claims of self-exaltation were a threat to the well-being of the
state, and for both men, readers were assured that in fact these
self-claims were completely justified.

Philostratus indicates that there were different reports of
Apollonius's "death." In one version he is said to have died on the
island of Crete. He had allegedly gone to a sanctuary dedicated
to a local god that was guarded by a group of vicious watchdogs.
But rather than raising a ruckus, the dogs greeted Apollonius in
a friendly manner. The sanctuary officials discovered him and
placed him in chains, thinking he must have used sorcery to get
by the dogs. But at midnight Apollonius set himself free, calling
to the jailers to watch what was to happen next. He ran up to
the doors of the sanctuary, which flew open of their own accord.
He then entered the sanctuary, the doors shut by themselves,
and from inside the (otherwise empty) sanctuary were heard the
voices of girls singing: "Proceed from earth! Proceed to heaven!
Proceed!" Apollonius was being told, in other words, to ascend
to the realm of the gods. He evidently did so, as he was no more
to be found on earth. Here again, the parallels to the stories of
Jesus are clear: at the end of his life Jesus caused a disturbance in
a temple, he was arrested and brought up on charges, and after
leaving this earthly realm he ascended to heaven, where he continues to live.

As a philosopher Apollonius taught that the human soul is
immortal; the flesh may die, but the person lives on. Not everyone believed him. But after he departed to heaven he appeared in

a vision to a follower who doubted him. Apollonius convinced this follower that he was still alive and was still present among them. Jesus too, of course, appeared to his disciples after his resurrection and convinced them, including doubting Thomas, of his ongoing reality and life in heaven.

Apollonius and Jesus

Modern scholars have debated the significance of the obvious connections between Jesus and Apollonius, but it is not merely a recent debate. In the early fourth century CE, a pagan author named Hierocles wrote a book called *The Lover of Truth* that contained a comparison between these two alleged Sons of God and celebrated the superiority of the pagan version. We no longer have the book in its entirety. But some years after it was written, it was explicitly refuted in the writings of the fourth-century church father Eusebius—sometimes known as the "father of church history" because he was the first to produce a history of Christianity from the time of Jesus up to his own day. Another of Eusebius's books was directed against Hierocles and his celebration of Apollonius. Luckily for us latter-day readers, Eusebius quotes in places the actual words of his opponent. Near the outset of his book, for example, Hierocles wrote:

> In their anxiety to exalt Jesus, they run up and down prating of how he made the blind to see and worked certain other miracles of the kind. . . . Let us note, however, how much better and more sensible is the view which we take of such matters, and explain the conception which we entertain of men gifted with remarkable powers. . . . During the reign of Nero there flourished Apollonius of Tyana . . . [who] worked any number of miracles, of which I will omit the greater number and only mention a few. (Life of Apollonius 2)[2]

Hierocles mocks the Gospels of the New Testament, as they contain tales of Jesus that were "vamped up by Peter and Paul and a few others of the kind—men who were liars and devoid of education and wizards." Reports about Apollonius, on the other hand, were written by highly educated authors (not lower-class peasants) and eyewitnesses to the things they saw. Because of his magnificent life, and the manner of his "death"—as "he went to heaven in his physical body accompanied by the gods"—"we must surely class the man among the gods." The Christian Eusebius's response was direct and vitriolic. Apollonius was not divine, but evil; he was not a son of God, but a man empowered by a demon.

If this little debate is looked at from a historical perspective, there can be little doubt that Eusebius ended up winning. But that would not have been a foregone conclusion when Hierocles wrote his book, before Christianity had become more powerful. Apollonius and Jesus were seen as competitors for divine honors: one a pagan worshiper of many gods, the other a Jewish worshiper of the one God; one a promoter of pagan philosophy, the other the founder of the Christian religion. Both of them were declared to be God on earth, even though they both were also, obviously, human. In a sense, they were thought of as divine men.[3]

What is striking is that they were not the only two. Even though Jesus may be the only miracle-working Son of God that people know about today, there were lots of people like this in the ancient world. We should not think of Jesus as "unique," if by that term we mean that he was the only one "like that"—that is, a human who was far above and very different from the rest of us mere mortals, a man who was also in some sense divine. There were numerous divine humans in antiquity. As will become clear, I'm not dealing with whether or not they were *really* divine; I'm saying that's how they were *understood*. Recognizing how this could be so is the first step in seeing how Jesus came to be thought of in these terms. But as we will see, Jesus was not originally thought of in this way—any more than Apollonius was during his lifetime. It was only after his death that the man Jesus came to be thought of as God on earth. How did that happen? The place to start is with an understanding of how other humans came to be considered divine in the ancient world.

Three Models of the Divine Human

CHRISTIANITY AROSE IN THE Roman empire immediately after the death of Jesus around the year 30 CE. The eastern half of the empire was thoroughly infused with Greek culture—so much so that the common language of the eastern empire, the language in fact in which the entire New Testament was written, was Greek. And so to understand the views of the early Christians we need to situate them in their historical and cultural contexts, which means in the Greek and Roman worlds. Jews of the time had many distinctive views of their own (see the next chapter), but in many key respects of concern for our study, they shared (in their own ways) many of the views of their Roman friends and neighbors. This is important to know because Jesus himself was a Jew, as were his immediate followers—including the ones who first proclaimed that he was not a mere mortal, but was actually God.

But how was it possible for God, or a god, to become, or to appear to become, a human? We have seen one way with Apollonius of Tyana. In his case, his mother was told before his birth that he would be the incarnation—the "coming in the flesh"—of a preexistent divine being, the god Proteus. This is very similar to later theological interpretation of Jesus—that he was God who became incarnate by being born of his mother Mary. I don't know of any other cases in ancient Greek or Roman thought of this kind of "god-man," where an already existing divine being is said to be born of a mortal woman. But there are other conceptions that are *close* to this view, and here we consider three of them.

Gods Who Temporarily Become Human

One of the greatest Roman poets was Ovid, an older contemporary of Jesus (his dates: 43 BCE–17 CE). His most famous work is his fifteen-volume *Metamorphoses,* which celebrates changes or transformations described in ancient mythology. Sometimes these changes involve gods who take on human form in order to interact, for a time, with mortals.

One of the most intriguing tales found in Ovid involves two elderly peasants, Philemon and Baucis, who live in Phrygia (a region of what is now Turkey). In this short account, the gods Jupiter and Mercury are traveling in the region disguised as mortals. Despite coming to a thousand homes, they can find no one who will take them in to give them a meal and allow them to rest. They finally happen upon the poor cottage of Philemon and Baucis, who bear their poverty well, "thinking it no shame." The elderly couple bid the visitors welcome, invite them into their poor home, prepare for them the best meal they can, and bathe their weary feet with warm water. In response, the grateful gods ensure that the wine bowl is never empty; as much as they all drink, it remains full.

Then the gods make their announcement: "We two are gods."[4] In response to their treatment in Phrygia, the gods declare:

> *This wicked neighborhood shall pay*
> *Just punishment; but to you there shall be given*
> *Exemption from this evil.*

Jupiter asks the couple what they most desire. After they talk it over, Philemon tells the king of the gods that he and his wife want to be made priests who will guard the gods' shrine, and when it is time for them to die, they want to die together:

> *Since in concord we have spent our years,*
> *Grant that the selfsame hour may take us both,*
> *That I my consort's tomb may never see,*
> *Nor may it fall to her to bury me.*

Jupiter grants their wishes. The neighborhood is destroyed. The shrine appears, and Philemon and Baucis become its guardians. When it comes time for them to die, the two are simultaneously turned into two trees that grow from one trunk, so that just as they had long harmonious lives as a couple, so they are joined in death. Later worshipers at the shrine not only acknowledge the ongoing "life" of the pair, but they also believe that the two have in effect been divinized and deserve to be worshiped:

> *They now are gods, who served the Gods;*
> *To them who worship gave is worship given.*

This beautiful and moving tale of love in life and death is also a tale of gods who temporarily become—or appear to become—human, and humans who become gods. When Philemon and Baucis are worshiped as gods, it is not because they are now as mighty as great Jupiter and Mercury. They are thought of as very low-level divinities, mortals who have been elevated to the divine plane. But divine they are. This is a key and important lesson for us. Divinity came in many shapes and sizes; the divine realm had many levels.

Today, we think of the realm of divinity, the realm of God, as completely Other and separate from our human realm. God is up there in heaven, we are down here on earth, and there is an infinite gulf between us. But most ancient people did not see the divine and earthly realms this way. The divine realm had numerous strata. Some gods were greater, one might say "more divine," than others, and humans sometimes could be elevated to the ranks of those gods. Moreover, the gods themselves could and occasionally did come down to spend time with us mere mortals. When they did so, it could lead to interesting or even disastrous consequences, as the inhospitable inhabitants of Phrygia learned to their great discomfort.

The lesson was not lost on later inhabitants of the region, as we learn from the pages of the New Testament itself. In the book of Acts we have an account of the Apostle Paul on a missionary journey with his companion Barnabas in this same region, visiting the town of Lystra (Acts 14:8–18). Paul sees a man who is crippled, and through the power of God he heals him. The crowds who have seen this miracle draw what for them is the natural conclusion: "The gods have come down to us in the likeness of men" (Acts 14:11). It is striking that they call Barnabas Zeus and Paul—the one who has been doing all the talking—Hermes. These identifications are no accident. Zeus was the Greek counterpart of the Roman Jupiter, and Hermes was the counterpart of Mercury. The people in Lystra know the tale of Philemon and Baucis and think that the two gods have appeared once again in their midst. So convinced are they of this that the local priest of Zeus brings out oxen and garlands to offer sacrifices to the two apostles, who have a very difficult time persuading everyone that they are only human, "of like nature with you." Paul uses the occasion, as was his wont, to preach his gospel message in order to convert the people. Even so, not everyone was convinced: "With these words they scarcely restrained the people from offering sacrifice to them" (14:18).

It is no wonder these worshipers of Zeus at Lystra were so eager to recognize that the gods temporarily become human among them; they remembered well what happened another time they refused to offer worship where worship was due. Whether the story in Acts is a historical recollection of Paul's missionary activities or simply an intriguing legend that sprang up in later times (like the story of Philemon and Baucis itself) is immaterial for our consideration here: in the Roman world it was widely thought that gods could take on human guise, such that some of the people one might meet on occasion may well indeed be divine. The ancient Greek and Roman mythologies are full of such stories.

Divine Beings Born of a God and a Mortal

Even though Apollonius was understood to be a preexistent god come in the flesh, this was not the normal Greek or Roman way of understanding how a divine human could be born of a mortal. By far the more common view was that a divine being came into the world—not having existed before birth—because a god had sex with a human, and the offspring then was in some sense divine. In Greek myths it was Zeus who most frequently engaged in these morally dubious activities, coming down from heaven and having a rather exotic sexual encounter with an attractive woman he had to have, which led to a highly unusual pregnancy. But tales of Zeus and his mortal lovers were not simply a matter of entertaining mythology. Sometimes such tales were told of actual historical figures, such as Alexander the Great (356–323 BCE).

According to his later biographer, the Greek scholar Plutarch, whose book on famous Greek and Roman men provides us with biographies of many of the greatest figures of the time, many people believed that Alexander was one of Zeus's offspring. Alexander's actual father was the famous and powerful Philip, king of Macedonia, who had fallen in love with a woman named Olympias. According to Plutarch, the night before the two were to consummate their marriage, Olympias dreamed that a thunderbolt came down from heaven and entered her. Presumably, this was Zeus doing his magic. Philip, in the meantime, apparently looked in on his wife that night and saw a serpent engaged in conjugal embrace with her. As Plutarch indicates, and as one might understand, this sight very much cooled Philip's passion for his bride. In ancient times Zeus was often represented in the form of a snake, and so, for those who believed this tale, the child—Alexander—was no mere mortal. He was the son of a god.

In mythology we have even more striking accounts of Zeus, or his Roman counterpart, Jupiter, engaging in such nocturnal activities. No story is more intriguing than the tale of the birth of Hercules. The tale takes many forms in antiquity, but perhaps the most memorable is the hilarious recounting found among the plays of the Roman comic playwright Plautus, in his work *Amphytrion*. The play is named after one of the main characters, a military general of Thebes who is married to an extraordinarily beautiful woman named Alcmena. Amphytrion has gone away to war, leaving his pregnant wife at home. Jupiter casts his lustful gaze upon her from heaven and decides that he has to have her. And he knows just how to do it.

Jupiter disguises himself as Amphytrion and tells Alcmena that he has come home from battle. She welcomes him with open arms and takes him to bed. So much does Jupiter enjoy the ensuing activities that he orders the constellations to stop in their circuit. In other words, he makes time stand still until he—even he, the mighty god with divine capacity for enjoyment—has his fill. The constellations resume their motion, Jupiter returns to his heavenly home, and Alcmena is obviously worn out from the very long frolic.

As it turns out, the real Amphytrion returns home that morning. And he is more than a little surprised and dismayed to find that his wife does not welcome him with all the enthusiasm that one might expect after such an extended absence. From her perspective, of course, this is completely understandable: she thinks that she has just spent a very long night in her husband's arms. Be that as it may, there is an interesting gestational result of this episode. Alcmena had already been made pregnant by Amphytrion. But she becomes pregnant yet again by Jupiter (some of these mythological tales were not strong on anatomy or biology).[5] The result is that she bears twins. One is the divine Hercules, the son of Jupiter; the other is his twin brother, a mortal, Iphicles.

The tale of Amphytrion and Alcmena, of course, is a myth, and it is not clear that anyone actually "believed" it. It was instead a great story. Still, the idea behind it—that a mortal woman could give birth to a child spawned by a god—was plausible to many people of the ancient world. It would not be unusual for them to think that some of the great beings who stride the earth—great conquerors like Alexander, for example, or even great philosophers with superhuman wisdom such as Plato[6]—may well have been conceived in ways different from us mere mortals. They may have had a divine parent so that they themselves were, in some sense, divine.

I should stress that when Alcmena gave birth to Hercules, the son of Jupiter, it was not an instance of a virgin birth. Quite the contrary. She had already had sex with her husband, and she had what you might call divine sex with Jupiter. In none of the stories of the divine humans born from the union of a god and a mortal is the mortal a virgin. This is one of the ways that the Christian stories of Jesus differ from those of other divine humans in the ancient world. It is true that (the Jewish) God is the one who makes Jesus's mother Mary pregnant through the Holy Spirit (see Luke 1:35). But the monotheistic Christians had far too an exalted view of God to think that he could have temporarily become human to play out his sexual fantasies. The gods of the Greeks and Romans may have done such things, but the God of Israel was above it all.

A Human Who Becomes Divine

The third model of understanding divine humans in Greek and Roman circles provided the most important conceptual framework that the earliest Christians had for conceiving how Jesus could be both human and divine. It is not a view about how a divine being could become human—through a temporary incarnation or a sexual act—but about how a human being could become divine. As it turns out, this allegedly happened numerous times in Greek and Roman antiquity.

Romulus

One of the most striking examples involves the legendary founder of Rome, Romulus. We have several accounts of the life of Romulus, including one produced by a great early historian of Rome, Livy (59 CE–17 CE), who in one place states the opinion that Romulus was a "god born of a god" (*History of Rome* 1.16). The event that most interests us involves the end of Romulus's life.

There were, to be sure, rumors of divine involvement in Romulus's conception. His mother was a Vestal Virgin, a sacred office that required—as the name indicates—a woman to abstain from sexual relations. But she became pregnant. Obviously, something went wrong with her vows. She claimed that the god Mars was responsible, and possibly some people believed her. If so, it simply shows again how a divine-human union could be taken to explain the appearance of remarkable humans on earth.

But it was Romulus's *dis*appearance from life that was even more astonishing. According to Livy, by the end of Romulus's life Rome had been established, the Roman government had been formed with the Senate in place and Romulus as king, the army was fully functioning, and everything was well positioned for the beginnings of the greatest city in history. During the final episode of his life, Romulus had gathered with members of the

Senate to review the military troops at the Campus Martius. Suddenly a huge thunderstorm arose. After major claps of thunder, Romulus was enveloped by fog. When the fog lifted, he was nowhere to be seen.

As it turns out, two reports circulated about his death. One of them—the one that apparently Livy and presumably most other skeptical observers believed—indicated that the senators had taken the opportunity of the moment to get rid of a despot: they had torn Romulus to shreds and hidden his remains. The other report, which the masses believed, was one that the senators themselves propagated—that Romulus "had been caught up on high in the blast." In other words, he had been taken up to heaven to live with the gods. The result was a sudden acclamation of Romulus's divine status: "Then, when a few men had taken the initiative, they all with one accord hailed Romulus as a god and a god's son, the king and Father of the Roman City, and with prayers besought his favor that he would graciously be pleased forever to protect his children" (*History of Rome* 1.16).[7]

Here we have a view of divine humans in a nutshell: a human can be honored by the gods by being made one of them; this happens because of the person's great merit; as a divinity, the person deserves worship; and in his role as a god, he can protect those who bring to him their supplications.

It is interesting that Livy reports that the ascension of Romulus was later verified by a man named Proculus Julius, who declared to the assembly of the Roman people that Romulus had appeared to him alive after his death. He is recorded as saying that "the Father of this City, Romulus, descended suddenly from the sky at dawn this morning and appeared to me. Covered with confusion I stood reverently before him. . . . 'Go,' he said, 'and declare to the capital of the world; so let them cherish the art of war, and let them know and teach their children that no human strength can resist Roman arms.' So saying . . . Romulus departed on high" (*History of Rome* 1.16).

Romans heartily and enthusiastically embraced the divinity of the man Romulus. A trio of gods—Jupiter, Mars, and Quirinus—lived at the heart of ancient Rome, on the ancient hill, the Capitoline. Originally, Quirinus may have been a god worshiped among one of the groups of people, the Sabines, who were incorporated into the Roman state early in its history. But by the time of Livy's writing, Quirinus was understood to be the divinized Romulus, worshiped right up there with the great father of the gods himself.

Julius Caesar

The traditional date for the founding of Rome is 753 BCE. If we move the calendar forward about seven centuries, we still find men who are proclaimed to have become gods. Few are better known than Julius Caesar, the self-declared dictator of Rome who was assassinated on the Ides of March, 44 BCE, by political enemies who preferred not having a dictator when all was said and done. The Roman biographer Suetonius provided a life of Julius Caesar in his *Lives of the Caesars,* published in 115 CE. According to Suetonius, already during his lifetime Caesar had declared that he had a divine heritage. In a funeral oration he delivered for his aunt he stated that one side of his family descended from the ancient Roman kings—through the legendary Marcus Ancius, the fourth king of Rome—and the other side descended from the gods. His family line, in fact, could be traced back to the goddess Venus.

At Caesar's death a vicious power struggle ensued between his enemies and supporters, the latter including Mark Antony (of Antony and Cleopatra fame) in league with Caesar's adopted son Octavian, who later became Caesar Augustus. At Caesar's funeral, Antony decided not to deliver the customary funerary oration. Instead, he had a herald cry out the Senate's decision "to render Caesar all honors, both human and divine." In effect, Julius Caesar was voted into divinity by the ruling authorities. This is a process known as *deification*—the recognition that, in this instance, a person had been so great that he had been taken up at death into the ranks of the gods. The "common people" and even the heavens seemed to support Caesar's deification, as Suetonius tells us: "[Caesar] died in the fifty-sixth year of his life and was included in the ranks of the gods, not only by formal decree but also by the conviction of the common people. Indeed at the first games which were given after his deification by his heir Augustus, a comet shone, appearing around the eleventh hour for seven days in succession, and it was believed to be the soul of Caesar who had been received into heaven" (*The Deified Julius Caesar* 88).[8]

Looking at the matter from a purely human and political point of view, there is little question about why the heir and adopted son Octavian wanted the Roman people to agree that Caesar was not only descended from a divine line, but had himself been made a divine being. If Julius Caesar was a god, what would that make his son? As New Testament scholar Michael Peppard has recently pointed out, to our knowledge only two people in the ancient world were actually called "Son of God." Other people were, to be sure, named after their divine fathers: son of Zeus, son of Apollo, and so on. But only two people known by name were also called "Son of God." One was the Roman emperor—starting with Octavian, or Caesar Augustus—and the other was Jesus. This is probably not an accident. When Jesus came on the scene as a divine man, he and the emperor were in competition.

Caesar Augustus

Julius Caesar may have been considered a god after he died, but his adopted son Octavian (emperor from 27 BCE to 14 CE) was sometimes considered a god while he was still alive. Considering a living ruler to be divine was not unheard of in the ancient world. The Egyptians had long revered their pharaohs as living representatives of deities, and the conqueror Alexander the Great, mentioned earlier, was offered and accepted the kind of obeisance reserved for the gods. But this was not done in the Roman world until the beginning of the worship of the emperor.

Legends indicated that Octavian did not have a normal human birth but, like others before him, was born of the union of a mortal and a god. According to Suetonius, Octavian's mother, Atia, was said to have been made pregnant by the god Apollo in the form of a snake (reminiscent, of course, of the conception of Alexander the Great). Atia had been attending the sacred rites of Apollo in a temple, and in the middle of the night, while she was asleep on her litter in the temple, a snake slid up to her and then quickly departed. When she awoke, she purified herself as she would have done after having sex with her husband, and miraculously the image of a snake permanently appeared on her body. Suetonius tells us that "Augustus was born ten months later and for this reason is believed to be the son of Apollo" (*The Deified Augustus* 94).

Moreover, that very night, Atia's husband, who was off at war in Thrace (northern Greece), had a dream in which he "saw his son of greater than mortal size with a thunderbolt and scepter and emblems of Jupiter Best and Greatest and a radiant crown drawn by twelve brilliantly white horses" (*The Deified Augustus* 94). Clearly, these were portents that this child was a divine figure, a great god on earth.

Unlike some of the later emperors, while in office Augustus was not enthusiastic about being worshiped as a god. Suetonius says that he would not allow temples in the Roman provinces to be dedicated to him unless they were jointly dedicated to the goddess Roma—the patron goddess of Rome. Sometimes cities got around this imperial reluctance by building a temple and dedicating it to the "genius" of Augustus. The word *genius* in this case does not mean his intellectual brilliance, but the guardian spirit that watched over his family and, especially, him as its leader, making him who he was. In a sense, by worshiping Augustus's genius, these cities revered him in a depersonalized but highly divinized sense.

Moreover, despite his reluctance, Octavian was hailed as the "Son of God" as early as 40 BCE—years before he was emperor—and this title is found on coins as early as 38 BCE. A decree from the Greek city of Cos hails Augustus as the god Sebastos (a Greek term equivalent to the Latin "Augustus") and indicates that he has "by his benefactions to all people outdone even the Olympian gods." That's pretty stiff competition for a mere mortal, but for his reverential followers, he was far more than that. After his death Augustus was deified and called "divine," or "one who has been made divine," or "one who has been accounted among the gods." When his body was cremated, according to Suetonius, a high-ranking Roman official claimed that he "saw Augustus's image ascending to the sky." He continued to be worshiped as a god by later Romans, including later Roman emperors.[9]

The Emperor Cult

For an ancient historian, the word *cult* does not have the kind of negative connotations it may have today—referring to a wild sectarian religion with bizarre beliefs and practices. It is simply a shortened version of the term *cultus deorum,* which means "care of the gods," a close equivalent to what today we would call "religion" (just as "agri*cul*ture" means "care of the fields"). The Roman cult of the emperor started with Augustus and continued through the emperors who followed him, many of whom lacked his reticence in being considered a manifestation of the divine on earth.[10]

In a speech by the famous Roman orator Quintilian (35–100 CE), we are told how the gods are to be praised by speakers giving a public address: "Some [gods] . . . may be praised because they were born immortal, others because they won immortality by their valour, a theme which the piety of our sovereign [the emperor Domitian] has made the glory even of these present times" (*Institutes of Oratory* 3.7.9).[11] Quintilian tells us that some gods were born that way (such as the great gods of Greek and Roman mythology), but others have "won immortality by their valour"— that is, some humans have *become* divine because of their amazing deeds. And he refers to those for whom this has happened in "these present times." Here, he is meaning the two previous emperors, Domitian's father, the emperor Vespasian, and Domitian's brother, the emperor Titus, both of whom were deified.

Normally, the emperor was officially declared a god at his death by a vote of the Roman Senate. This may seem a bit odd to us today, and it is perhaps best to think of the Senate *recognizing* a divine figure who had been in their midst rather than *making* someone divine. The recognition was based on the fact that the person was powerful and beneficent. And who could be more powerful and beneficent than the Roman emperor? So-called bad emperors (there were a number of them) did not receive divine honors at death, but the good ones did. As with Octavian, many were worshiped as divine even while alive. So we find an inscription (a text carved on stone) in the city of Pergamon that gives honor to "the God Augustus Caesar," and another in the city of Miletus dedicated to Gaius, otherwise known to history as Caligula (later considered a very bad emperor—but this inscription was made during his lifetime), which read "Gaius Caesar Germanicus, Son of Germanicus, God Sebastos." While he was alive, at least, Caligula was sometimes considered divine.

Over the years scholars have wrestled with the problem of how to understand the development of the emperor cult throughout the Roman empire—in particular with the idea that a living person was revered as a god. Couldn't everyone see that the man was human like everyone else? He had to eat and drink; he had other bodily functions; he had personal weaknesses as well as strengths—he was altogether mortal. In what sense could he seriously be considered a god?

As a rule, older scholarship was skeptical on this point, arguing that in fact most people didn't really think the emperor was a god and that the bestowal of divine honors was mostly a form of flattery.[12] This scholarly view was largely based on ancient writings that were produced by the literary elite, that is, the upper echelon of society. Moreover, from this perspective it looked as if the emperor cult was sponsored by the ruling authorities themselves as a kind of imperial propaganda, to make everyone in the Roman provinces understand and appreciate whom they were dealing with when they were dealing with the Roman authorities. Ultimately, they were dealing with a god. In this view, everyone knew that of course the emperor was just a mortal, as all his predecessors had been, but members of the empire participated in the imperial cult to remain on Rome's good side.

So cities built temples dedicated not simply to one of the great gods or goddesses of Rome—Jupiter, his wife Juno, Mars, Venus, or even "Roma"—but also to the "god" emperor. And sacrifices were made to the image of the emperor, just as to the gods. Still, in this former view of things the emperor was a lower-class divinity, and the worship of these human divinities was restricted to those who had already been deified at their deaths.

This older scholarly view is no longer the consensus, however. More recent scholarship has been less interested in what the literary elite of the upper classes had to say about Roman religion and more interested in what we can learn about what most Romans—the vast majority of whom could not read, let alone write, great works of biography or history—may have thought and certainly did practice. In this newer scholarship, the category of "belief" has come to be recognized as rather complicated with regard to Roman religion. Unlike Christianity, Roman religions did not stress belief or the "intellectual content" of religion. Instead, religion was all about *action*—what one *did* in relation to the gods, rather than what one happened to think or believe about them. From this perspective, the emperors—both dead and living—were indeed treated in the ways gods were treated, sometimes in virtually identical ways.[13]

More recent scholarship does not consider worship of the emperor as a top-down act of propaganda, promoted by Roman officials among the poor dupes who couldn't know any better. It was instead a series of local movements usually initiated by city officials of the provinces as a way of revering the power of the empire. Moreover, this worship happened within Rome itself, not simply out in the boonies. Many people quite likely did believe that the emperor was a god. And whether they believed it or not, they certainly *treated* the emperor as a god. Not only did they perform sacrifices to the (other) gods on *behalf* of the emperor, they also performed sacrifices *to* the emperor, as a god—or at least to his genius, or to his "numen"—the power within him that made him who he was, a divine being.

I have already alluded to the reason a powerful ruler would be considered divine. He was capable of doing many things, but he also put his abilities to good use, by bestowing benefits on people under his rule. Throughout the Roman world we find this emphasis on "benefaction" in the inscriptions dedicated to rulers—chiefly, but not only, the emperors. An example from a realm outside of but obviously related to the emperor cult is an inscription dedicated to the Syrian ruler Antiochus III from the second century BCE. Antiochus had freed the town of Teas from the oppression of a foreign power. In response, the town set up cult statues of Antiochus and his wife Laodice and performed sacrifices at an official public ceremony. The two statues were dedicated beside the statue of Dionysus, who was the chief god in the city, within his temple and were accompanied by the following inscription honoring Antiochus and Laodice: "Having made the city and its territory sacred . . . and having freed us from tribute . . . they should receive honours from everyone to the greatest possible extent and, by sharing in the temple and other matters with Dionysus, should become the common saviors of our city and should give us benefits in common."[14] The political benefactors are considered "religious" heroes. They have statues and a place in the temple, and sacrifices are made in their honor. In a very real sense they are the "saviors" and so are treated as such.

So too the emperors. Already we find with Augustus the province of Asia deciding to celebrate his birthday every year, as explained in an inscription in gratitude for his "benefaction of mankind" and for being "a savior who put an end to war and established all things." Augustus had "surpassed the benefactors born before him," so that "the birthday of the god marked for the world the beginning of good tidings through his coming."[15]

If all this sounds familiar to Christian readers, it should. This man—here, the emperor—is a god whose birthday is to be celebrated because it brought "good tidings" to the world; he is the greatest benefactor of humans, surpassing all others, and is to be considered a "savior." Jesus was not the only "savior-God" known to the ancient world.

A Nonruler: The Passing of Peregrinus
To this point, in exploring humans who were thought to have become divine, I have focused principally on powerful rulers.

But other great humans also had this capacity. Of course, lots of people among us are reasonably powerful, wise, or virtuous. Others are remarkably powerful, wise, or virtuous. And others are *unbelievably* powerful, wise, or virtuous. If someone's power, wisdom, or virtue is almost beyond belief, it may be because the person is not a lower life-form—a mortal like the rest of us. That person may be a god in human form. Or so it was widely believed in the Greek and Roman worlds.

One of the clearest ways to evaluate the common beliefs of a society is to consider the satires that arise within it. Satire makes fun of standard assumptions, perspectives, views, and beliefs. For satire to work, it has to be directed against something that is widely accepted. This is one reason that satire is such a perfect tool for unpacking the beliefs of other cultures. As it turns out, we have some brilliant satires from the Roman world.

One of the most entertaining satirists of ancient times was the second-century CE Lucian of Samosata, a Greek-speaking wit who proved to be the gadfly of all pretension, especially philosophical and religious. Among Lucian's many surviving works is a book called *The Passing of Peregrinus*. Peregrinus was a self-styled philosopher of the Cynic mode. In ancient philosophy being a Cynic did not mean simply being cynical; it was a style of philosophy. Cynic philosophers were adamant that you shouldn't live for the "good things" in life. You shouldn't care what you possess, what you wear, or what you eat. You shouldn't care for anything, in fact, that is external to you, anything that is ultimately beyond your ability to control. If your house burns down, that's outside your control, so you shouldn't be personally invested in your house. If you get fired from your job, that's outside your control, so you shouldn't be personally invested in your job. If your spouse divorces you or your child unexpectedly dies, those things are outside your control, so you shouldn't be personally invested in your family. What you *can* control are your attitudes about the things in your life. And so it is your inner self, your attitudes, that you should be concerned about.

People who hold such views are not going to be interested in having a nice, comfortable life (since it can be taken away), in how other people respond to them (no way to control that), or in social convention (why should anyone care?). Cynic philosophers who acted out their convictions had no possessions, no personal loves, and often no manners. They didn't have permanent homes and performed bodily functions in public. That's why they were called Cynics. The word *cynic* is from the Greek word for *dog*. These people lived like dogs.

Some people from outside the ranks of Cynics highly respected them. Some people thought they could be brilliant philosophers. And some people who wanted to be *thought of* as brilliant philosophers became Cynics. In a sense, it was easy enough to do. All you had to do was give up everything and declare such a choice to be a virtue.

Lucian thought the whole Cynic business was a sham, an attention-grabbing ploy with no serious substance behind it. And so he mocked Cynics and their ways. No one earned his opprobrium more than a Cynic named Peregrinus. In *The Passing of Peregrinus* (meaning, the death of Peregrinus) Lucian tells the real story behind this famous Cynic whom others in his time considered to be so deeply profound and philosophical that they suspected he was in fact a divine being—which is precisely what Peregrinus wanted, in Lucian's view. Lucian gives a hilarious account of Peregrinus's life, but here I'm interested in the events surrounding his death. In a sense, the entire book is looking forward to the death of this self-aggrandizing proponent of selfless debasement.

Peregrinus reportedly presented himself as being the god Proteus in the flesh. And he wanted to demonstrate his divine virtue by the way he died. As a Cynic he proclaimed—hypocritically, in

Lucian's view—the need to abstain from all the pleasure and joy of this life. He decided to prove his point by voluntarily undergoing a violent and painful death, so as to show how he thought that people should in fact live. He planned, and proclaimed, that he would immolate himself. According to Lucian, he did just that, before a large crowd that had gathered to observe the event.

After announcing his intentions and hyping the event at great length (itself a form of self-aggrandizement, as Lucian portrays it), at a set time, around midnight, and near the Olympic games (where crowds would be sure to gather), Peregrinus and his followers built an enormous pyre and lit it. According to Lucian, Peregrinus hoped to be stopped by those who could not bear to see him pass from human existence, but when it came to the moment, Peregrinus realized he had no choice but to go through with the deed. He cast himself into the raging fire and so ended his life.

Lucian claims to have witnessed the event and thought the entire episode was ridiculous and absurd. He says that on the way back from the scene he met people who were coming—too late—to see the great man display his godlike courage and resilience to pain. Lucian informed them that they had missed the festivities, but he told them what happened, and did so as if he himself were a believer:

> For the benefit of the dullards, agog to listen, I would thicken the plot a bit on my own account, saying that when the pyre was kindled and Proteus flung himself bodily in, a great earthquake first took place, accompanied by a bellowing of the ground, and then a vulture, flying up out of the midst of the flames, went off to Heaven, saying, in human speech, with a loud voice, "I am through with the earth; to Olympus I fare." (The Passing of Peregrinus 39)[16]

And so Peregrinus, in the shape of a bird (not the noble eagle but the scavenger vulture), allegedly ascended to Mount Olympus, home of the gods, to live there, divine man that he was. To Lucian's unmitigated amusement, he then met another man who was also telling about the event. This man claimed that after it was all over, he had met the supposedly dead Peregrinus, who was wearing a white garment and a garland of wild olive. Moreover, this man indicated that before this meeting, when Peregrinus had met his fiery fate, a vulture had arisen from the fire and flown off to heaven. This was the vulture that Lucian himself had invented! And so stories go, as they are invented, told by word of mouth, and then come to be taken as gospel truth.

Lucian, of course, mocked the entire proceeding and concluded his account by speaking not of Peregrinus's divinity, but of his utter, and rather lowly, humanity: "So ended that poor wretch Proteus, a man who (to put it briefly) never fixed his gaze on the truth but always did and said everything with a view to glory and the praise of the multitude, even to the extent of leaping into fire, when he was sure not to enjoy the praise because he could not hear it" (*The Passing of Peregrinus* 42).

Divine Humans in the Greek and Roman Worlds

FROM THESE EXAMPLES, WE can see a variety of ways in the ancient world that divine beings could be thought to be human and that humans could be thought to be divine. Again, this way of looking at things stands considerably at odds with how most people today understand the relationship of the human and the divine, at least people who stand in the western religious traditions (Jews, Christians, Muslims). As I have noted already, in our world it is widely thought that the divine realm is separated from the human by an unbridgeable chasm. God is one thing; humans are another—and never the twain shall meet. Well, almost never:

in the Christian tradition they did meet once, in the person of Jesus. Our question is how that was thought to have happened. At the root of that idea is a different sensibility about the world, one in which divinity is not absolutely but only relatively remote from humanity.

In this ancient way of thinking, both humanity and divinity are on a vertical continuum, and these two continuums sometimes meet at the high end of the one and the low end of the other. By contrast, most modern people, at least in the West, think that God is above us all in every respect and in infinite degree. He is completely Other. And there is no continuum in God. For one thing, there aren't any other gods that could provide a continuum. There is only one God, and he is infinitely beyond what we can think, not just relatively better in every way. True, some humans are more "godlike" than others—and in some traditions there does appear to be some crossover to the divine (e.g., with Roman Catholic saints). But even there, at the end of the day, God is wholly Other compared with everyone and everything else and is on an entirely different plane, by himself.

But not for most ancient people. Apart from Jews in the ancient world—whom I will address in the next chapter—everyone was a polytheist. There were lots of gods, and they were on graded levels of divinity. This can be seen in the way ancient people talked about divine beings. Consider the following inscription from the city of Mytilene, which wanted to honor the emperor as a god. This decree speaks of those humans who "have attained heavenly glory and possess the eminence and power of gods."[17] But then it goes on to say that the divine status can always be heightened for the divine emperor: "If anything more glorious than these provisions is found hereafter, the enthusiasm and piety of the city will not fail in anything that can further deify him." It is these last words that are the most important: "can further deify him." How can they *further* deify someone who is already a deity?

They cannot if being a deity means being at a fixed, certain level of divinity. But they can if being a deity placed a person on a continuum of divinity, say, at the lower end. Then the person could be moved up. And how is the person to be moved up? The decree is quite clear: the reason the emperor has been regarded as divine in the first place is because of what he has done for the people of Mytilene, "the provisions" that he has made for them. If he comes through with even more benefactions, then he will become even more divine.

When ancient people imagined the emperor—or any individual—as a god, it did not mean that the emperor was Zeus or one of the other gods of Mount Olympus. He was a divine being on a much lower level.

The Divine Pyramid

INSTEAD OF A CONTINUUM, possibly it is helpful to understand the ancient conception of the divine realm as a kind of pyramid of power, grandeur, and deity.[18] Some ancient people—for example, some of those more philosophically inclined—thought that at the very pinnacle of the divine realm was one ultimate deity, a god who was over all things, who was infinitely, or virtually infinitely, powerful and who was sometimes thought to be the source of all things. This god—whether Zeus, or Jupiter, or an unknown god—stood at the apex of what we might imagine as the divine pyramid.

Below this god, on the next lower tier, were the great gods known from tales and traditions that had been passed down from antiquity, for example, the twelve gods on Mount Olympus described in the ancient myths and in Homer's *Iliad* and *Odyssey,* gods such as Zeus, Hera, Apollo, Athena, Mercury, and so on. These gods were fantastically powerful, far beyond what we can imagine. The myths about them were entertaining stories, but many people thought these myths were just that, stories—not historical narratives of things that actually happened. Philosophers tried to "demythologize" the myths, that is, to strip them of their obvious literary features to see how, apart from a literal reading, they told deeper truths about the world and reality. At any rate, these gods were worshiped as the most powerful beings in the universe. Many of them were adopted by cities and towns as their patron gods; some were acknowledged and worshiped by the state as a whole, which had clear and compelling reasons to want the mighty gods to look favorably upon it in times of both war and peace.

But they were not the only divine beings. On a lower tier of the pyramid were many, many other gods. Every city and town had its local gods, who protected, defended, and aided the place. There were gods of every imaginable function: gods of war, love, weather, health, childbirth—you name it. There were gods for every locale: gods of forests, meadows, mountains, and rivers. The world was populated with gods. This is why it made no sense to ancient people—apart from Jews—to worship only one God. Why would you worship *one* god? There were lots of gods, and all of them deserved to be worshiped. If you decided to start worshiping a new god—for example, because you moved to a new village and wanted to pay respect to its local divinity—that did not require you to stop worshiping any of the other gods. If you decided to perform a sacrifice to Apollo, that didn't stop you from also offering a sacrifice to Athena, or Zeus, or Hera. This was a world of lots of gods and lots of what we might call religious tolerance.

Below these levels of gods there were still other tiers. There was a group of divine beings known as *daimones*. Sometimes this word gets translated as "demons," but that word as we think of it today gives the wrong connotation. Some of these beings could be malevolent, to be sure, but not all of them were; and they were not fallen angels or wicked spirits that could possess people and make them do hurtful things such as fling themselves in harm's way or twist their heads 360 degrees or projectile vomit (as in the movie *The Exorcist*). The daimones instead were simply a lower level of divinity, not nearly as powerful as the local gods, let alone the great gods. They were spiritual beings far more powerful than humans. But being closer in power to humans, they had more to do with humans than the more remote great gods and could often help people through their lives, as in the famous daimon that the Greek philosopher Socrates claimed guided his actions. If displeased, they could do harmful things. It was important to keep them happy by paying them their due in reverence and worship.

In the divine pyramid a yet lower tier, near or at the bottom, would be inhabited by divine humans. This is where the "pyramid" analogy breaks down because we should not think that these divine humans were more numerous than the other deities above them. In fact, it was relatively rare to run across people who were so mighty, wise, or gorgeous that they must in some sense be divine. But it did happen on occasion. A great general, a king, an emperor, a great philosopher, a fantastic beauty—these could be more than human. Such people could be superhuman. They could be divine. Maybe their father was a god. Maybe they were a god temporarily assuming a human body. Maybe because of their own virtue, power, or physical features they were thought to have been accepted into the divine realm. But they were not like the rest of us lowly humans.

We too, as I have pointed out, are on a continuum. Some among us are quite lowly—those whom the likes of Lucian of Samosata, for example, would consider the scum of the earth. Others of us are about average in every way. Others of us think that we, and our entire families, are well above average. Some of us recognize that there are fellows among us who are superior in remarkable ways. For ancient people, some of us are so vastly superior that we have begun to move into the realm of the divine.

Jesus and the Divine Realm

THIS VIEW OF THE divine realm did not change significantly until later Christians changed it. It is hard to put a finger on when exactly it changed, but change it did. By the time of the fourth Christian century—some three hundred years after Jesus lived, when the empire was in the process of converting from paganism to Christianity—many of the great thinkers of the Roman world had come to believe that a huge chasm separated the divine and human realms. God was "up there" and was the Almighty. He alone was God. There were no other gods and so there was no continuum of divinity. There was just us down here, the lowly sinners, and God up there, the supreme sovereign over all that is.

Jesus himself eventually came to be thought of as belonging not down here with us, but up there with God. He himself was God, with a capital G. But how could he be God, if God was God, and there were not a number of gods, not even two gods, but only one God? How could Jesus be God and God be God and yet there be only one God? That, in part, is the question that drives this book. But the more pressing and immediate question is about how this perception started in the first place. How did Jesus move from being a human to being God—in *any* sense?

I should stress those final three words. One of the mistakes that people make when thinking about the question of Jesus as God involves taking the view that eventually was widely held by the fourth Christian century—that a great chasm exists between the human and divine realms—and assuming that this view was in place during the early days of the Christian movement. This mistake is made not only by laypeople, but also, widely, by professional theologians. And not just theologians, but scholars of all sorts—including biblical scholars (or maybe, *especially* biblical scholars) and historians of early Christianity. When people who make this mistake ask "how did Jesus become God?," they mean, how did Jesus move from the realm of the purely human—where there are millions of us with varying degrees of talent, strength, beauty, and virtue—to the realm of God, God himself, the one and only Almighty Creator and Lord of all that is? How did Jesus become GOD?[19]

This is indeed an interesting question—because it did indeed happen. Jesus became God in that major fourth-century sense. But he had been seen as God before that, by people who did not have this fourth-century understanding of the relationship of the human and divine realms. When we talk about earliest Christianity and we ask the question, "Did Christians think of Jesus as God?," we need to rephrase the question slightly, so that we ask, "In what *sense* did Christians think of Jesus as God?" If the divine realm is a continuum rather than an absolute, a graduated pyramid rather than a single point, then it is the *sense* in which Jesus is God that is the main issue at the outset.

It will become clear in the following chapters that Jesus was not originally considered to be God in any sense at all, and that he eventually became divine for his followers in some sense before he came to be thought of as equal with God Almighty in an absolute sense. But the point I stress is that this was, in fact, a development.

One of the enduring findings of modern scholarship on the New Testament and early Christianity over the past two centuries is that the followers of Jesus, during his life, understood him to be human through and through, not God. People saw Jesus as a teacher, a rabbi, and even a prophet. Some people thought of him as the (very human) messiah. But he was born like everyone else and he was "like" everyone else. He was raised in Nazareth and was not particularly noteworthy as a youth. As an adult—or possibly even as a child—he became convinced, like many other Jews of his time, that he was living near the end of the age, that God was soon to intervene in history to overthrow the forces of evil and to bring in a good kingdom here on earth. Jesus felt called to proclaim this message of the coming apocalypse, and he spent his entire public ministry doing so.

Eventually Jesus irritated the ruling authorities during a trip he made to Jerusalem, and they had him arrested and tried. He was brought before the governor of Judea, Pontius Pilate, and after a short trial he was convicted on charges of political insurgency: he was claiming to be the Jewish king when only the Roman overlords who were in charge of Palestine and the rest of the Mediterranean could appoint a king. As a political troublemaker he was condemned to a particularly ignominious death, by crucifixion. And as far as the Romans were concerned, that's where his story ended.

But in fact, that's not where his story ended. And so we return to the driving question of our study: How did an apocalyptic prophet from the backwaters of rural Galilee, crucified for crimes against the state, come to be thought of as equal to the One God Almighty, maker of all things? How did Jesus—in the minds and hearts of his later followers—come to be God?

An obvious place to start to find an answer would be with the life and teachings of Jesus. But first we need to consider the religious and cultural matrix of first-century Judaism within which he lived his life and proclaimed his message. As we will see, even though Jews were distinct from the pagan world around them in thinking that only one God was to be worshiped and served, they were not distinct in their conception of the relationship of that realm to the human world we inhabit. Jews also believed that divinities could become human and humans could become divine.

CHAPTER 2

Divine Humans in Ancient Judaism

WHEN I FIRST STARTED my teaching career in the mid-1980s I was offered an adjunct position at Rutgers University. Since part-time adjunct faculty members rarely make much money, I worked other jobs to make ends meet, including one at the Institute for Advanced Study at Princeton. A long-term project was under way there called the Princeton Epigraphy Project. It involved collecting, cataloguing, and entering into a computer database all of the Greek inscriptions in major urban centers throughout the ancient Mediterranean. These were eventually published in separate volumes for each location. I was the research grunt for the person in charge, who, unlike me, was a highly trained classicist who could read an inscription like a newspaper. I had the job of entering and editing the inscriptions. One of the localities that I had responsibility for was the ancient city of Priene, on the west coast of Turkey. I had never heard of Priene before that, but I collected and catalogued all the inscriptions that had ever been found there and previously published.

Move the calendar up to 2009 and my life was very differ-

ent indeed. As a tenured professor at the University of North
Carolina, I had the ability to travel far and wide. And I did. That
summer, I decided to tour around Turkey with my good friend
Dale Martin, professor of New Testament at Yale, and check out
various archaeological sites. We spent two weeks there, with very
few advance plans, simply going wherever we wanted to go. It
was terrific.

One of the highlights was going to the ruins of ancient Priene.
It's an amazing site, in a striking mountain setting. Over the years
German archaeologists have made significant digs there, but it is
for the most part still deserted. There are ruins of temples, houses,
shops, and streets. There is a theater that could seat five thousand. An interesting bouleuterion—a council house, where the
local governing council members gathered for their meetings—
still stands in its square shape with seats on three sides. A temple
of Athena Pollis is a major structure, its columns fallen and the
drums that once made up columns scattered on the ground. And
there are lots of Greek inscriptions, just sitting out here and there
waiting to be read.

That afternoon, looking at one of the inscriptions, I had a
blinding realization. It was one of those thoughts that was completely obvious—an idea that scholars had discussed for many
years but that had never hit me, personally, with full force. How
could that be? Why had it never impressed me before? I had to
sit down and think hard for fifteen minutes before I could move
again.

At that time I had been making some initial sketches for this
book and was planning on writing about how Jesus became God
as a purely internal Christian development, as a logical outgrowth
of the teachings of Jesus as they developed after some of his followers came to believe he had been raised from the dead (as I'll
explain in later chapters). But I didn't have a single thought of
putting that development in relationship to what was going on

beyond the bounds of the Christian tradition. And then I read an inscription lying outside a temple in Priene. The inscription referred to the God (Caesar) Augustus.

And it hit me: the time when Christianity arose, with its exalted claims about Jesus, was the same time when the emperor cult had started to move into full swing, with its exalted claims about the emperor. Christians were calling Jesus God directly on the heels of the Romans calling the emperor God. Could this be a historical accident? How could it be an accident? These were not simply parallel developments. This was a competition. Who was the *real* god-man? The emperor or Jesus? I realized at that moment that the Christians were not elevating Jesus to a level of divinity in a vacuum. They were doing it under the influence of and in dialogue with the environment in which they lived. As I said, I knew that others had thought this before. But it struck me at that moment like a bolt of lightning.

I decided then and there to reconceptualize my book. But an obvious problem also hit me. The first Christians who started speaking about Jesus as divine were not pagans from Priene. They were Jews from Palestine. These Jews, of course, also knew about the emperor cult. In fact, it was practiced in some of the more Greek cities of Palestine during the first century. But the first followers of Jesus were not particularly imbued with Greek culture. They were Jews from rural and village parts of Galilee. It may be the case that later, after the Christian church became more heavily gentile, with pagan converts making up the majority of its members, the heightened emphasis on Jesus as God (rather than the emperor as God) made sense. But what about at the beginning?

So I started thinking about divine humans within Judaism. Here was an immediate enigma. Jews, unlike their pagan neighbors, were monotheists. They believed in only one God. How could they say that Jesus was God and still claim there was only one God? If God was God and Jesus was God, doesn't that make *two* Gods? I realized that I needed to do some research into the matter to figure it out.

Judaism in the Ancient World

THE FIRST STEP, OF course, must be to lay out in basic terms what Judaism was in the ancient world, around the time of Jesus. My focus is on what Jews at the time "believed" since I am interested in the question of how belief in Jesus as God could fit into Jewish thinking more broadly. I should stress that Judaism was not principally about belief per se; for most Jews, Judaism was a set of practices every bit as much, or even more, than a set of beliefs. Being Jewish meant living in certain ways. It meant engaging in certain "religious" activities, such as performing sacrifices and saying prayers and hearing scripture read; it meant certain kinds of lifestyles such as observing food regulations and honoring the Sabbath day; it meant certain ritual practices, such as circumcising baby boys and observing Jewish festivals; it meant following certain ethical codes, such as can be found in the Ten Commandments. All of this and much more is what it meant to be Jewish in antiquity. But for the purposes of this chapter, I am principally interested in what Jews of the time thought about God and the divine realm, since it is these thoughts that can make sense of how a man like Jesus could be considered divine.

Saying what Jews thought is itself highly problematic, since lots of different Jews thought lots of different things. It would be like asking what Christians think today. Someone may well say that Christians believe that Christ is fully divine and fully human. And that would be true—except for those Christians who continue to think that he really was God and was human only in appearance, or for those Christians who think that he was an inordinately religious man but was not really God. You can pick almost any doctrine of the Christian church and find lots of people who identify themselves as Christians thinking something different from what other Christians think about it. It's like what some Episcopalians say about themselves today: get four in a room and you'll find five opinions. So too with ancient Jews.

Widespread Jewish Beliefs

WITH ALL THESE CAVEATS in mind, I can try to explain briefly what most Jews at the time of Jesus appear to have believed. (A full treatment, of course, would require a very large book of its own.)[1] Jews on the whole were monotheists. They knew that the pagans had lots of gods, but for them there was only one God. This was their God, the God of Israel. This God had created the world and all that was in it. Moreover, he had promised the ancestors of Israel an enormous body of descendants who made up Israel. He had called Israel to be his people and made a covenant—a kind of pact, or peace treaty—with them: he would be their God if they would be his people. Being his people meant following the law he had given them—the law of Moses, which is now found in the first five books of the Hebrew Bible: Genesis, Exodus, Leviticus, Numbers, and Deuteronomy, which together are sometimes called the Torah (the Hebrew word for law).

This was the law that God had revealed to his prophet Moses after he saved the people of Israel from their bondage in Egypt, as described in the book of Exodus. The law included instructions on how to worship God (for example, through sacrifices), how to be distinct as a social group from other peoples (for example, through the kosher food laws), and how to live together in community (for example, through the ethical injunctions of the Ten Commandments). At the heart of the Jewish law was the commandment to worship the God of Israel alone. The very beginning of the Ten Commandments states: "I am the Lord your God, who brought you out of the land of Egypt, out of the house of slavery; you shall have no other gods before me" (Exod. 20:2–3).

By the days of Jesus, most (but not all) Jews considered other ancient books to be sacred along with the Torah. There were writings of prophets (such as Amos, Isaiah, and Jeremiah) that described the history of ancient Israel and proclaimed the word of God to the dire situations people had faced during difficult times. There were other writings such as the books of Psalms and Proverbs that were invested with special divine authority. Some of these other books restated the teachings of the Torah, speaking the words of the law to a new situation. The book of Isaiah, for example, is emphatic in its monotheistic assertions: "I am the LORD, and there is no other; besides me there is no god" (Isa. 45:5); or as can be found later in the same chapter of the prophet:

> Turn to me and be saved,
>> All the ends of the earth!
>> For I am God, and there is no other.
> By myself I have sworn,
>> From my mouth has gone forth in righteousness
> A word that shall not return:
>> "To me every knee shall bow,
>> Every tongue shall swear." (Isa 45:22–23)

Isaiah is here expressing a view that became important later in the history of Judaism. Not only is God the only God there is, but eventually everyone will realize it. All the peoples of earth will, in the future, bow down in worship before him alone and confess his name.

Can There Be a Spectrum of Divinity in Judaism?

WITH THE STRESS ON the oneness of God throughout scripture, how is it possible to imagine that Jews could have something like a divine pyramid? Within the pagan system it was possible to imagine not only that divine beings temporarily became human, but also that humans in some sense could be divine. But if there is only one God, how could that be possible?

In this chapter I argue that it was in fact possible and that Jews also thought there were divine humans. Before going into detail about how this could happen, however, I need to make two general points about Jewish monotheism. The first is that not every ancient Israelite held a monotheistic view—the idea that there is only one God. Evidence for this can be seen already in the verse I quoted from the Torah above, the beginning of the Ten Commandments. Note how the commandment is worded. It does not say, "You shall believe that there is only one God." It says, "You shall have no other gods before me." This commandment, as stated, presupposes that there *are* other gods. But none of them is to be worshiped ahead of, or instead of, the God of Israel. As it came to be interpreted, the commandment also meant that none of these other gods was to be worshiped alongside of or even *after* the God of Israel. But that does not mean the other gods don't exist. They simply are not to be worshiped.

This is a view that scholars have called *henotheism,* in distinction from the view I have thus far been calling *monotheism.* Monotheism is the view that there is, in fact, only one God. Henotheism is the view that there are other gods, but there is only one God who is to be worshiped. The Ten Commandments express a henotheistic view, as does the majority of the Hebrew Bible. The book of Isaiah, with its insistence that "I alone am God, there is no other," is monotheistic. It represents the minority view in the Hebrew Bible.

By the time of Jesus, many, possibly most, Jews had moved into the monotheistic camp. But doesn't that view preclude the possibility of other divine beings in the divine realm? As it turns out—this is my second point—that is not the case either. Jews may not (usually) have called other superhuman divine beings "God" or "gods." But there were other superhuman divine beings. In other words, there were beings who lived not on earth but in the heavenly realm and who had godlike, superhuman powers, even if they were not the equals of the ultimate God himself. In the Hebrew Bible, for example, there are angels, cherubim, and seraphim—attendants upon God who worship him and administer his will (see, for example, Isa. 6:1–6). These are fantastically powerful beings far above humans in the scale of existence. They are lower-level divinities. By the time of the New Testament we find Jewish authors referring to such entities as principalities, dominions, powers, and authorities—unnamed divine beings in the heavenly realm who are active as well here on earth (e.g., Eph. 6:12; Col. 1:16). And these divinities stand in a hierarchical scale, a continuum of power. Some cosmic beings are more powerful than others. So Jewish texts speak of the great angels Michael, Gabriel, and Raphael. These are divine powers far above humans, though far below God as well.

The point is this: even within Judaism there was understood to be a continuum of divine beings and divine power, comparable in many ways to that which could be found in paganism. This was true even among authors who were strict monotheists. They may have believed that there was only one supreme being who could be called God Almighty, just as some pagan philosophers thought there was only one ultimate true god above all the others at the top of the "pyramid." And some, possibly most, Jews insisted that this one God alone was to be worshiped. But there were other Jews whom we know about who thought it was altogether acceptable and right to worship other divine beings, such as the great angels. Just as it is right to bow down before a great king in obeisance to him, they believed it is right to bow down before an even greater being, an angel, to do obeisance.

We know that some Jews thought it was right to worship angels in no small part because a number of our surviving texts insist that it *not* be done.[2] You don't get laws prohibiting activities that are never performed. No city on earth would have a law against jaywalking or against speeding if no one had ever done either. Ancient authors insisted that angels *not* be worshiped precisely because angels *were* being worshiped. Even those who were worshiping angels may have thought that doing so was not a violation of the Ten Commandments: God was the ultimate source of all that was divine. But there were lower divinities as well. Even within monotheistic Judaism.

It is within this context that I move to my central concern here: divine beings who become human within Judaism, and humans who become divine. I consider three categories roughly corresponding to the three ways a human could be divine in the pagan world. Within Judaism we find divine beings who temporarily become human, semidivine beings who are born of the union of a divine being and a mortal, and humans who are, or who become, divine.

Divine Beings Who Temporarily Become Human

ANGELS IN ANCIENT JUDAISM were widely understood to be superhuman messengers of God who mediated his will on earth. It is striking that various angels sometimes appeared on earth in human guise. More than that, in some ancient Jewish texts there is a figure known as "the Angel of the Lord," who is regarded as the "chief" angel. How exalted is this figure? In some passages he is identified as God himself. And yet sometimes he appears as a human. This is the Jewish counterpart to the pagan view that the gods could assume human guise to visit the earth.

The Angel of the Lord as God and Human
An example early in scripture can be found in Genesis 16. The situation is this. God has promised Abraham that he will have

many descendants, that he will, in fact, be the father of the nation of Israel. But he is childless. His wife Sarah hands her servant Hagar over to him so he can conceive a child with her. Abraham willingly complies, but then Sarah becomes jealous of Hagar and mistreats her. Hagar runs away.

"The Angel of the Lord" then finds Hagar in the wilderness and speaks to her (Gen. 16:7). He tells her to return to her mistress and lets her know that she, Hagar, will have a son who will be the ancestor of a (different) great people. But then, after referring to this heavenly visitant as the Angel of the Lord, the text indicates that it was, in fact, "the LORD" who had spoken with her (16:13). Moreover, Hagar realizes that she has been addressing God himself and expresses her astonishment that she had "seen God and remained alive after seeing him" (16:13). Here there is both ambiguity and confusion: either the Lord appears as an angel in the form of a human, or the Angel of the Lord is the Lord himself, God in human guise.

A similar ambiguity occurs two chapters later, this time with Abraham. We are told in Genesis 18:1 that "the LORD appeared to Abraham by the oaks of Mamre." But when the episode is narrated, we learn that "three men" come to him (18:2). Abraham plays the good host and entertains them, preparing for them a very nice meal, which they all three eat. When they talk to him afterward, one of these three "men" is identified explicitly as "the LORD" (18:13). At the end of the story we are informed that the other two were "angels" (19:1). So here we have a case where two angels and the Lord God himself have assumed human form—so much so that they appear to Abraham to be three men, and they all eat the food he has prepared.

The most famous instance of such ambiguity is found in the story of Moses and the burning bush (Exod. 3:1–22). By way of background: Moses, the son of Hebrews, had been raised in Egypt by the daughter of Pharaoh, but he has to escape for murdering an Egyptian and is wanted by the Pharaoh himself. He goes to Midian where he marries and becomes a shepherd for his father-in-law's flocks. One day, while tending to his sheeply duties, Moses sees an astonishing sight. We are told that he arrives at Mount Horeb (this is Mount Sinai, where later, after the exodus, he is given the law) and there, "the angel of the LORD appeared to him in a flame of fire out of a bush" (Exod. 3:2). Moses is amazed because the bush is aflame but is not being consumed by the fire. And despite the fact that it is the Angel of the Lord who is said to have appeared to him, it is "the Lord" who sees that Moses has come to the bush, and it is "God" who then calls to him out of the bush. In fact, the Angel of the Lord tells Moses, "I am the God of your father, the God of Abraham, the God of Isaac, and the God of Jacob" (Exod. 3:6). As the story continues, the Lord God continues to speak to Moses and Moses to God. But in what sense was it the Angel of the Lord that appeared to him? As a helpful note in the *HarperCollins Study Bible* puts it: "Although it was an *angel* that appeared in v. 2, there is no substantive difference between the deity and his agents."[3] Or as New Testament scholar Charles Gieschen has expressed it, this "Angel of the Lord" is "either indistinguishable from God as his visible manifestation" or he is a distinct figure, separate from God, who is bestowed with God's own authority.[4]

Other Angels as God and Human

There are numerous other examples both in the Bible and in other Jewish texts in which angels are described as God and, just as important, in which angels are described as humans. One of the most interesting is Psalm 82. In this beautiful plea that justice be done for those who are weak and needy, we are told, in v. 1, that "God has taken his place in the divine council; in the midst of the gods he holds judgment." Here, God Almighty is portrayed as having a divine council around him; these are angelic beings with whom God consults, as happens elsewhere in the Bible—most famously in Job 1, where the Satan figure is himself reckoned among these divine beings.[5] In the Job passage the divine beings making up God's council are called "sons of God." Here in Psalm 82 they are called "children of the Most High." But more than that, they are called "Elohim" (82:6)—the Hebrew word for "God" (it is a plural word; when not referring to God, it is usually translated as "gods"). These angelic beings are "gods." Here in the psalm they are rebuked because they have no concern for people who are lowly, weak, and destitute. Because of the failures of these "gods," God bestows upon them the ultimate punishment: he makes them mortal, so that they will die and cease to exist (82:7).

Thus angelic beings, children of God, can be called gods. And in a variety of texts we find that such beings become human. Here I might turn to some instances outside the Bible. In a Jewish text that probably dates to the first Christian century, the *Prayer of Joseph,* we find the Jewish ancestor Jacob speaking in the first person and indicating that he is in fact an angel of God: "I, Jacob, who is speaking to you am also Israel, an angel of God. . . . I am the first born of every living thing to whom God gives life."[6] "Uriel, the angel of God, came forth and said that I, Jacob, descended to earth and tabernacled [dwelled in a tent] among people and that I have been called by the name Jacob." He is further called "the archangel of the power of the Lord" and is said to be the "chief captain" among the sons of God. Here again, the chief angel appears as a human being on earth—in this case, as the patriarch Jacob, otherwise known from the book of Genesis.

As a second example I turn to another Jewish book from about the same time, called the *Apocalypse of Abraham.* This book describes a vision allegedly experienced by the patriarch Abraham, father of the Jews. Abraham hears a voice but does not see anyone who is speaking; in astonishment he falls to the ground, as if lifeless (10.1–2). And while facedown on the ground he hears the voice of God saying to an angel named Jaoel to go and strengthen him. Jaoel appears to Abraham "in the likeness of a man" (10.4) and raises and strengthens him. He tells Abraham that he is the angel who brings peace to warring factions in heaven and who works miracles not only on earth, but also in Hades, the realm of the dead. When Abraham looks at the angel, he sees a body like sapphire, a face like chrysolite, hair like snow, a rainbow on his head, royal purple garments, and a golden staff in his hand (11.2–3). Here then is a mighty angel, who temporarily becomes incarnate, in order to effect God's will on earth—in this instance to be with Abraham in his various activities on earth.

Humans Who Become Angels

Other Jewish texts speak not only of angels (or even God) as becoming human, but also of humans who become angels. Many people today have the view that when people die, they become angels (well, at least if they've been "good"). This is a very old belief indeed. In the book of *2 Baruch,* one of the great apocalypses that has come down to us from early Judaism (an *apocalypse* is a vision of heavenly secrets that can make sense of earthly realities), we learn that righteous believers will be transformed "into the splendor of angels . . . for they will live in the heights of that world and they will be like the angels and be equal to the stars. . . . And the excellence of the righteous will then be greater than that of the angels" (*2 Bar.* 51.3–10).[7] Here, then, those who are righteous become angels who are greater than other angels—greater even than the stars, which many ancient people believed to be fantastically great angels.

Some ancient Jewish texts portray particular individuals as being transformed into angels at death. One of the supremely mysterious characters in the Hebrew Bible is the ancient figure Enoch. We do not learn much about him in the terse comments of the principal passage that mentions him in the Hebrew Bible, Genesis 5. We learn that he was the father of Methuselah, the oldest man who ever lived in scripture (969 years, according to Gen 5:27), and the great-grandfather of Noah. But what is most striking is that when Enoch was 365 years old, he passed from this earth—but without dying: "Enoch walked with God; then he was no more, because God took him" (Gen. 5:24). This laconic statement generated enormous speculations and speculative literature throughout ancient Judaism. Several ancient apocalypses are attributed to Enoch. Who better to know about the future course of history or of the heavenly realm than one who was transported to heaven without dying first?

In a book called *2 Enoch,* written possibly around the time of Jesus, we learn one opinion about what happened to Enoch when he was taken up into the divine realm (*2 En.* 22.1–10). We are told that he came into the presence of the Lord himself and did obeisance to him. God tells him to stand up and says to his angels, "Let Enoch join in and stand in front of my face forever."[8] God then tells the angel Michael: "Go, and extract Enoch from his earthly clothing. And anoint him with my delightful oil, and put him into the clothes of my glory." Michael does so. Enoch reflects on his transformation in the first person: "And I looked at myself and I had become like one of his glorious ones, and there was no observable difference." As a result of this angelification, if we can call it that, Enoch's face became so bright that no one could look at it (37.2), and he no longer needed to eat or sleep (23.3; 56.2). In other words, he became identical to an angel.

Something similar is said to have happened to Moses. The death of Moses is described in cryptic terms in the Bible where we learn that he died alone and no one ever knew the location of his grave (Deut. 34:5–6). Later Jewish writers maintained that he was taken up to heaven to dwell. And so, for example, in the apocryphal book of Sirach we learn that God made Moses "equal in glory to the holy ones, and made him great, to the terror of his enemies" (45.1–5). He thus is equal to the angels. Some authors think of him as even greater than the angels, as in a book attributed to a person known as Ezekiel the Tragedian, who indicates that Moses was given a scepter and summoned to sit on a throne, with a diadem placed on his head, so that the "stars" bowed down to him. Recall: stars were considered superior angels. Here they bow down in worship to Moses, who has been transformed into a being even greater than they.

To summarize our findings to this point: the Angel of the Lord is sometimes portrayed in the Bible as being the Lord God himself, and he sometimes appears on earth in human guise. Still other angels—the members of God's divine council—are called gods and are made mortals. And yet other angels make their appearances on earth in human form. Still more important, some Jewish texts talk about humans becoming angels at death—or even superior to angels and worthy of worship. The ultimate relevance of these findings for our question about how Jesus came to be considered divine should already begin to become apparent. In one of the important studies of early Christian Christology, New Testament scholar Larry Hurtado states a key thesis: "I propose the view that the principal angel speculation and other types of divine agency thinking . . . provided the earliest Christians with a basic scheme for accommodating the resurrected Christ next to God without having to depart from their monotheistic tradition."[9] In other words, if humans could be angels (and angels humans), and if angels could be gods, and if in fact the chief angel could be the Lord himself—then to make Jesus divine, one simply needs to think of him as an angel in human form.

Divine Beings Who Beget Semidivine Beings

IN CHAPTER 1 WE saw a common theme in pagan mythology: divine men who were born of the union of a mortal and a god (such as the lusty Zeus). There is nothing exactly like this in ancient Jewish texts, probably because such human passions as sexual desire and lust were regularly deemed completely unsuitable for the God of Israel. Anger and wrath, yes; sexual love, no. Especially if it involved such scandalous activities as rape.

But there is something roughly analogous even in Judaism—not with God himself, but with some of his divine minions, the sons of God, the angels, who are occasionally said to have had sex with mortals and had superhuman offspring. We find the first intimation of some such thing in the early chapters of Genesis.

In a tantalizingly terse passage in Genesis 6, we learn that the "sons of God" looked down upon the earth and saw beautiful women whom they desired. "And they took wives for themselves of all that they chose" (6:2). More specifically, "the sons of God went in to the daughters of humans, who bore children to them" (6:4). God was not pleased with this state of affairs, so he decided to limit human life to 120 years and, immediately afterward, decided further to be rid of the whole lot of them by bringing the flood, which only Noah and his family survived. And who were the offspring of these unions of the sons of God and human women? We are told that the "Nephilim" were on the earth in those days. These are the offspring, "the heroes that were of old, warriors of renown" (6:4). The word *Nephilim* means "those who have fallen." In the book of Numbers they are said to have been the giants who originally inhabited the land of Canaan (13:3). Putting all this together, one can see that divine beings—the sons of God—had sex with women on earth, and their semidivine offspring were giants. I am calling them "semidivine" both because they were born of the unions of divine beings and mortals and because they do not actually live in the heavenly realm like other divinities. But they are superior to other humans—giants who made fantastic warriors, for rather obvious reasons. As a side note, I think we can assume that in order for the sons of God to make these women their wives, they had to assume human shape. Here again, then, we have divine beings appearing as humans; and what is more, we have them generating yet other superhuman beings. This is a Jewish version of the pagan myths.

A fuller exposition of this account in the book of Genesis can be found in another Jewish apocalypse attributed to that mysterious figure of biblical history Enoch. The noncanonical book of *1 Enoch* is a complicated collection of different texts that have been spliced together by later editors. The first portion of the book, called the Book of the Watchers, comprises chapters 1–36. It originally appears to have existed independently of *1 Enoch* itself; scholars typically date it to the third century BCE. A good portion of the Book of the Watchers is an exposition of the brief but suggestive episode about the sons of God in Genesis 6; in *1 Enoch* these figures are called the Watchers (chaps. 6–16). Unlike in Genesis 6, here they are also explicitly called "angels."

We are told that there were two hundred of these errant angels, and we actually learn the names of their leaders, such angelic greats as Semyaz, Ram'el, and Tam'el. In this account the two hundred descend to earth onto Mount Hermon, they each choose a wife, and they have sex with her. The offspring who result are giants indeed: we are told that they were 450 feet tall. As such huge beings, these giants have ravenous appetites; they eventually run out of food and so start eating humans. No wonder God was not pleased.

The angelic beings, the Watchers, perform other illicit activities. They teach people magic, medicine, and astrology—some of the forbidden arts—and they instruct them in metallurgy, so they can make both jewelry and weapons. Three of the angels up in heaven—Michael, Surafel, and Gabriel—look down, see what is happening on earth, and issue a complaint to God about it. God responds by sending the flood to destroy the giants (and everyone else). The Watchers are then bound and cast into a pit in the desert where they are to live in darkness for seventy generations until they are sent into eternal fire on the day of judgment. Enoch is instructed to pronounce judgment upon them: "you used to be holy, spiritual, the living ones, possessing eternal life; but now you have defiled yourselves with women and with the blood of the flesh of begotten children, you have lusted with the blood of the people" (5.4).[10] In this Jewish version, the divine beings are condemned for doing what Zeus did in the pagan stories.

The text goes on to explain that "now the giants who are born from the union of the spirits and the flesh shall be called evil spirits upon the earth. . . . Evil spirits have come out of their bodies" (15.8–9). This appears to be an explanation of where the beings who were later called demons came from. And so here we have a view even closer to that found in the pagan myths: the offspring of the union of divine and human beings are more divine beings—in this case the demonic forces that plague the world.

Other Nonhuman Divine Figures

THERE ARE OTHER FIGURES—APART from God himself—who are sometimes described as divine in ancient Jewish sources, both the Bible and later writings from near the time of Jesus and his followers. The first is modeled on a figure found in an enigmatic passage of scripture, Daniel 7, a figure that came to be known as "the Son of Man."

The Son of Man
The book of Daniel is something like a Hebrew Bible version of the book of Revelation—a book that modern fundamentalists

think sets out a blueprint of human history, down to our own time. Critical scholars see it as something very different indeed, as a book of its own time and place. The ostensible setting of the book of Daniel is in the sixth century BCE—although scholars have long been convinced that the book was not actually written then, but centuries later in the second century BCE. In this book Daniel is portrayed as a Judean captive who has been taken into exile to Babylon, the world empire that destroyed his homeland in 586 BCE. In chapter 7 Daniel describes a wild vision in which he sees four beasts arising out of the sea, one after the other. Each is awe-inspiring and truly terrible, and they wreak havoc on the earth. Then he sees "one like a son of man" coming on the "clouds of heaven" (Dan. 7:13). Here is a figure that is not beastly, but is in human form; and rather than coming from the turbulent sea of chaos, he arrives from the realm of God. The beasts that had caused such destruction on earth are judged and removed from power, and the kingdom of the earth is delivered over to the one "like a son of man."

Daniel is unable to make heads or tails of the vision, but luckily—as typically happens in these apocalyptic texts that are disclosing sublime heavenly truths—an angel is standing by to interpret it for him. The beasts each represent a kingdom that will come, in succession to one another, to rule the earth. At the end, after the fourth beast, a humanlike one will be given dominion over the earth. In the angel's interpretation of the vision, we are told that this dominion will be given to the "people of the holy ones of the Most High" (Dan. 7:27). This may mean that just as the beasts each represented a kingdom, so too did the "one like a son of man." The beasts were the successive kingdoms of Babylonia, Media, Persia, and Greece, which would each achieve world domination. The one like a son of man, then, would be the kingdom of Israel, which will be restored to its proper place and given authority over all the earth. Some interpreters have thought that since the beasts can also be taken to represent kings (at the head of the kingdoms), so too the one like a son of man—possibly he is an angelic being who is head of the nation of Israel.[11]

However one interprets Daniel in its original second-century BCE context, what is clear is that eventually in some Jewish circles it came to be thought that this "one like a son of man" was indeed a future deliverer, a cosmic judge of the earth, who would come with divine vengeance against God's enemies and with a heavenly reward for those who had remained faithful to him. This figure came to be known as "the Son of Man." Nowhere is he described more fully than in the book of *1 Enoch*, which we have already considered in relation to the Book of the Watchers (*1 En.* 1–36). The Son of Man, on the other hand, is a prominent figure in a different portion of the final edition of *1 Enoch*, chapters 37–71, which are usually called the Similitudes.

There are debates about the date of the Similitudes. Some scholars put this part of the book near the end of the first century CE; probably more date it earlier, to around the time of Jesus himself.[12] For our purposes a precise date is not particularly important. What matters is the exalted character of the Son of Man. Many great and glorious things are said in the Similitudes about this person—who now is thought of as a divine being, rather than, say, as the nation of Israel. We are told that he was given a name "even before the creation of the sun and the moon, before the creation of the stars" (*1 En.* 48.2–3). We are told that all the earth will fall down and worship him. Before the creation he was concealed in the presence of God himself; but he was always God's chosen one, and it is he who has revealed God's wisdom to the righteous and holy, who will be "saved in his name," since "it is his good pleasure that they have life" (48.2–7).

At the end of time, when all the dead are resurrected, it is he, the "Elect One," who will sit on God's throne (51.3). From this "throne of glory" he will "judge all the works of the holy ones in heaven above, weighing in the balance their deeds" (61.8). He himself is eternal: "He shall never pass away or perish before the face of the earth." And "all evil shall disappear before his face" (69.79). He will "remove the kings and the mighty ones from their thrones. He shall loosen the reins of the strong and crush the teeth of sinners. He shall depose the kings from their thrones and kingdoms. For they do not extol and glorify him and neither do they obey him, the source of their kingship" (46.2–6).

At one point this cosmic judge of the earth is called the messiah—a term we will consider more fully in the next chapter. For now, it is enough to say that it comes from the Hebrew word for *anointed* and was originally used of the king of Israel, God's anointed one (i.e., the one chosen and favored by God). Now the ruler anointed by God is not a mere mortal; he is a divine being who has always existed, who sits beside God on his throne, who will judge the wicked and the righteous at the end of time. He, in other words, is elevated to God's own status and functions as the divine being who carries out God's judgment on the earth. This is an exalted figure indeed, as exalted as one can possibly be without actually being the Lord God Almighty himself. It is striking that a later addition to the Similitudes, chapters 70–71, identifies this Son of Man as none other than Enoch. In this somewhat later view, it is a man, a mere mortal, who is exalted to this supreme position next to God.[13] As this exalted being, the Son of Man is worshiped and glorified by the righteous.

The Two Powers in Heaven

Earlier I pointed out that the injunctions against worshiping angels scattered throughout early Jewish texts suggest that indeed angels were worshiped—otherwise, there would be no reason to forbid the practice. Now we have seen that the Son of Man also was worshiped. One could easily argue that anyone or anything seated beside God on a throne in the heavenly realm deserves worship. If you're willing to bow down and prostrate yourself in the presence of an earthly king, then surely it's appropriate to do so in the presence of the cosmic judge of the earth.

In an interesting and compelling study, Alan Segal, a scholar of ancient Judaism, argues that early rabbis were particularly concerned about a notion, which was evidently widespread in parts of Judaism, that along with God in heaven there was a second power on the divine throne. Following these Jewish sources, Segal refers to these two—God and the other—as the "two powers in heaven."[14] The Son of Man figure whom we have just examined would be one such divine figure, as he shares the status and power of God. But there evidently were others who were candidates for this celestial honor, and the rabbis who were concerned about regulating what Jews should think and believe found such views unnerving, so much so that they went on the attack against them. Their attacks were effective, more or less silencing those who ascribed to these views.

Segal's careful analysis shows that those who held to the "heretical" notion of two powers maintained that the second power was either some kind of angel or a mystical manifestation of a divine characteristic thought to be in some sense equal with God (discussed more below). They subscribed to this notion because of their interpretations of certain passages in the Bible, such as those that describe the Angel of the Lord as bearing the divine name himself, or Daniel 7 and its reference to "the one like a son of man"—a figure independent of God who is given eternal power and dominion. Yet other passages could lead to a "two-powers" doctrine, such as Genesis 1:26, in which God, in creating humans, says, "Let us make humankind in our image, according to our likeness." Why is God speaking in the plural: "us" and "our"? According to the two-powers heresy, it was because another divine figure was with him. This also could be the person that the "elders of Israel" saw sitting on the divine throne in Exodus

24:9–10. This figure is called the God of Israel, but the people actually *saw* him. Elsewhere, even within the book of Exodus, it is explicitly stated that no one can see God and live (Exod. 33:20). Yet they did see God and they did live. They must, then, have seen the second power, not God.

The rabbis of the second, third, fourth, and following centuries CE condemned any such notion as a heresy. But, again, the fact that they condemned it shows that it was a view held by other Jews, and since the rabbis condemned it so thoroughly, it was probably held by a large number of Jews. Segal argues that this heresy can be traced back to the first Christian century and to Palestine itself. He maintains that one obvious target for such views were the Christians, who elevated Christ—as we will see—to the level of God. But it wasn't only Christians who held to the two-powers heresy. Non-Christian Jews did as well, on the basis of their interpretation of passages from the Hebrew Bible.

Divine Hypostases

Scholars sometimes use technical terms for no good reason, other than the fact that they are the technical terms scholars use. When I was in graduate school we used to ask, wryly, why we should use a perfectly good English term when we had an obscure Latin or German term that meant the same thing? But there are some rare terms that simply don't have satisfactory, simple words that adequately express the same thing, and the word *hypostasis* (plural: *hypostases*) is one of them. Possibly the closest common term meaning roughly the same thing would be *personification*—but even that doesn't quite get it, and it too isn't a word you normally hear as you stand in line at the grocery store.

The term *hypostasis* comes from Greek and refers to the essence or substance of something. In the context in which I'm using the term here, it refers to a feature or attribute of God that comes to take on its own distinct existence apart from God. Imagine, for example, that God is wise. That means he has wisdom. This in turn means that wisdom is something that God "has"—that is, it is something independent of God that he happens to have possession of. If that's the case, then one could imagine "wisdom" as a being apart from God; and since it is God's wisdom, then it is a kind of divine being alongside God that is also within God as part of his essence, a part of who he is.

As it turns out, some Jewish thinkers imagined that Wisdom was just that, a hypostasis of God, an element of his being that was distinct from him in one sense, but completely his in another. Wisdom was with God as a divine being and could be thought of as God (since it was precisely his wisdom). Other hypostases are discussed in ancient Jewish writings, but here I restrict myself to two—Wisdom and what was sometimes thought of as the outward manifestation of Wisdom, the Word (Greek, *Logos*) of God.

Wisdom

The idea that Wisdom could be a divine hypostasis—an aspect of God that is a distinct being from God that nonetheless is itself God—is rooted in a fascinating passage of the Hebrew Bible, Proverbs 8. Here, Wisdom is portrayed as speaking and says that it was the first thing God created:

> *The LORD created me at the beginning of his work,*
> > *The first of his acts of long ago.*
> *Ages ago I was set up,*
> > *at the first, before the beginning of the earth . . .*
> *Before the mountains had been shaped,*
> > *before the hills, I was brought forth. (8:22–23, 25)*

And then, once Wisdom was created, God created the heavens and the earth. In fact, he created all things with Wisdom, who worked alongside him:

When he established the heavens, I was there,
When he drew a circle on the face of the deep,
When he made firm the skies above,
When he established the fountains of the deep . . .
Then I was beside him, like a master worker;
And I was daily his delight,
Rejoicing before him always,
Rejoicing in his inhabited world
And delighting in the human race. (8:27–28, 30–31)

God made all things in his wisdom, so much so that Wisdom is seen as a co-creator of sorts. Moreover, just as God is said to have made all things live, so too life comes through Wisdom:

For whoever finds me finds life,
And obtains favor from the LORD;
But those who miss me injure themselves;
All who hate me love death. (8:35–36)

This passage can be read, of course, without thinking of Wisdom as some kind of personification of an aspect of God that exists apart from and alongside him. It could simply be a meta-phorical way of saying that the world is an astounding place and that the creation of it is rooted in the wise foreknowledge of God, who made all things just as they ought to be. Moreover, if you understand the wisdom of the way things are made, and live in accordance with this knowledge, you will live a happy and fulfilled life. But some Jewish readers read the passage more liter-ally and took Wisdom to be an actual being that was speaking, a being alongside God that was an expression of God.

This view led some Jewish thinkers to magnify Wisdom as a divine hypostasis. Nowhere is this seen more clearly than in a book of the Jewish Apocrypha called the Wisdom of Solomon.

The book is attributed to King Solomon himself—who is acclaimed in the Bible as the wisest man ever to have lived—but it was actually written many centuries after he had been laid to rest. Especially in chapters 7–9 we find a paean to Wisdom, which is said to be "a pure emanation of the glory of the Almighty . . . for she is a reflection of eternal light, a spotless mirror of the working of God, and an image of his goodness" (Wis. 7:25–26; Wisdom is referred to as "she"—or even as "Lady Wisdom"—because the Greek word for wisdom is feminine); "she is an initiate in the knowledge of God, and an associate in his works" (8:4).

Here too we are told that Wisdom "was present when you [God] made the world" (9:9)—but more than that, she actually is beside God on his throne (9:10). It was Wisdom who brought salvation to Israel at the exodus and afterward throughout the history of the nation (chaps. 10–11). Interestingly, Wisdom is said to have done not only what the Hebrew Bible claims God did (creation; exodus), but also what the "angel" of God did—for example, rescuing Abraham's nephew Lot from the fires that destroyed Sodom and Gomorrah in Genesis 19 (10:6).

In a sense, then, Wisdom could be seen as an angel, even a highly exalted angel, or indeed the Angel of the Lord; but as a hypostasis it is something somewhat different. It is an aspect of God that is thought to exist alongside God and to be worthy, as being God's, of the honor and esteem accorded God himself.

The Word

In some ways the most difficult divine hypostasis to discuss is the Word—in Greek, the *Logos*. That's because the term had a long, distinguished, and complex history outside the realm of Judaism among the Greek philosophers. Full treatment of the philosophical reflections on Logos would require an entire study,[15] but I can say enough here to give an adequate background to its use in the philosophical circles of Judaism, especially regarding the most famous Jewish philosopher of antiquity, Philo of Alexandria (20 BCE–50 CE).

The ancient Greek philosophers known as the Stoics had extensive discussions of the divine Logos. The word *Logos* does mean "word"—as in the thing you speak—but it could carry much deeper and richer connotations and nuances. It is, obviously, the word from which we get the English term *logic*—and that's because Logos can also mean *reason*—as in, "there is a reason for that" and "that view is quite reasonable." Stoics believed that Logos—reason—was a divine element that infused all of existence. There is, in fact, a logic to the way things are, and if you want to understand this world—and more important, if you want to understand how best to live in this world—then you will seek to understand its underlying logic. As it turns out, this is possible because Logos is not only inherent in nature, it resides in us as human beings. We ourselves have a portion of Logos given to us, and when we apply our minds to the world, we can understand it. If we understand the world, we can see how to live in it. If we follow through on that understanding, we will indeed lead harmonious, peaceful, and enriched lives. But if we don't figure out the way the world works and is, and if we don't live in harmony with it, we will be miserable and no better off than the dumb animals.

Thinkers who saw themselves standing directly in the line of the great fifth-century BCE Plato took the idea of the Logos in a different direction. In Platonic thinking, there is a sharp divide between spiritual realities and this world of matter. God, in this thinking, is pure spirit. But how can something that is pure spirit have any contact with what is pure matter? For that to happen, some kind of link is needed, some kind of go-between that connects spirit and matter. For Platonists, the Logos is this go-between. The divine Logos is what allows the divine to interact with the nondivine, the spirit with matter.

We have Logos within our material bodies, so we too can connect with the divine, even though we are thoroughly entrenched in the material world. In some sense, the way to happiness and fulfillment is to escape our material attachments and attain to spiritual heights. Among other things, this means that we should not be too attached to the bodies we inhabit. We become attached by enjoying physical pleasures and thinking that pleasure is the ultimate good. But it's not. Pleasure simply makes us long for more and keeps us attached to matter. We need to transcend matter if we are to find true meaning and fulfillment, and this means accessing the Logos of the universe with that part of the Logos that is within us.

In some respects it was quite simple for Jewish thinkers who were intimately familiar with their scriptures to connect them with some of these Stoic and Platonic philosophical ideas. In the Hebrew Bible, God creates all things by speaking a "word": "And God *said,* Let there be light. And there was light." Creation happened by means of God uttering his Logos. The Logos comes from God, and since it is God's Logos, in a sense it is God. But once he emits it, it stands apart from God as a distinct entity. This entity was sometimes thought of as a person distinct from God. The Logos came to be seen in some Jewish circles as a hypostasis.

Already in the Hebrew Bible the "word of the Lord" was sometimes identified as the Lord himself (see, for example, 1 Sam. 3:1, 6). In the hands of Philo of Alexandria, who was heavily influenced especially by the Platonic tradition, the Logos became a key factor in understanding both God and the world.

Philo maintained that the Logos was the highest of all beings, the image of God according to which and by which the universe is ordered. God's Logos was, in particular, the paradigm according to which humans were created. It is easy to see here that Logos is taking on the function also assigned to Wisdom, which was thought to be the creator and ordering factor of all things. In some sense the Logos is in fact "born" of Wisdom. If wisdom is something that people have within themselves, then Logos is the outward manifestation of the wisdom when the person speaks. And so, in this understanding, Wisdom gives birth to Logos, which is, in fact, what Philo himself believed. Moreover, as the mind is to the body, so the Logos is to the world.

Since the Logos is God's Logos, it is itself divine and can be called by divine names. Thus Philo calls Logos the "image of God" and the "Name of God" and the "firstborn son" (e.g., *Agriculture* 51).[16] In one place he indicates that God "gives the title of 'God' to his chief Logos" (*Dreams* 1.230). Because the Logos is God, and God is God, Philo sometimes speaks of "two gods" and in other places speaks of Logos as "the second God" (*Questions on Genesis* 2.62). But there is a difference for Philo between "the God" and "a god" (in Greek between *o theos*—meaning "God"—and *theos*—meaning "god"). Logos is the latter.

As a divine being apart from God, Logos obviously sounds a lot like the Angel of the Lord discussed at the beginning of this chapter. And in fact, Philo sometimes maintained that Logos was indeed this Angel of the Lord (e.g., *Changing of Names* 87, *Dreams* 239). When God was manifest to humans, it was his Logos that made the appearance. Here we see Philo's Platonic thought at work and combining with his knowledge of scripture. God does not have direct contact with the world of matter; his contact with the world is by means of his Logos. God does not speak directly to us; he speaks to us through his Logos.

In sum, for Philo the Logos is an incorporeal being that exists outside God but is his faculty of thinking; on occasion it becomes the actual figure of God who appears "like a man" so that people can know, and interact with, its presence. It is another divine being that is distinct from God in one sense, and yet is God in another.

Humans Who Become Divine

FOR THOSE WHO WANT to know how Jesus could become God in a Jewish religion that insisted on remaining monotheistic, even more important are Jewish texts which indicate that not just angels, hypostases, and other divine entities could be called God, but humans could be as well. As it turns out, such passages can be found even in the Bible. Just as within pagan circles the emperor was thought to be both the son of god and, in some sense, himself god, so too in ancient Judaism the king of Israel was considered both Son of God and—astonishingly enough—even God.

The King of Israel

There is nothing controversial in the claim that the king of Israel was thought of as standing in a uniquely close relationship to God and was in that sense considered the Son of God. This view is found scattered throughout the Hebrew Bible. A key passage occurs in 2 Samuel 7. At this point in the narrative, Israel has already had two kings: the first king, treated with considerable ambivalence in the narrative, Saul, and the great king of Israel's golden age, David. Despite David's many virtues, he had a number of vices as well, and for that reason, when he expressed his wish to build a temple for God, God refused to allow it. The backstory is that since the days of the exodus, more than two centuries earlier, Israel had worshiped God in a portable facility, a large tent, the tabernacle. Now that Israel is firmly ensconced in the land, David wants to build a permanent dwelling place, a house, for God. But God tells him no. Instead, he himself will build a (metaphorical) "house" for David. David will have a son (referring to Solomon) who will build God's temple, and from this son God will raise a house—a dynasty—to David. Moreover, this son of David will be chosen by God himself, adopted as it were, to be his own son: "I will raise up your offspring after you, who shall come forth from your body, and I will establish his kingdom. He shall build a house for my name; and I will establish the throne of his kingdom forever. I will be a father to him, and he shall be a son to me" (2 Sam. 7:12–14).

This idea that God has adopted the king to be his son is consonant with other usages of the term "Son of God" in the Hebrew Bible. We have already seen that angelic beings, the members of God's divine council, were called sons of God. These were divine beings who stood in a specially close relationship with God as his advisors, servants, and ministers—even if some of them did fall from grace on occasion, as in that little episode in Genesis 6. Moreover, the nation of Israel itself is sometimes called the "Son of God," as in Hosea 11:1—"Out of Egypt I called my son." Here again, Israel is God's Son because it stands in a uniquely close relationship with God and as such is the object of his love and special favor; moreover, it is through Israel that God mediates his will on earth.

So too with the king, who stands at the head of Israel and so in an even more special sense is "the" Son of God. In Psalm 89, in which the psalmist indicates that David was anointed by God (that is, literally anointed with oil as a sign of God's special favor; v. 20), he is said to be God's "firstborn, the highest of the kings of earth" (v. 27). Even more remarkable is Psalm 2, in words spoken by God to the king, probably at his coronation ceremony (when he received the anointing with oil): "You are my son; today I have begotten you" (v. 7). In this case the king is not only adopted by God, he is actually *born* of God. God has brought him forth.

The son of a human is human, just as the son of a dog is a dog and the son of a cat is a cat. And so what is the son of God? As it turns out, to the surprise of many casual readers of the Bible, there are passages in which the king of Israel is referred to as divine, as God.

Hebrew Bible scholar John Collins points out that this notion ultimately appears to derive from Egyptian ways of thinking about their king, the Pharaoh, as a divine being.[17] Even in Egypt, where the king was a god, it did not mean that the king was on a par with the great gods, any more than the Roman emperor was thought to be on a par with Jupiter or Mars. But he was a god. As we have seen, in Egyptian and Roman circles, there were *levels* of divinity, and so too in Jewish circles. Thus we find highly exalted terms used of the king of Israel, terms that may surprise readers who think—on the basis of the kind of thinking that developed in the fourth Christian century—that there is an unbridgeable chasm between God and humans. Nonetheless, here it is, in the Bible itself, the king is called both Lord and God.

For example, Psalm 110:1: "The LORD says to my Lord, 'Sit at my right hand until I make your enemies your footstool.'" The first term, LORD—traditionally printed in capital letters in English—is the Hebrew name of God YHWH, often spelled Yahweh. The four Hebrew letters representing that name were considered so special that in traditional Judaism they were not (and are not) pronounced. They are sometimes called the *Tetragrammaton* (Greek for "four letters"). The second term, "Lord," is a different word, *adn* (= *adonai,* or *adoni*), which is a common term for the Lord God but is also a term that could be used, for example, by a slave for his master. What is striking here is that YHWH is speaking to "my Lord" and telling him to "sit at my right hand." Any being enthroned with God is sharing the glory, status, and honor due to God himself. There is not a question of identity or absolute parity here—the king, sitting at God's right hand—is not God Almighty himself. That is clear from what is said next: God will conquer the king's enemies for him and put them under his feet. But he is doing so for one whom he has exalted up to the level of his own throne. The king is being portrayed as a divine being who lives in the presence of God, above all other creatures.

Even more stark is Psalm 45:6–7, in which the king is addressed in the following remarkably exalted terms, as a God:

> *Your throne, O God, endures forever and ever.*
>> *Your royal scepter is a scepter of equity;*
>> *You love righteousness and hate wickedness.*
> *Therefore God, your God, has anointed you*
>> *With the oil of gladness beyond your companions.*

It is clear that the person addressed as "O God" (Elohim) is not God Almighty but the king, because of what is said later: God Almighty is the king's own God and has "anointed" him with oil—the standard act of the king's coronation ceremony in ancient Israel. And so God has both anointed and exalted the king above all others, even to a level of deity. The king is in some sense God. Not equal with God Almighty, obviously (since the differentiation is made clearly, even here), but God nonetheless.

A yet more astonishing example comes in the prophet Isaiah, chapter 9, which celebrates a new king who has been given to the people. Anyone who knows Handel's *Messiah* will recognize the words; but unlike in Handel, the passage in its original context in Isaiah appears to be referring not merely to the birth of the king, but to the birth of the king as the son of God—in other words, it is about his coronation. At this coronation, a "child" has been given to the people—that is, the king has been made the "son of God." But what is said about the king is truly remarkable:

> *For a child has been born for us,*
>> *A son given to us;*
> *Authority rests upon his shoulders;*
>> *And he is named*
> *Wonderful Counselor, Mighty God [El],*
>> *Everlasting Father, Prince of Peace.*

His authority shall grow continually,
And there shall be endless peace
For the throne of David and his kingdom. (Isa 9:6–7)

That this passage is referring to the king of Israel is obvious by the final line. This is a king from the line of David: most scholars think it is a reference to the king at the time of Isaiah's prophecy, King Hezekiah. He is acclaimed as the "son" of God, one with great authority and one who will bring endless peace. Clearly, this person is not God Almighty himself, since his authority is said to "grow continually," and one can hardly imagine God not having final, ultimate, and complete authority from the outset. Nonetheless, the epithets delivered for the king are astounding. He is called "Mighty God" and "Everlasting Father." As the son of God, he is exalted to the level of God and so has God's status, authority, and power—so much so that he can be called God.

Moses as God

It is interesting to note that not only the king of Israel, human as he was, is lauded with divine status and even the term "God," but so too in ancient Jewish texts was that great savior and lawgiver of the people, Moses. The root of this tradition is in the Torah itself, from an intriguing passage in Exodus 4. God is commissioning Moses to go to the Egyptian Pharaoh and demand that he set free the enslaved people of Israel. Moses resists God's demands and says that he is not an eloquent speaker but is "slow of speech and slow of tongue" (Exod. 4:10). God does not accept the excuse: he himself is the one who gives speech to humans. Moses continues to resist, and God finally strikes a compromise: Moses's brother Aaron will accompany him, and Aaron will do all the talking, based on what Moses instructs him. And then God makes this remarkable statement: "[Aaron] indeed shall speak for you to the people; he shall serve as a mouth for you, and you shall serve as

God for him" (Exod. 4:16). Here, Moses is not said actually to *be* God, but he will *function* as God. He will be the one who tells Aaron God's message to be delivered to Pharaoh, and in that sense he will "serve as God."

Some later Jews took this message a step further and claimed that Moses was, in fact, divine. The clearest expression of this view comes in the works of the aforementioned Philo of Alexandria. Philo was deeply imbued in Greek philosophical thought, as we have seen, and was particularly invested in showing how the Jewish scripture, if properly understood by means of allegorical, or figurative, modes of interpretation, presents and supports the teachings of the great Greek philosophers (or rather, how the teachings of the Greek philosophers are already found in the Hebrew Bible). Judaism, for Philo, presented the best of what the greatest philosophers of the world had ever taught.

Philo was highly prolific, and we still have a number of his writings, including a biography of Moses that praises the great lawgiver of the Jews as a highly learned and insightful man. In these and other writings Philo celebrates both Moses and the deeply philosophical law that he proclaimed. For Philo, Moses was "the greatest and most perfect man that ever lived" (*Life of Moses* 1.1). In interpreting the passage laid out above, Exodus 4:16, Philo indicates that Moses appeared to others as a god — but he was not really God in essence (*The Worse Attacks the Better* 161–62). Here, Philo is playing with the idea that there are levels of divinity. In fact, he thought that through his life, Moses "was gradually becoming divine" (*Sacrifices of Abel and Cain* 9–10). Since Moses was a prophet and friend of God, "then it follows that he would naturally partake of God himself and of all his possessions as far as he had need" (*Life of Moses* 1.156). That is why some people had wondered whether Moses did not have a merely human mind but rather "a divine intellect" (*Life of Moses* 1.27).

In the Hebrew Bible, Moses receives the law directly from the hand of God, as he alone ascends Mount Sinai to commune with God (Exod. 19–20). Philo maintained that because of Moses's contemplation of God, "he also enjoyed an even greater communion with the Father and Creator of the universe" (*Life of Moses* 1.158). As a result, Moses was to be God's heir: he would have as his inheritance "the whole world" (*Life of Moses* 1.157). Moreover, even though he was not God Almighty himself, Moses, according to Philo, "was called the god and king of the whole nation" (*Life of Moses* 1.158). Here then we see Moses called what the king of Israel is called—and what, in a different context, the emperor of the Romans was called: god.

Like other specially favored humans who had a particularly close relationship with God—so close that Moses himself could be considered in some sense divine—at the end of his life Moses was highly exalted by God and made immortal: "When he was about to depart from hence to heaven, to take up his abode there, and leaving this mortal life to become immortal, having been summoned by the Father, who now changed him, having previously been a double being composed of soul and body, into the nature of a single body, transforming him wholly and entirely into a most sun-like mind" (*Life of Moses* 2.228).

Or as Philo states even more forcefully elsewhere: "Having given up and left behind all mortal kinds, he is changed into the divine, so that such men become kin to God and truly divine" (*Questions on Exodus* 3.29). Here, then, is a close Jewish analogy to what we have found in pagan sources: a powerful, wise, and great man rewarded after his life by being made divine. At times, Philo goes even further and imagines Moses as a kind of preexistent divine being sent to earth for a time: "And even when [God] sent him as a loan to the earthly sphere and caused him to dwell there, he fitted him with no ordinary excellence, such as that which kings and rulers have, . . . but he appointed him as god, placing all the bodily region and the mind which rules it in subjection and slavery to him" (*Sacrifices* 8–10).

Jewish Divine Men

IT MAY NOT HAVE come as a huge surprise to learn that pagans who held to a range of polytheistic religions sometimes imagined that humans could be divine in some sense. It is more surprising, for most people, to learn that the same is true within Judaism. It is absolutely the case that by the time of Jesus and his followers most Jews were almost certainly monotheists. But even as they believed that there was only one God Almighty, it was widely held that there were other divine beings—angels, cherubim, seraphim, principalities, powers, hypostases. Moreover, there was some sense of continuity—not only discontinuity—between the divine and human realms. And there was a kind of spectrum of divinity: the Angel of the Lord, already in scripture, could be both an angel and God. Angels were divine, and could be worshiped, but they could also come in human guise. Humans could become angels. Humans could be called the Son of God or even God. This did not mean that they were the One God who created heaven and earth; but it did mean that they could share some of the authority, status, and power of that One God.

Thus, even within a strict monotheism, there could be other divine beings and the possibility of a gradation of divinity. And even among Jews at the time of Jesus there was not a sense of an absolute break, a complete divide, an unbridgeable chasm between the divine and the human. So, if one wants to know whether an angel could be thought of as a god, one has to ask, "in what sense?" The same is true with humans. If the king, or Moses, or Enoch as the Son of Man, or anyone else is said or thought to be God, it needs to be explained in what sense this is the case. Is this a person who was adopted by God to be his son? Who was born to a human by divine intervention? Who was made into an angel? Who was exalted to God's throne to be his co-ruler? Or something else?

We will have to ask such questions when exploring early

Christian views of Jesus. Yes, I will argue, soon after Jesus's death, the belief in his resurrection led some of his followers to say he was God. But in what sense? Or rather, in whatever *senses*—plural—since, as we will see, different Christians meant different things by it.

But before we go there, we need first to explore the man Jesus himself—the historical Jesus. Did his followers think he was divine while he was still treading the dusty paths of Galilee? Did he himself think he was divine?

CHAPTER 3

Did Jesus Think He Was God?

W HEN I ATTENDED Moody Bible Institute in the mid-1970s, every student was required, every semester, to do some kind of Christian ministry work. Like most of my fellow students, I was completely untrained and unqualified to do what I did, but I think Moody believed in on-the-job training. And so during one semester we had to devote maybe two to three hours a week to "door-to-door evangelism," trying to convert people cold-turkey, a fundamentalist version of the Mormon missionary, also carried out two-by-two. Another semester I was a late-night counselor on the Moody Christian radio station. People would call up with questions about the Bible or with problems in their lives, and I would, well, give them "all the answers." I was all of eighteen years old. One semester I was a chaplain during one afternoon a week at Cook County Hospital. I was way out of my depth with that one.

Then, when I was a senior, my roommate Bill and I decided that we wanted to do our ministry as youth pastors in a church. Through Moody, we were hooked up with a terrific church in

Oak Lawn, a southern suburb of Chicago. It was Trinity Evangelical Covenant Church—part of a small denomination that
originated as a Swedish pietist movement that split from the Lu-
therans.

Bill and I went to the church on Wednesday evenings, Saturday evenings, and all day Sundays to do the youth pastor sorts of
things—lead prayer groups, Bible studies, social events, retreats,
and so on. Bill did this for a year; I stayed on through my final
two years of college at Wheaton, and so did it for three years altogether. It was a great group of kids (high school and college). I
still have extremely fond memories of those days.

The pastor of the church was pious, wise, and energetic, a
dynamic preacher and a real care-er for souls. His name was Evan
Goranson, and for three years he was my mentor, teaching me the
ropes of ministry. My only problem with Pastor Goranson was
that I thought he was a shade too liberal. (Even Billy Graham was
too liberal for me in those days.) But as a minister, Pastor Goranson was one of the most loving people on the planet, and he was
far more focused on helping people in need (there are always lots
of them in any church of any size) than in fretting and arguing
about religion. And in fact, I now know he had a very traditional,
conservative theology.

Years later, when I was working on an advanced degree at
Princeton Theological Seminary, this form of traditional theology had come to seem less than satisfying to me, as I had begun to
entertain doubts about some of the most fundamental aspects of
the faith, including the question of the divinity of Jesus. During
those intervening years I had come to realize that Jesus is hardly
ever, if at all, explicitly called God in the New Testament. I realized that some of the authors of the New Testament do not
equate Jesus with God. I had become impressed with the fact that
the sayings of Jesus in which he claimed to be God were found
only in the Gospel of John, the last and most theologically loaded

of the four Gospels. If Jesus really went around calling himself God, wouldn't the other Gospels at least mention the fact? Did they just decide to skip that part?

In the throes of my theological doubt, I returned to Chicago to visit Trinity Church and Pastor Goranson. I remember the moment vividly. We were driving in his car, and I began to tell him the doubts I was having about the Bible and about what I had formerly held to be sacrosanct. He was sympathetic, since he had always been a bit more liberal and a whole lot less doctrinaire. His view was that we simply had to hold on to the basics. He told me to remember that Jesus had said, "I am the way, the truth, and the life; no one comes to the Father but by me" (John 14:6). That was all that mattered.

Then I asked him, "But what if Jesus never said that?" He was taken aback and stunned, and, good pastor that he was, tears started to well up in his eyes. It hurt me to see, but what could I do? You can't believe something just because someone else desperately wants you to.

The question in this chapter is, Did Jesus say that? Or other things that are attributed to him? Did he claim to be the one who came down from heaven who could lead people back to the Father? Did he claim that he preexisted? Did he claim that he was equal with God? If he did, then there is a very good reason that his followers did so as well—this is what he taught them. But if he did not claim to be God, then we need to find some other explanation for why his followers did so later, after his death.

The Historical Jesus: Problems and Methods

FOR AN EXHAUSTIVE STUDY of the historical Jesus, we would need not just an entire book, but a whole series of books, such as the massive and impressive four-volume (and counting) set by New Testament scholar and Notre Dame professor John Meier, *A Mar-*

ginal Jew. For readers who prefer something shorter and quicker, there is my book *Jesus: Apocalyptic Prophet of the New Millennium,* or superb treatments by such stalwarts as E. P. Sanders, Geza Vermes, Dale Allison, Paula Fredriksen, and many others.[1] These books all vary in a number of ways, in no small part because their authors are so different from one another in religious persuasion (or lack of persuasion), personality, background, and training. But one thing they all agree on: Jesus did not spend his ministry declaring himself to be divine.

The reason we need books like these is that the Gospels cannot simply be taken at face value as giving us historically reliable accounts of the things Jesus said and did. If the Gospels were those sorts of trustworthy biographies that recorded Jesus's life "as it really was," there would be little need for historical scholarship that stresses the need to learn the ancient biblical languages (Hebrew and Greek), that emphasizes the importance of Jesus's historical context in his first-century Palestinian world, and that maintains that a full understanding of the true character of the Gospels as historical sources is fundamental for any attempt to establish what Jesus really said and did. All we would need to do would be to read the Bible and accept what it says as what really happened. That, of course, is the approach to the Bible that fundamentalists take. And that's one reason why you will not find fundamentalists at the forefront of critical scholarship.

In a few short paragraphs I want to explain both why critical scholars think differently and what approaches to the Gospels they have urged, in view of the fact that the New Testament does not provide stenographic records of Jesus's words or picture-perfect accounts of his life.

Problems with the Gospels
The first thing to stress is that if we want to know about any figure from the past, we need to have sources of information. This may seem obvious enough, but for some reason, when it comes

to Jesus, people seem to think that they simply know who he was, what he said, or what he did—almost as if they gained this knowledge by osmosis from the environment. In fact, however, anything you know about Jesus, or think you know, has come to you from a source—either someone has told you, or you have read what someone has written. But where did these people get their information, what makes them authorities, and why should you think they are right? Every story about Jesus (or any other historical figure) either is historically accurate (something he really said or did) or is made up, or is a combination of the two. And the only way to know whether a detail from Jesus's life is historically accurate is to investigate our sources of information. The sources available to you, me, and your Sunday school teacher are all the same. Stories about Jesus have circulated by word of mouth and in writing since he lived and died. Obviously, stories that began to be told last year for the first time were made up. So too the stories that first began to circulate a hundred years ago. What we want, if we want historically reliable accounts, are sources that can be traced back to Jesus's own time. We want ancient sources.

We do, of course, have ancient sources, but they are not as ancient as we would like. Our very first Christian author is the Apostle Paul, who was writing twenty to thirty years after Jesus's death. A number of Paul's letters are included in the New Testament. Other Christian authors may have been writing earlier than Paul, but none of their works survive. The problems with Paul are that he didn't actually know Jesus personally and that he doesn't tell us very much about Jesus's teachings, activities, or experiences. I sometimes give my students an assignment to read through all of Paul's writings and list everything Paul indicates Jesus said and did. My students are surprised to find that they don't even need a three-by-five card to list them. (Paul, by the way, never says that Jesus declared himself to be divine.)

Our next earliest sources of information about the historical Jesus are the Gospels of the New Testament. As it turns out, these are our best sources. They are best not because they happen to be in the New Testament, but because they are also the earliest narratives of Jesus's life to survive. But even though they are the best sources available to us, they really are not as good as we might hope. This is for several reasons.

To begin with, they are not written by eyewitnesses. We call these books Matthew, Mark, Luke, and John because they are named after two of Jesus's earthly disciples, Matthew the tax collector and John the beloved disciple, and two of the close companions of other apostles, Mark the secretary of Peter and Luke the traveling companion of Paul. But in fact the books were written anonymously—the authors never identify themselves—and they circulated for decades before anyone claimed they were written by these people. The first certain attribution of these books to these authors is a century after they were produced.

There are good reasons for thinking that none of these attributions is right. For one thing, the followers of Jesus, as we learn from the New Testament itself, were uneducated lower-class Aramaic-speaking Jews from Palestine. These books are not written by people like that. Their authors were highly educated, Greek-speaking Christians of a later generation. They probably wrote after Jesus's disciples had all, or almost all, died. They were writing in different parts of the world, in a different language, and at a later time. There's not much mystery about why later Christians would want to *claim* that the authors were in fact companions of Jesus, or at least connected with apostles: that claim provided much needed authority for these accounts for people wanting to know what Jesus was really like.

Scholars typically date the New Testament Gospels to the latter part of the first century. Most everyone would agree that Jesus died sometime around 30 CE. Mark was the first Gospel to be written, probably around 65–70 CE; Matthew and Luke were written about fifteen to twenty years after that, say, 80–85 CE;

and John was written last, around 90–95 CE. What is significant here is the time gap involved. The very first surviving account of Jesus's life was written thirty-five to forty years after his death. Our latest canonical Gospel was written sixty to sixty-five years after his death. That's obviously a lot of time.

If the authors were not eyewitnesses and were not from Palestine and did not even speak the same language as Jesus, where did they get their information? Here again, there is not a lot of disagreement among critical scholars. After Jesus died, his followers came to believe he was raised from the dead, and they saw it as their mission to convert people to the belief that the death and resurrection of Jesus were the death and resurrection of God's messiah and that by believing in his death and resurrection a person could have eternal life. The early Christian "witnesses" to Jesus had to persuade people that Jesus really was the messiah from God, and to do that they had to tell stories about him. So they did. They told stories about what happened at the end of his life—the crucifixion, the empty tomb, his appearances to his followers alive afterward. They also told stories of his life before those final events—what he taught, the miracles he performed, the controversies he had with Jewish leaders, his arrest and trial, and so on.

These stories circulated. Anyone who converted to become a follower of Jesus could and did tell the stories. A convert would tell his wife; if she converted, she would tell her neighbor; if she converted, she would tell her husband; if he converted, he would tell his business partner; if he converted, he would take a business trip to another city and tell his business associate; if he converted, he would tell his wife; if she converted, she would tell her neighbor . . . and on and on. Telling stories was the only way to communicate in the days before mass communication, national media coverage, and even significant levels of literacy (at this time only about 10 percent of the population could read and write, so most communication was oral).

But who, then, was telling the stories about Jesus? Just the apostles? It can't have been just the apostles. Just the people whom the apostles authorized? No way. Just people who checked their facts to make sure they didn't change any of the stories but only recounted events that really happened and as they happened? How could they do that? The stories were being told by word of mouth, year after year, decade after decade, among lots of people in different parts of the world, in different languages, and there was no way to control what one person said to the next about Jesus's words and deeds. Everyone knows what happens to stories that circulate this way. Details get changed, episodes get invented, events get exaggerated, impressive accounts get made even more impressive, and so on.

Eventually, an author heard the stories in his church—say it was "Mark" in the city of Rome. And he wrote his account. And ten or fifteen years later another author in another city read Mark's account and decided to write his own, based partially on Mark but partially on the stories he had heard in his own community. And the Gospels started coming into existence.

Those are the Gospels we now have. Scholars for three hundred years and more have studied them in minute detail, and one of the assured results of this intensive investigation is the certainty that the Gospels have numerous discrepancies, contradictions, and historical problems.[2] Why would that be? It would be better to ask, "How could that *not* be?" Of course, the Gospels contain nonhistorical information and stories that have been modified and exaggerated and embellished. These books do not contain the words of someone who was sitting at Jesus's feet taking notes. They are nothing like that. They are books that are intending to tell the "good news" of Jesus (the word *gospel* means "good news"). That is, their authors had a vested interest both in what they were telling and in how they were telling it. They wanted to preach Jesus. They were not trying to give biographical information that would pass muster among critical historians living two thousand years later who have developed significantly different standards of writing history, or *historiography*. They were writing for their own day and were trying to convince people about the truth—as they saw it—about Jesus. They were basing their stories on what they had heard and read. What they had read was based on what the authors of these other writings had heard. It all goes back to oral tradition.

Some people today claim that cultures rooted in oral tradition are far more careful to make certain that traditions that are told and retold are not changed significantly. This turns out to be a modern myth, however. Anthropologists who have studied oral cultures show that just the opposite is the case. Only literary cultures have a concern for exact replication of the facts "as they really are." And this is because in literary cultures, it is possible to check the sources to see whether someone has changed a story. In oral cultures, it is widely expected that stories will indeed change—they change anytime a storyteller is telling a story in a new context. New contexts require new ways of telling stories. Thus, oral cultures historically have seen no problem with altering accounts as they were told and retold.[3]

So of course there are discrepancies, embellishments, made-up stories, and historical problems in the Gospels. And this means that they cannot be taken at face value as giving us historically accurate accounts of what really happened. Does this mean that the Gospels are useless as historical sources? No, it means that we need to have rigorous historical methods to help us examine books that were written for *one* purpose—to proclaim the "good news" of Jesus—to achieve a *different* purpose: to know what Jesus really said and did.

Methods

Here I can give only a brief summary of the methods that New Testament scholars have devised for dealing with sources of this kind. I should stress that the Gospels are in fact virtually our only available sources.[4] We do not have any accounts of Jesus from Greek or Roman (pagan) sources of the first century, no mention even of his name until more than eighty years after his death. Among non-Christian Jewish sources we have only two brief comments by the Jewish historian Josephus. We do have other Gospels from outside the New Testament, but these were all written later than the New Testament Gospels and as a rule are highly legendary in character. There are a couple of Gospels that may provide us with some additional information—such as the *Gospel of Thomas* and the *Gospel of Peter,* both discovered in modern times—but at the end of the day they actually do not give us much. And so we more or less have our four Gospels.

Nearly everyone agrees that even though these canonical Gospels are highly problematic as sources for the historical Jesus, they nonetheless do contain some historically accurate recollections of what he said, did, and experienced amid all the embellishments and changes. The question is how to ferret out the historically accurate information from the later alterations and inventions.

Scholars have determined that some of our written accounts are independent of one another—that is, they inherited all or some of their stories from independent streams of oral transmission. It is widely thought, for example, that the Gospel of John did not rely on the other three Gospels for its information. The other three, Matthew, Mark, and Luke, are called the *Synoptic Gospels* because they are so much alike. The word *synoptic* means "seen together": these three can be placed in parallel columns on the same page and be seen together, because they tell so many of the same stories, usually in the same sequence and often in the same words. This is almost certainly because the authors were copying each other, or rather—as scholars are almost universally convinced—because two of them, Matthew and Luke, copied the earlier Mark. That is where Matthew and Luke got a lot of their stories. But they share other passages not found in Mark. Most of these other passages are sayings of Jesus. Since the nineteenth century, scholars have mounted formidable arguments that this is because Matthew and Luke had another source available to them that provided them with these non-Markan passages. Since this other source was mainly made up of sayings, these (German) scholars called it the *Sayings Source*. The word for *source* in German is *Quelle,* and so scholars today speak about "Q"—the lost source that provided Matthew and Luke with much of their sayings material.

Matthew has stories not found in any of the other Gospels, and he obviously got them from somewhere, so scholars talk about his M source. So too Luke has unique stories, and the alleged source then is called L. M and L may have each been a single written document; they may have been multiple written documents; they may have been a combination of written and oral sources. But for simplicity's sake, they are just called M and L.

And so among our Gospels we have not only Matthew, Mark, Luke, and John (and, say, the Gospels of Thomas and Peter); we also can isolate Q, M, and L. These three were probably independent of each other and independent of Mark, and John was independent of all of them.

In other words we have numerous streams of tradition that independently all go back, ultimately, to the life of Jesus. In light of this fact—taken as a fact by almost all critical scholars—we are in a position to evaluate which of the Gospel stories are more likely to be authentic than others. If a story is found in several of these independent traditions, then it is far more likely that this story goes back to the ultimate source of the tradition, the life of Jesus itself. This is called the *criterion of independent attestation.* On the other hand, if a story—a saying, a deed of Jesus—is found in only one source, it cannot be corroborated independently, and so it is less likely to be authentic.

Let me give a couple of examples. There is a reference to John the Baptist—a fiery apocalyptic preacher—in close association with Jesus in Mark, John, and Q, all independently. Conclusion? Jesus probably associated with John the Baptist, a fiery apocalyptic preacher. Or an obvious one: Jesus is said to have been crucified under Pontius Pilate in both Mark and John, and there are independent aspects of the story reported in M and L. And so that's probably what happened: he was crucified on order of the Roman governor Pilate. Or take a counterexample. When Jesus was born, we are told in Matthew (this comes from M) that wise men followed a star to come worship him as an infant. Unfortunately, this story is not corroborated by Mark, Q, L, John, or anything else. It *might* have happened, but it can't be *established* as having happened following the criterion of independent attestation.

A second criterion is predicated on the fact that the accounts found in all these independent sources came down to their authors through the oral tradition, in which the stories were changed in the interests of the storytellers—as they were trying to convert others or to instruct those who were converted in the "true" view of things. But if that's the case, then any stories in the Gospels that do not coincide with what we know the early Christians would have wanted to say about Jesus, or indeed, any stories that seem to run directly counter to the Christians' self-interests in telling them, can stake a high claim to being historically accurate. The logic should be obvious. Christians would not have made up stories that work against their views or interests. If they told stories like that, it was simply because that's just the way something actually happened. This methodological principle is sometimes called the *criterion of dissimilarity*. It states that if a tradition about

Jesus is dissimilar to what the early Christians would have wanted to say about him, then it more likely is historically accurate.

Let me illustrate. Jesus is said to have grown up in Nazareth in Mark, M, L, and John; so it is multiply attested. But it also is not a story that a Christian would have been inclined to make up, because it proved to be an embarrassment to later Christians. Nazareth was a small village—a hamlet, really—that no one had ever heard of. Who would invent the idea that the Son of God came from *there*? It's hard to see any reason for someone to make it up, so Jesus probably really did come from there. A second example: the idea that Jesus was baptized by John the Baptist proved discomforting for Christians, because John was baptizing people to show that their sins had been forgiven ("for the remission of sins," as the New Testament puts it). Moreover, everyone knew in the early church that the person doing the baptizing was spiritually superior to the person being baptized. Who would make up a story of the Son of God being baptized because of his sins, or in which someone else was shown to be his superior? If no one would make up the story, why do we have it? Because Jesus really was baptized by John. Or take a counterexample. In Mark, Jesus three times predicts that he has to go to Jerusalem, be rejected, be crucified, and then be raised from the dead. Can you imagine a reason that a Christian storyteller might claim that Jesus said such things in advance of his passion? Of course you can. Later Christians would not have wanted anyone to think Jesus was caught off guard when he ended up being arrested and sent to the cross; they may well have wanted him to predict just what was going to happen to him. These predictions show both that he was raised—as Christians believed—and that he knew he was going to be raised—as they also believed. Since this is precisely the kind of story a Christian would want to make up, we cannot establish that Jesus really made these kinds of predictions. He may have done so, but following this methodological principle of dissimilarity, these predictions cannot be *shown* to have happened.

Finally, scholars are especially keen to consider whether traditions about Jesus can actually fit in a first-century Palestinian Jewish context. Some of the later Gospels from outside the New Testament portray Jesus teaching views that are starkly different from what we can plausibly situate in Jesus's own historical and cultural milieu. Such teachings cannot obviously be accepted as ones that a first-century Palestinian Jew would have spoken. This is called the *criterion of contextual credibility*.

This final criterion insists that we understand Jesus's historical context if we want to understand what he said and did during his life. Any time you take something out of context, you misunderstand it. For situating any historical personage, context is everything. And so, before proceeding further, I need to say a few things about Jesus's context and then about what we can know about his message and proclamation from within that context, applying the methods I have just recounted, in order to see whether he talked about himself as God.

Jesus's Historical and Cultural Context

IN BROADEST TERMS, JESUS needs to be understood as a first-century Jew. In Chapter 2, I discussed the basic religious views of Judaism at the time. Like most Jews, Jesus would have believed that there was one true God, the creator of heaven and earth, who had chosen Israel to be his special people and given them his law. Keeping the law of Moses would have been of paramount importance to Jesus, as it was to all religious Jews of his time. Later controversies are reported in the Gospels when Jesus is said to have violated the law—for example, the law of Sabbath—but in fact it is very difficult to find any instance in which he actually did what the law forbade. What he violated was the understanding and interpretation of the law by other Jewish leaders of his day, especially the Pharisees, who had developed complex rules to be adopted in order to be sure the law was kept. Most Jews didn't follow these additional rules, and Jesus didn't either. To that extent he was probably like most Jews. (The Pharisees were not hypocritical in developing these rules: they simply believed that one should do everything possible to do what God had required and so formulated policies to help make that happen.)[5]

One of the most important aspects of Judaism for understanding the historical Jesus is a widespread worldview shared by many Jews of his time that scholars have called *apocalypticism*. This term comes from the word *apocalypse,* which means a "revealing" or an "unveiling." Jewish apocalypticists believed that God had revealed to them the heavenly secrets that could make sense of earthly realities. In particular, they were convinced that God was very soon to intervene in this world of pain and suffering to overthrow the forces of evil that were in control of this age, and to bring in a good kingdom where there would be no more misery or injustice. This apocalyptic worldview is well attested from Jewish sources around the time of Jesus: it is a view that is prominent among the Dead Sea Scrolls—a collection of writings discovered in 1947, produced by Jews from about the time of Jesus and not far from where he lived—and among other Jewish texts not in the Bible; it was the view of John the Baptist; it was the view of the Pharisees; it was the view widely held throughout Jesus's world. Here I summarize four of the major tenets of this view, before showing that Jesus almost certainly held this view himself.

Dualism

Jewish apocalypticists were dualists—by which I mean that they believed there were two fundamental components of reality: the forces of good and the forces of evil. God, of course, was in charge of all that was good; but for these Jews, God had a personal opponent, the devil, who was in charge of all that was evil. God had angels on his side; the devil had his own evil spirits on his. God had the power to give life and to bestow righteousness; the devil had the power to dispense death and to promote sin. The powers of good and evil, for Jewish apocalypticists, were engaged in a cosmic battle, and everything, and everyone, had to take a side. There was no neutral territory. Everyone was on the side of either good and God or evil and the devil.

This cosmic dualism worked itself out in a historical scenario. The history of this world was divided into two phases: the present age, which was controlled by the forces of evil, and the age to come, in which God would rule supreme. It is not hard to see that the present is an evil age. Just consider all the wars, famines, droughts, hurricanes, earthquakes, birth defects, hatred, oppression, and injustice. The powers of evil are in charge, and they are gaining in strength. But God will intervene to overthrow the forces of evil in a cataclysmic act of judgment, to bring in his good kingdom.

Pessimism

Jewish apocalypticists were pessimistic about the possibilities of improving things in this current evil age. The powers of evil were far more powerful than we mortals, and even though people could resist them, they could not overcome them. No one could make this world, ultimately, a better place—no matter how many good deeds were performed, no matter how many wise political decisions were made, no matter how many helpful technologies were developed. Things were bad in this age, and they were only going to get worse until its end, when literally all hell was going to break loose.

Judgment

But apocalypticists believed that when things got just as bad as they possibly could get, God would intervene in a mighty act of judgment. In the previous chapter we saw that *1 Enoch* described the powerful Son of Man who would be a future cosmic judge of the earth. *First Enoch* embraces this apocalyptic worldview and maintains that indeed a time will come when God will judge all the powers of evil on earth and in heaven through his representative the Son of Man. Other apocalypticists too thought that judgment was coming, that God would destroy the evil powers aligned against him and his people, and that he would vindicate those who had chosen to side with him and had suffered as a result. He would send a savior from heaven, and a new kingdom would arrive to replace the wicked kingdoms of this age. In this kingdom of God there would be no more pain, misery, or suffering, and those who entered the kingdom would live an eternal utopian existence.

This coming judgment would not affect only the people who happened to be living at the time. It would affect both the living and the dead. Apocalypticists came up with the idea that at this climactic act of history, with the arrival of the end of the age, the dead would be resurrected. All people would be brought back into their bodies to face judgment, either punishment or reward. This was a comforting idea for those who had sided with God and were being oppressed by the forces of evil and their earthly representatives as a result. A reward was coming. Moreover, people should not think that they could side with the forces of evil, prosper as a result (since these are the forces in charge of this age), oppress others, become mighty and powerful, and then die and get away with it. No one could get away with it. God was going to raise all people from the dead in order to judge them, whether they were willing or not.

But when would this promised end of the age come? In fact, it was coming very soon.

Imminence

Jewish apocalypticists believed that the world had gotten just about as bad as it could get. The powers of evil were out in full force making life a cesspool of misery for the righteous who sided with God. But they were very near the end. People needed to hold on for just a little while longer and keep the faith. God would soon intervene and set up his good kingdom. But when? How long did they need to wait? "Truly I tell you, some of you standing here will not taste death before they see that the kingdom of God has come in power." Those are the words of Jesus, Mark 9:1. He thought the apocalyptic end would arrive very soon, before his disciples had all died. Or as he says elsewhere, "Truly I tell you, this generation will not pass away before all these things take place" (Mark 13:30).

Jesus is portrayed in our earliest Gospels, the Synoptics, as being an apocalypticist anticipating the imminent end of the age and the arrival of God's good kingdom. But how do we know that this portrayal is right? If the Gospels contain traditions of Jesus that were invented or altered in the course of oral transmission, how can we tell that the apocalyptic traditions were not simply foisted on him by his later followers?

There are in fact good grounds for thinking that Jesus himself, and not just his followers, was thoroughly apocalyptic in his outlook. Recall: we need to apply our rigorous methodological principles to the Gospels to see what is historically accurate in them. When we do so, it becomes clear that Jesus held very strongly to an apocalyptic view, that in fact at the very core of his earthly proclamation was an apocalyptic message. This will be a key factor in seeing how he understood himself, whether as divine or otherwise. Let me explain some of the evidence.[6]

Jesus as an Apocalypticist

I EARLIER POINTED OUT that when establishing historically authentic tradition from the Gospels we are looking for lots of independently attested sayings and deeds. I should add here that in particular we are looking for such independently attested traditions from our earliest sources. Since stories were getting changed over time, the more time that had passed between Jesus's life and the source that narrates his life, the more chance that traditions had been changed and even invented. And so we want our earliest sources. John is the last of the Gospels to be written, some sixty to sixty-five years after Jesus lived. The Synoptic Gospels are earlier. And the *sources* of the Synoptics are even earlier than the Synoptics. If we find traditions independently attested in, say, Mark, our earliest Gospel, and Q, the source for parts of Matthew and Luke, and M and L, the two independent sources (or group of sources) these other two Gospels used, then we have early, independent traditions. And that is as good as it gets.

The Independent Attestation of Jesus's Apocalyptic Message
As it turns out, this is precisely what we have with respect to apocalyptic declarations by Jesus. They are independently attested in all our earliest sources.

From Mark
> And in those days, after that affliction, the sun will grow dark and the moon will not give its light, and the stars will be falling from heaven, and the powers in the sky will be shaken; and then they will see the Son of Man coming on the clouds with great power and glory. And then he will send forth his angels and he will gather his elect from the four winds, from the end of earth to the end of heaven . . . Truly I tell you, this generation will not pass away before all these things take place. (Mark 13:24–27, 30)

From Q

For just as the flashing lightning lights up the earth from one part of the sky to the other, so will the Son of Man be in his day. . . . And just as it was in the days of Noah, so will it be in the days of the Son of Man. They were eating, drinking, marrying, and giving away in marriage, until the day that Noah went into the ark and the flood came and destroyed them all. . . . So too will it be on the day when the Son of Man is revealed. (Luke 17:24, 26–27, 30; see Matt. 24:27, 37–39)

From M

Just as the weeds are gathered and burned with fire, so will it be at the culmination of the age. The Son of Man will send forth his angels, and they will gather from his Kingdom every cause of sin and all who do evil, and they will cast them into the furnace of fire. In that place there will be weeping and gnashing of teeth. Then the righteous will shine forth as the sun, in the Kingdom of their Father. (Matt. 13:40–43)

From L

But take care for yourselves so that your hearts are not overcome with wild living and drunkenness and the cares of this life, and that day come upon you unexpectedly, like a sprung trap. For it will come to all those sitting on the face of the earth. Be alert at all times, praying to have strength to flee from all these things that are about to take place and to stand in the presence of the Son of Man. (Luke 21:34–36)

These are just samples. And I should stress, selecting them to illustrate my point is not simply a matter of willy-nilly picking and choosing the verses that I want. I'm looking for a message that is found independently attested in all our early sources, and it turns out, that's precisely what we find with the apocalyptic proclamations of Jesus.

It is also striking and worth noting that this apocalyptic message comes to be toned down, and then virtually eliminated, and finally preached *against* (allegedly by Jesus!) in our later sources. And it is not hard to figure out why. If Jesus predicted that the imminent apocalypse would arrive within his own generation, before his disciples had all died, what was one to think a generation later when in fact it had not arrived? One might conclude that Jesus was wrong. But if one wanted to stay true to him, one might change the message that he proclaimed so that he no longer spoke about the coming apocalypse. So it is no accident that our final canonical Gospel, John, written after that first generation, no longer has Jesus proclaim an apocalyptic message. He preaches something else entirely. Even later, in a book like the *Gospel of Thomas,* Jesus preaches directly against an apocalyptic point of view (sayings 2, 113). As time went on, the apocalyptic message came to be seen as misguided, or even dangerous. And so the traditions of Jesus's preaching were changed. But in our earliest multiply attested sources, there it is for all to see. Jesus almost certainly delivered some such message. As we will see, this is a significant key for understanding who Jesus actually thought he was: not God, but someone else.

I stress again that it is important that any tradition of Jesus be placed in a plausible first-century Palestinian Jewish context. And there is no doubt that these apocalyptic sayings of Jesus do just that. Apocalypticism was very much in the air, as we know from the Dead Sea Scrolls and other Jewish writings from around the time, such as *1 Enoch* and other apocalypses that have survived. Jesus's message was not altogether unusual for his day. Other Jewish preachers were declaring similar things.

But can this apocalyptic message pass our criterion of dissimilarity? Some scholars have claimed it cannot, that in fact these are words placed on Jesus's lips by his later followers who, unlike him, thought the history of the world was soon to come to a crashing halt. I think this view is flat-out wrong, for two reasons: one is that some of the apocalyptic sayings absolutely do pass the criterion of dissimilarity; the other—this one is a bit more involved—is that the apocalyptic character of Jesus's proclamation can be demonstrated by considering in tandem both how he began his ministry and what happened in its wake.

Dissimilarity and the Message of Jesus

A number of the apocalyptic sayings in our earliest Synoptic sources are not the kinds of things that early Christians would have wanted to place on Jesus's lips. I give you three examples.

First, in the sayings about the "Son of Man" that I quoted above, there is a peculiarity that many people gloss over without thinking about it. This is somewhat complicated, but the issue is this. Early Christians, including the authors of the Gospels, thought that Jesus was the Son of Man, the cosmic judge of the earth who was to return from heaven very soon. The Gospels in fact identify Jesus as the Son of Man in a number of places. Do such identifications pass the criterion of dissimilarity? Obviously not: if you think Jesus is the cosmic judge, you would have no difficulty coming up with sayings in which Jesus is identified as the Son of Man. But what if you have sayings in which Jesus is actually *not* identified as the Son of Man? Even better, what if you have sayings in which it appears that Jesus is talking about someone other than *himself* as the Son of Man? Those are sayings that Christians would have been less likely to make up, since they thought he *was* the Son of Man.

Look again at the sayings given above. In none of them is there any hint that Jesus is talking about himself when he refers to the Son of Man coming in judgment on the earth. Readers naturally assume that he is talking about himself either because they believe that Jesus is the Son of Man or because they know that elsewhere the Gospels identify him as the Son of Man. But nothing in these sayings would lead someone to make the identification. These sayings are not phrased the way early Christians would have been likely to invent if they, rather than Jesus, had come up with them.

Or consider another saying, from Mark 8:38. Pay close attention to the wording: "Whoever is ashamed of me and of my words in this adulterous and sinful generation, of that one will the Son of Man be ashamed when he comes in the glory of his Father with the holy angels." Now, anyone who already thinks that Jesus is the Son of Man may casually assume that here he is talking about himself—whoever is ashamed of Jesus, Jesus will be ashamed of him (that is, he will judge him) when he comes from heaven. But that's not actually what the saying says. Instead, it says that if anyone is ashamed of Jesus, of that person the Son of Man will be ashamed when *he* comes from heaven. Nothing in this saying makes you think that Jesus is talking about himself. A reader who thinks Jesus is talking about himself as the Son of Man has brought that understanding to the text, not taken it from the text.

This is probably not the way an early Christian would have made up a saying about the Son of Man. You can imagine someone inventing a saying in which it is crystal clear that Jesus is talking about himself: "If you do this to me, then I, the Son of Man, will do that to you." But it is less likely that a Christian would make up a saying that seems to differentiate between Jesus and the Son of Man. This means the saying is more likely authentic.

My second example is from one of my favorite passages of the entire Bible, the story of the last judgment of the sheep and the goats (Matt. 25:31–46; this is from M). We are told that the

Son of Man has come in judgment on the earth, in the presence of the angels, and he sits on his throne. He gathers all people before him and separates them "as a shepherd separates the sheep from the goats" (25:32). The "sheep" are on his right side and the "goats" on his left. He speaks first to the sheep and welcomes them to the kingdom of God that has been prepared especially for them. And why are they allowed to enter this glorious kingdom? "Because I was hungry and you gave me food, I was thirsty and you gave me drink, I was a stranger and you welcomed me, I was naked and you clothed me, I was sick and you visited me, I was in prison and you came to me" (25:35–36). The righteous are taken aback and don't understand: they have never done these things for him—in fact they have never even seen him before. The judge tells them, "Truly, I say to you, as you did it to one of the least of these my brethren, you did it to me" (25:40). He then speaks to the "goats" and sends them away to the "eternal fire prepared for the devil and his angels" (25:41), and he tells them why. They didn't feed him when he was hungry, give him a drink when he was thirsty, welcome him as a stranger, clothe him when he was naked, visit him when he was sick and in prison. They too don't understand—they have never seen him before either, so how could they have refused to help him? And to them he says, "Truly, I say, to you, as you did it not to one of the least of these, you did it not to me" (25:45). And so we are told that the sinners go off to eternal punishment and the righteous off to eternal life.

It is a spectacular passage. And it almost certainly is something very close to what Jesus actually said. And why? Because it is not at all what the early Christians thought about how a person gains eternal life. The early Christian church taught that a person is rewarded with salvation by believing in the death and resurrection of Jesus. The Apostle Paul, for example, was quite adamant that people could not earn their salvation by doing the things the law required them to do, or in fact by doing anything at all. If that were possible, there would have been no reason for Christ to have died (see, for example, Gal. 2:15–16, 21). Even in Matthew's Gospel the focus of attention is on the salvation that Jesus brings by his death and resurrection. In this saying of Jesus, however, people gain eternal life not because they have believed in Christ (they have never even seen or heard of the Son of Man), but because they have done good things for people in need. This is not a saying that early Christians invented. It embodies the views of Jesus. The Son of Man will judge the earth, and those who have helped others in need will be the ones who will be rewarded with eternal life.

My third example of a saying that almost certainly passes the criterion of dissimilarity is an apocalyptic saying that will be important for our discussion later in this chapter. In a saying preserved for us in Q, Jesus tells his twelve disciples that in the "age to come, when the Son of Man is seated upon his glorious throne, you also will sit upon twelve thrones judging the twelve tribes of Israel" (Matt. 19:28; see Luke 22:30). It doesn't take much reflection to see why this is something that Jesus is likely to have said—that it was not put on his lips by his later followers after his death. After Jesus died, everyone knew that he had been betrayed by one of his own followers, Judas Iscariot. (That really did happen: it is independently attested all over the map, and it passes the criterion of dissimilarity. Who would make up a story that Jesus had such little influence over his own followers?) But to whom is Jesus speaking in this saying? To all the Twelve (meaning the twelve disciples). Including Judas Iscariot. He is telling them that they all, Judas included, will be rulers in the future kingdom of God. No Christian would make up a saying that indicated that the betrayer of Jesus, Judas Iscariot himself, would be enthroned as a ruler in the future kingdom. Since a Christian would not have made the saying up, it almost certainly goes back to the historical Jesus.

The Beginning and End as the Keys to the Middle

The combination of all these arguments I have mustered have persuaded the majority of critical scholars of the New Testament for more than a century that Jesus is best understood to have proclaimed an apocalyptic message. The final argument that I give now is, in my judgment, the most convincing of them all. It is so good that I wish I had come up with it myself.[7] The argument is that we know with relative certainty how Jesus began his ministry, and we know with equal certainty what happened in its aftermath. The only thing connecting the beginning and the end is the middle—the ministry and proclamation of Jesus himself.

Let me explain. I earlier pointed out that we have good evidence—independent attestation and dissimilarity—of how Jesus began his public life—by being baptized by John the Baptist. And who was John the Baptist? A fiery, apocalyptic preacher proclaiming that the end of the age was coming very soon and that people needed to repent in preparation for it. John's words are best recorded for us in a statement found in the Q document, delivered to the crowds: "Who warned you to flee from the wrath to come? Bear fruits worthy of repentance. . . . Even now the ax is lying at the root of the trees; every tree therefore that does not bear good fruit is cut down and thrown into the fire" (Luke 3:7–9). This is a thoroughly apocalyptic message. Wrath is coming. People need to prepare (by "bearing good fruit"). And if they don't? They will be cut down like a tree and tossed into the fire. When will this happen? It is ready to start at any moment: the ax is already at the root of the tree, and the chopping is ready to begin.

Jesus associated with John the Baptist at the outset of his ministry. Most scholars think Jesus started out as a disciple or follower of John before he broke off on his own. Jesus of course had lots of religious options to him in the religiously diversified world of first-century Judaism—he could have joined the Pharisees, for example, or moved to Jerusalem to focus on the worship in the temple, or joined up with some other religious leader. But he chose to associate with an apocalyptic preacher of coming destruction. It must have been because he agreed with his message. Jesus started out his ministry as an apocalypticist.

But the key to this particular argument is that the aftermath of Jesus's ministry was also apocalyptic in its orientation. What happened immediately after Jesus's life? The Christian church started. His disciples started converting people to believe in him. And what did these early Christians believe? All of our evidence suggests that they too were apocalypticists. They thought that Jesus was soon to return from heaven in judgment on the earth. Our earliest Christian author, as I've pointed out, was Paul. He was thoroughly entrenched in apocalyptic thinking. He was so sure that the end was coming soon that he thought he himself would be alive when judgment day arrived (thus 1 Thess. 4:17; 1 Cor. 15:51–53).

Jesus began his ministry by associating with a fiery apocalyptic preacher, and in the wake of his death enthusiastically apocalyptic communities of followers emerged. The beginning was apocalyptic and the end was apocalyptic. How could the middle not be? If only the beginning were apocalyptic, one could argue that Jesus shifted away from John the Baptist's apocalyptic message— which is why his followers did not subscribe to an apocalyptic view. But they did subscribe to such a view, so that doesn't work. Or if only the end were apocalyptic, one could argue that Jesus himself did not hold such views but that his followers came to subscribe to them afterward, and so they read their views back onto his life. But in fact the beginning of Jesus's ministry *was* heavily apocalyptic, so that doesn't work either. Since Jesus associated with the Baptist at the beginning of his ministry and since apocalyptic communities sprang up in the wake of his ministry, the ministry itself must have been characterized by an apocalyptic proclamation of the imminent arrival of the Son of Man, who would judge the earth and bring in God's good kingdom.

Who Did Jesus Think He Was?

THROUGHOUT THIS DISCUSSION I have been focusing on the character of Jesus's message. I do not, by any stretch of the imagination, want to suggest that his message was all that mattered to the historical Jesus or all that matters to scholars trying to understand his life. But one could argue that the various deeds that Jesus is known to have performed, the various controversies that he was involved with, the various events that led up to his death—all of them make sense within an apocalyptic framework in particular, as fuller studies have shown.[8] My interest in this book, however, is on a theological/religious question of how (and when) Jesus came to be thought of as God. And my argument is that this is not what Jesus himself spent his days teaching and preaching during his public ministry. Quite the contrary, the burden of his message was an apocalyptic proclamation of coming destruction and salvation: he declared that the Son of Man would be coming on the clouds of heaven, very soon, in judgment on the earth, and people needed to prepare for this cataclysmic break in history, as a new kingdom would arrive in which the righteous would be vindicated and rewarded for remaining true to God and doing what God wanted them to do, even when it led to suffering.

But what about Jesus, the messenger himself? What was his role in that coming kingdom? The way I want to begin reflecting on this question is by considering what we know about what Jesus's earliest followers said about him.

The single most common descriptive title that was applied to Jesus in the early years of the Christian movement was the term *Christ*. Sometimes I have to tell my students that Christ was not Jesus's last name. Most people at the time Jesus lived, apart from the upper-crust Roman elite, did not have last names, so he was not Jesus Christ, born to Joseph and Mary Christ. Christ is a title and is, in fact, the Greek translation of the Hebrew word for messiah. Saying Jesus Christ means saying Jesus is the messiah.

There are reasons for thinking that some of Jesus's followers thought of him as the messiah during his lifetime, not simply afterward. And there are further reasons for thinking that Jesus himself said he was the messiah. But to get to these reasons, we first have to examine briefly what the term *messiah* meant to first-century Palestinian Jews.

The Jewish Messiah

We know from various Jewish writings of a number of ways the term *messiah* could be understood.[9] To begin with, I should stress what I mentioned: the word *messiah* in Hebrew means "one who is anointed." And *anointed* in this context always means something like "chosen and specially honored by God." It usually carries with it the connotation "in order to fulfill God's purposes and mediate his will on earth." As we have seen, *1 Enoch* speaks of the Son of Man as the anointed one. This is a somewhat unusual interpretation of the term, in that it applies to the future cosmic judge of the earth; but it makes sense that some Jews would interpret it in this way. Who better could be described as God's special chosen one than that divine, possibly angelic being who would come to destroy the forces of evil and to set up God's kingdom? From *1 Enoch* we know that some Jews clearly did think of this future judge—whether he was called the Son of Man or something else—as God's messiah.

More commonly, though, the term was used to refer not to a divine angelic being, but to a human being. We know from the Dead Sea Scrolls, for example, that some Jews—especially those deeply committed to the ritual laws given in the Torah—had the idea that a future ruler of Israel would be a great and powerful priest; in the Dead Sea Scrolls this priestly ruler is understood to be a messiah. He would be anointed by God and would be an authoritative interpreter of scripture who would rule the people by explaining to them God's laws and enforcing them as need be. This priestly interpretation of the term *messiah* also makes sense because in the Hebrew Bible priests were sometimes said to be anointed by God.

But a much more common understanding of the term did not involve an angelic judge of the earth or an authoritative priest, but a different kind of ruler. Again, as we have already seen: it was the king of Israel who was understood to be God's "anointed one" par excellence. Saul was made the first king of Israel through a ritual ceremony of anointing (1 Sam. 10:1). So too the second king, the great David (1 Sam. 16:13). And so too the successors in his family line.

The key to this most widespread understanding of "messiah" is the promise that God is said to have made to David in 2 Samuel 7, as discussed earlier: he promised that he would "be a father" to the son of David, Solomon. In that sense, the king was the "son of God." But a second thing God promised is just as significant, as he tells David: "Your house and your kingdom shall be made sure forever before me; your throne shall be established forever" (2 Sam. 7:16). This is about as plain as God could make it. David would always have a descendant on the throne. God promised.

As it turns out, descendants of David were on the throne for a very long time—for some four centuries. But sometimes history gets in the way of expectations, and that happened in 586 BCE. That is when the rising political power of Babylon destroyed the nation of Judea—and its capital city Jerusalem, along with the temple of God originally built by Solomon—and removed the Davidic king from his throne.

Later Jews looking back at this disaster wondered how it could have happened. God had promised that even if David's "son" should be disobedient, God would still honor him, and there would always be a king from David's line ruling Israel. But that was no longer the case. Had God gone back on his word? Some Jewish thinkers came to believe that the promise of God was not null and void, but that it was to find fulfillment in some future time. The Davidic king had been temporarily removed from the throne, but God would remember his promise. And so an anointed one was still to come—a future king like David, one of his descendants, who would reestablish the Davidic kingdom and make Israel once more a great and glorious independent state, the envy of all the other nations. This future anointed one—the messiah—would be like his greatest ancestor, a mighty warrior and skilled politician. He would overthrow the oppressors who had taken over the promised land and reestablish both the monarchy and the nation. It would be a glorious time.

It appears that some Jews who had this expectation of the future messiah saw him in political terms: as a great and powerful king who would bring about the restored kingdom through military force, taking up the sword to dispose of his enemies. Other Jews—especially of a more apocalyptic bent—anticipated that this future event would be more miraculous: as an act of God when he personally intervened in the course of history to make Israel once more a kingdom ruled through his messiah. Those who were most avidly apocalyptic believed that this future kingdom would be no ordinary run-of-the-mill political system with all its bureaucracies and corruption, but would in fact be the kingdom of God, a utopian state in which there would be no evil, pain, or suffering of any kind.

Jesus as the Messiah

There is every good reason to think that Jesus's followers, during his lifetime, believed that he might be this coming anointed one. Two pieces of data must be seen in tandem to recognize their full force. The first is one I have already mentioned, that "Christ" (i.e., anointed one; i.e., messiah) was far and away the most common descriptive title the early Christians used for Jesus, so much so that they often called him Christ rather than Jesus (so that, despite my little joke earlier, it really did begin to function as his name). This is very surprising, given the fact that as far as we can tell, Jesus did nothing during his life to make anyone think that he was this anointed one. That is to say, he did not come on the clouds of heaven to judge the living and the dead; he was not a priest; and he never raised an army and drove the Romans out of the promised land to set up Israel as a sovereign state. So why did his followers so commonly designate him by a title that suggested that he had done one of these things?

This question relates to the second datum. Many Christians today assume that the earliest followers of Jesus concluded that he was the messiah because of his death and resurrection: if Jesus died for sins and was raised from the dead, he must be the messiah. But such thinking is precisely wrong, for reasons that you may already have inferred from what I have said to this point. Ancient Jews had no expectation—zero expectation—that the future messiah would die and rise from the dead. That was not what the messiah was supposed to do. Whatever specific idea any Jew had about the messiah (as cosmic judge, mighty priest, powerful warrior), what they all thought was that he would be a figure of grandeur and power who would be a mighty ruler of Israel. And Jesus was certainly not that. Rather than destroying the enemy, Jesus was destroyed by the enemy—arrested, tortured, and crucified, the most painful and publicly humiliating form of death known to the Romans. Jesus, in short, was just the *opposite* of what Jews expected a messiah to be.

At a later point, Christians began heated and prolonged arguments with Jews over this issue, with the Christians claiming that in fact the Hebrew Bible predicted that the future messiah would die and be raised from the dead. They pointed to passages in the Bible that talked about one who suffered and was then vindicated, passages such as Isaiah 53 and Psalm 22. Jews, though, had a ready response: these passages are not talking about the messiah. And you can see by reading them for yourself, in fact the word *messiah* never occurs in them.

Whether or not you choose to understand these passages as referring to the messiah, even though they make no explicit reference to the messiah, is beside my point at this stage. My point here is that no Jew before Christianity was on the scene ever interpreted such passages as referring to the messiah. The messiah was to be a figure of great strength who overwhelmed the enemy and set up God's kingdom; but Jesus was squashed by the enemy. For most Jews, this was decisive enough. Jesus wasn't the messiah, more or less by definition.

But this leads now to the problem. If belief that Jesus had died for sins and been raised from the dead would not make any Jew think that he therefore must be the messiah, how do we account for the fact that Christians immediately started proclaiming—not despite his death, but because of his death—that he was the messiah? The only plausible explanation is that they called Jesus this after his death because they were calling him this before his death.

Here is what many scholars take to be the most reasonable scenario. During his life, Jesus raised hopes and expectations that he might be the messiah. His disciples expected great things from him. Possibly he would raise an army. Possibly he would call down the wrath of God on the enemy. But he would do *something* and would be the future ruler of Israel. The crucifixion completely disconfirmed this idea and showed the disciples just how wrong they were. Jesus was killed by his enemies, so he wasn't the messiah after all. But then they came to believe that Jesus had been raised from the dead, and this reconfirmed what had earlier been disconfirmed. He really is the messiah. But not in the way we thought!

I will pursue this line of thinking in the next two chapters, as I explore belief in Jesus's resurrection. At this stage I want simply to make the most basic point. Jesus's followers must have considered him to be the messiah in some sense before his death, because nothing about his death or resurrection would have made them come up with the idea afterward. The messiah was not supposed to die or rise again.

Jesus's Messianic Self-Understanding

IN VIEW OF THIS discussion, what can we say about how Jesus most likely understood himself? Did he call himself the messiah? If so, what did he mean by it? And did he call himself God? Here I want to stake out a clear position: messiah, yes; God, no.

I think there are excellent reasons for thinking that Jesus imagined himself as the messiah, in a very specific and particular sense. The messiah was thought to be the future ruler of the people of Israel. But as an apocalypticist, Jesus did not think that the future kingdom was going to be won by a political struggle or a military engagement per se. It was going to be brought by the Son of Man, who came in judgment against everyone and everything opposed to God. Then the kingdom would arrive. And I think Jesus believed he himself would be the king in that kingdom.

I have several reasons for thinking so. First let me go back to my earlier point about the disciples. They clearly thought and talked about Jesus as the messiah during his earthly life. But in fact he did nothing to make a person think that he was the messiah. He may well have been a pacifist ("love your enemy," "turn the other cheek," "blessed are the peacemakers," etc.), which would not exactly make him a leading candidate to be general over the Jewish armed forces. He did not preach the violent over-throw of the Roman armies. And he talked about someone else, rather than himself, as the coming Son of Man. So if nothing in what Jesus was actively doing would make anyone suspect that he had messianic pretensions, why would his followers almost certainly have been thinking about him and calling him the messiah during his public ministry? The easiest explanation is that Jesus told them that he was the messiah.

But what he meant by "messiah" has to be understood within the broader context of his apocalyptic proclamation. This is where one of the sayings of Jesus that I earlier established as almost certainly authentic comes into play. As we have seen, Jesus told his disciples—Judas Iscariot included—that they would be seated on twelve thrones ruling the twelve tribes of Israel in the future kingdom. Well enough. But who would be the ultimate king? Jesus was their master (= lord) now. Would he not be their master (= Lord) then? He is the one who called them, instructed them, commissioned them, and promised them thrones in the kingdom. It is almost unthinkable that he did not imagine that he too would have a role to play in that kingdom, and if he was the leader of the disciples now, he certainly would be the leader of the disciples then. Jesus must have thought that he would be the king of the kingdom of God soon to be brought by the Son of Man. And what is the typical designation for the future king of Israel? Messiah. It is in this sense that Jesus must have taught his disciples that he was the messiah.

Two other considerations render this judgment even more certain. The first has again to do with Judas Iscariot, the Jewish bad guy in the stories of the Gospels; the second involves Pontius Pilate, the Roman bad guy. First, about Judas. There has been endless speculation about who Judas Iscariot was—to the extent of wondering what *Iscariot* is supposed to mean—and about why he betrayed Jesus.[10] As I pointed out, there is no doubt that Judas did betray Jesus (the betrayal passes all our criteria), but why did he do it? There are lots of theories about this, but they are not germane to the point I want to make here. Rather, I want to reflect on what it was that Judas actually betrayed.

According to the Gospels, it was very simple. When Jesus had come to Jerusalem during the last week of his life to celebrate the annual Passover meal in the capital city, he caused a disturbance in the temple—predicting in good apocalyptic fashion that it would be destroyed in the coming judgment. This made the local authorities sit up and take notice. The Jewish leaders who were in charge of the temple and of civil life within Jerusalem were known as the Sadducees. These were aristocratic Jews, many of them priests who ran the temple and its sacrifices; among their number was the chief official, the high priest. The priests were invested in maintaining order among the people, in no small measure because the Romans who were in charge allowed local aristocrats to run their own affairs and to do things as they wanted as long as there were no local disturbances. But Passover was an incendiary time; the festival itself was known to stir up nationalistic sentiment and thoughts of rebellion.

That's because the Passover feast commemorated that episode from the Hebrew Bible when God delivered the people of Israel from slavery in Egypt under the leadership of Moses. Every year the exodus event was celebrated as Jews from around the world remembered that God had intervened on their behalf in order to save them from foreign domination. The festival, climaxing with the special meal—the Passover seder, as it came to be called—was not simply celebrated out of antiquarian interests. Many Jews hoped and even anticipated that what God had done before, long ago, under Moses, he would do again, in their own day, under one of their own leaders. Everyone knew that uprisings could occur when nationalistic passions reached a fevered pitch. So this was one time of the year when the Roman governor of Judea, who normally lived in the coastal city of Caesarea, would come to Jerusalem with troops, to quell any possible riots. The Sadducees, who were willing to cooperate with the Romans in exchange for being able to maintain the worship of God in the temple as God had instructed in the Torah, were equally invested in keeping the peace.

So what were they to think when this outsider from Galilee, Jesus of Nazareth, appeared in town, preaching his fiery apocalyptic message of the coming destruction of the armed forces and predicting that their own beloved temple would be destroyed in the violent overthrow of everything that was opposed to God? They surely did not take kindly to the message or the messenger, and they kept a steady eye on him.

According to all our accounts, Jesus spent the week leading up to the Passover feast in Jerusalem preaching his apocalyptic message of coming destruction (see Mark 13; Matt. 24–25). It appears that he was gathering more and more crowds. People were listening to him. Some were accepting his message. The movement was growing. So the leaders decided to act.

This is where Judas Iscariot comes in. In the Gospels, Judas appears to have been hired to lead the authorities to Jesus so they could arrest him when the crowds were not around. I've always been suspicious of these accounts. If the authorities wanted to arrest Jesus quietly, why not just have him followed? Why did they need an insider?

There are reasons for thinking that in fact Judas betrayed something else. Here there are two facts to bear in mind. The first is to reaffirm that we have no record of Jesus ever proclaiming himself to be the future king of the Jews, the messiah, in a public context. This is never his message. His message is about the coming kingdom to be brought by the Son of Man. He always keeps himself out of it. The second fact is that when the authorities arrested Jesus and handed him over to Pontius Pilate, the consistent report is that the charge leveled against him at his trial was that he called himself the king of the Jews. If Jesus never preached in public that he was the future king, but this was the charge that was leveled against him at his trial, how did outsiders come to know of it?[11] The simplest answer is that this is what Judas betrayed.

Judas was one of the insiders to whom Jesus disclosed his vision of the future. Judas and the eleven others would all be rulers in the future kingdom. And Jesus would be the king. For some reason—we'll never know why—Judas became a turncoat and betrayed both the cause and his master.[12] He told the Jewish authorities what Jesus was actually teaching in private, and it was all they needed. They had him arrested and turned him over to the governor. Here was someone who was declaring himself to be king.

And now a word about Pontius Pilate. As governor of Judea, Pilate had the power of life and death. The Roman empire did not have anything like federal criminal law, such as can be found in many countries today. Governors were appointed to rule the various provinces and had two major tasks: to collect taxes for Rome and to keep the peace. They could achieve these two goals by any means necessary. So, for instance, anyone who was considered to be a troublemaker could be dealt with ruthlessly and swiftly. The governor could order his death, and the order would be immediately carried out. There was no such thing as due process, trial by jury, or the possibility of appeal. Problematic people in problematic times were dealt with by means of swift and decisive "justice," usually violent justice.

According to our accounts, the trial of Jesus before Pilate was short and to the point. Pilate asked him whether it was true that he was the king of the Jews. Almost certainly, this was the actual charge leveled against Jesus. It is multiply attested in numerous independent witnesses, both at the trial itself and as the charge written on the placard that hung with him on his cross (e.g., Mark 15:2, 26). Moreover, it is not a charge that Christians would have invented for Jesus—for a possibly unexpected reason. Even though Christians came to understand Jesus to be the messiah, they never ever, from what we can tell, applied to him the title "king of the Jews." If Christians were to *invent* a charge to put on Pilate's lips, it would be, "Are you the messiah?" But that's not how it works in the Gospels. The charge is specifically that he called himself "king of the Jews."

Evidence that Jesus really did think that he was the king of the Jews is the very fact that he was killed for it. If Pilate asked him whether he were in fact calling himself this, Jesus could have simply denied it, and indicated that he meant no trouble and that he had no kingly expectations, hopes, or intentions. And that would have been that. The charge was that he was calling himself the king of the Jews, and either he flat-out admitted it or he refused to deny it. Pilate did what governors typically did in such cases. He ordered him executed as a troublemaker and political pretender. Jesus was charged with insurgency, and political insurgents were crucified.

The reason Jesus could not have denied that he called himself the king of the Jews was precisely that he did call himself the king of the Jews. He meant that, of course, in a purely apocalyptic sense: when the kingdom arrived, he would be made the king. But Pilate was not interested in theological niceties. Only the Romans could appoint someone to be king, and anyone else who wanted to be king had to rebel against the state.

And so Pilate ordered Jesus crucified on the spot. According to our records, which are completely believable at this point, the soldiers roughed him up, mocked him, flogged him, and then led him off to be crucified. Evidently, two similar cases were decided that morning. Maybe a couple more the day after that and the day after that. In this instance, they took Jesus and the two others to a public place of execution and fixed them all to crosses. According to our earliest account, Jesus was dead in six hours.

Did Jesus Claim to Be God?

THIS, THEN, IN A nutshell is what I think we can say about the historical Jesus and his understanding of himself. He thought he was a prophet predicting the end of the current evil age and the future king of Israel in the age to come. But did he call himself God?

It is true that Jesus claims to be divine in the last of our canonical Gospels to be written, the Gospel of John. We will look at the relevant passages at length in Chapter 7. But here it is enough to note that in that Gospel Jesus does make remarkable claims about himself. In speaking of the father of the Jews, Abraham (who lived eighteen hundred years earlier), Jesus tells his opponents, "Truly I tell you, before Abraham was, I am" (8:58). This particular phrase, "I am," rings a familiar chord to anyone acquainted with the Hebrew Bible. In the book of Exodus, in the story of the burning bush that we considered in Chapter 2, Moses asks God what his name is, and God tells him that his name is "I am." Jesus appears to be claiming not only to have existed before Abraham, but to have been given the name of God himself. His Jewish opponents know exactly what he is saying. They immediately take up stones to stone him.

Later in the Gospel, Jesus is even more explicit, as he proclaims "I and the Father are one" (John 10:30). Once again, the Jewish listeners break out the stones. Still later, when Jesus is talking to his disciples at his last meal with them, his follower Philip asks him to show them who God the Father is; Jesus replies, "The one who has seen me has seen the Father" (14:9). And again later, during the same meal, Jesus prays to God and speaks about how God had "sent him" into the world and refers to "my glory that you gave me . . . before the foundation of the world" (17:24).

Jesus is not claiming to be God the Father here, obviously (since when he's praying, he is not talking to himself). So he is not saying that he is identical with God. But he is saying that he is equal with God and has been that way from before the world was created. These are amazingly exalted claims.

But looked at from a historical perspective, they simply cannot be ascribed to the historical Jesus. They don't pass any of our criteria. They are not multiply attested in our sources; they appear only in John, our latest and most theologically oriented Gospel. They certainly do not pass the criterion of dissimilarity since they express the very view of Jesus that the author of the Gospel of John happens to hold. And they are not at all contextually credible. We have no record of any Palestinian Jew ever saying any such things about himself. These divine self-claims in John are part of John's distinctive theology; they are not part of the historical record of what Jesus actually said.

Look at the matter in a different light. As I pointed out, we have numerous earlier sources for the historical Jesus: a few comments in Paul (including several quotations from Jesus's teachings), Mark, Q, M, and L, not to mention the finished Gospels of Matthew and Luke. In none of them do we find exalted claims of this sort. If Jesus went around Galilee proclaiming himself to be a divine being sent from God—one who existed before the creation of the world, who was in fact equal with God—could anything *else* that he might say be so breathtaking and thunderously important? And yet none of these earlier sources says any such thing about him. Did they (all of them!) just decide not to mention the one thing that was most significant about Jesus?

Almost certainly the divine self-claims in John are not historical. But is it possible that Jesus considered himself divine in some other sense? I have already argued that he did not consider himself to be the Son of Man, and so he did not consider himself to be the heavenly angelic being who would be the judge of the earth. But he did think of himself as the future king of the kingdom, the messiah. And we saw in the previous chapter that in some passages of scripture the king is talked about as a divine being, not a mere mortal. Isn't it possible that Jesus understood himself as divine in *that* sense?

It is of course possible, but I think it is highly unlikely for the following reason. In the Hebrew Bible, and indeed in the entire Jewish tradition, we do have instances in which mortals—for example, a king, or Moses, or Enoch—were considered to be divine beings in some sense. But that was always what someone else said about them; it was never what they were recorded as saying about themselves. This is quite different from the situation that we find in, say, Egypt, where the pharaohs claimed direct divine lineage; or with Alexander the Great, who accepted cultic veneration; or with some of the Roman emperors, who actively propagated the idea that they were gods. This never happens in Judaism that we know of. The idea that a king could be divine may have occurred to his followers later, as they began to think more about his eminence and significance. But we have no known instance of a living Jewish king proclaiming himself to be divine.

Could Jesus be the exception? Yes, of course; there are always exceptions to everything. But to think that Jesus is the exception in this case, one would need a good deal of persuasive evidence. And it just doesn't exist. The evidence for Jesus's claims to be divine comes only from the last of the New Testament Gospels, not from any earlier sources.

Someone may argue that there are other reasons, apart from explicit divine self-claims, to suspect that Jesus saw himself as divine. For example, he does amazing miracles that surely only a divine figure could do; and he forgives people's sins, which surely is a prerogative of God alone; and he receives worship, as people bow down before him, which surely indicates that he welcomes divine honors.

There are two points to stress about such things. The first is that all of them are compatible with human, not just divine, authority. In the Hebrew Bible the prophets Elijah and Elisha did fantastic miracles—including healing the sick and raising the dead—through the power of God, and in the New Testament so did the Apostles Peter and Paul; but that did not make any of them divine. When Jesus forgives sins, he never says "I forgive you," as God might say, but "your sins are forgiven," which means that *God* has forgiven the sins. This prerogative for pronouncing sins forgiven was otherwise reserved for Jewish priests in honor of sacrifices that worshipers made at the temple. Jesus may be claiming a priestly prerogative, but not a divine one. And kings were worshiped—even in the Bible (Matt. 18:26)—by veneration and obeisance, just as God was. Here, Jesus may be accepting the worship due to him as the future king. None of these things is, in and of itself, a clear indication that Jesus is divine.

But even more important, these activities may not even go back to the historical Jesus. Instead, they may be traditions assigned to Jesus by later storytellers in order to heighten his eminence and significance. Recall one of the main points of this chapter: many traditions in the Gospels do not derive from the life of the historical Jesus but represent embellishments made by storytellers who were trying to convert people by convincing them of Jesus's superiority and to instruct those who were converted. These traditions of Jesus's eminence cannot pass the criterion of dissimilarity and are very likely later pious expansions of the stories told about him—told by people who, after his resurrection, did come to understand that he was, in some sense, divine.

What we can know with relative certainty about Jesus is that his public ministry and proclamation were not focused on his divinity; in fact, they were not about his divinity at all. They were about God. And about the kingdom that God was going to bring.

And about the Son of Man who was soon to bring judgment upon the earth. When this happened the wicked would be destroyed and the righteous would be brought into the kingdom—a kingdom in which there would be no more pain, misery, or suffering. The twelve disciples of Jesus would be rulers of this future kingdom, and Jesus would rule over them. Jesus did not declare himself to be God. He believed and taught that he was the future king of the coming kingdom of God, the messiah of God yet to be revealed. This was the message he delivered to his disciples, and in the end, it was the message that got him crucified. It was only afterward, once the disciples believed that their crucified master had been raised from the dead, that they began to think that he must, in some sense, be God.

CHAPTER 4

The Resurrection of Jesus

What We Cannot Know

I GIVE A LOT OF lectures around the country every year, not just at colleges and universities, but also for civic organizations, divinity schools, and churches. When I get invited to speak at a conservative evangelical school or church, it is almost always for a public debate, in which I am asked to engage with a conservative evangelical scholar on some topic of mutual interest, such as: "Can Historians Prove That Jesus Was Raised from the Dead?" or "Do We Have the Original Text of the New Testament?" or "Does the Bible Adequately Explain Why There Is Suffering?" For obvious reasons, these kinds of audiences tend to be less interested in hearing what I have to say than in seeing how a scholar of their own theological persuasion can respond to and refute my views. I understand that and actually enjoy these venues: the debates tend to be lively, and the audiences are almost always receptive and gracious, even if they think I'm a dangerous spokesperson for the dark side.

In more liberal churches and secular contexts I typically have free reign and more receptive audiences, who are eager to hear what scholars have to say about the history of the early Christian religion and about the New Testament from a historical perspective. I often speak, in those contexts, about the historical Jesus, laying out the view summarized in the previous chapter—that Jesus is best understood as an apocalyptic prophet who was anticipating that God was soon to intervene in human affairs to overthrow the forces of evil and set up a good kingdom here on earth. As we have seen, this view was not unique to Jesus but could be found in the teachings of other apocalyptically minded Jews of his day.

When I deliver talks like this, I regularly and consistently get two questions from members of the audience. The first is, "If this is the view widely held among scholars, why have I never heard it before?" I'm afraid that this question has an easy but troubling answer. In most instances the view of Jesus that I have is similar to that taught—with variations here or there, of course—to ministerial candidates in the mainline denominational seminaries (Presbyterian, Lutheran, Methodist, Episcopalian, and so on). So why have their parishioners never heard it before? Because their pastors haven't told them. And why haven't their pastors told them? I don't know for sure, but from my conversations with former seminarians, I think that many pastors don't want to make waves; or they don't think their congregations are "ready" to hear what scholars are saying; or they don't think that their congregations *want* to hear it. So they don't tell them.

The second question is somewhat more intellectually challenging: "If other Jews in Jesus's day taught this apocalyptic view, then . . . why Jesus? Why is it that Jesus started Christianity, the largest religion in the world, when other apocalyptic teachers are forgotten to history? Why did Jesus succeed where others failed?"

It's a great question. Sometimes a person asking it thinks there is an obvious answer, namely, that Jesus must have been unique and completely *unlike* all the others who proclaimed this message.

He was God, and they were humans, so of course he started a new religion and they didn't. In this line of thinking, the only way to explain the enormous success of Christianity is to believe that God actually was behind it all.

The problem with this answer is that it ignores all the other great religions of the world. Do we want to say that all great and successful religions come from God himself and that their founders were "God"? Was Moses God? Mohammed? Buddha? Confucius? Moreover, the rapid spread of Christianity throughout the ancient Roman world is not necessarily an indication that God was on its side. Those who say so should think again about other religions of our world. Just as an example: the sociologist Rodney Stark has shown that during its first three hundred years, the Christian religion grew at a rate of 40 percent every decade. If Christianity started out as a relatively small group in the first century but had some three million followers by the early fourth century—that's a 40 percent increase every ten years. What is striking to Stark is that this is the same growth rate of the Mormon church since it started in the nineteenth century. So these mainline Christians who think that God must have been behind Christianity or it would not have grown as quickly as it did—are they willing to say the same thing about the Mormon church (which they in fact tend not to support)?

And so we are left with our question: What is it that made Jesus so special? In fact, as we will see, it was not his message. That did not succeed much at all. Instead, it helped get him crucified—surely not a mark of spectacular success. No, what made Jesus different from all the others teaching a similar message was the claim that he had been raised from the dead. Belief in Jesus's resurrection changed absolutely everything. Such a thing was not said of any of the other apocalyptic preachers of Jesus's day, and the fact that it was said about Jesus made him unique. Without the belief in the resurrection, Jesus would have been a mere footnote in the annals of Jewish history. With the belief in the resurrection, we have the beginnings of the movement to promote Jesus to a superhuman plane. Belief in the resurrection is what eventually led his followers to claim that Jesus was God.

You will notice that I have worded the preceding sentences very carefully. I have not said that the *resurrection* is what made Jesus God. I have said that it was the *belief* in the resurrection that led some of his followers to *claim* he was God. This is because, as a historian, I do not think we can show—historically—that Jesus was in fact raised from the dead. To be clear, I am not saying the opposite either—that historians can use the historical disciplines in order to demonstrate that Jesus was *not* raised from the dead. I argue that when it comes to miracles such as the resurrection, historical sciences simply are of no help in establishing exactly what happened.

Religious faith and historical knowledge are two different ways of "knowing." When I was at Moody Bible Institute, we affirmed wholeheartedly the words of Handel's *Messiah* (taken from the book of Job in the Hebrew Bible): "I know that my Redeemer liveth." But we "knew" this not because of historical investigation, but because of our faith. Whether Jesus is still alive today, because of his resurrection, or indeed whether any such great miracles have happened in the past, cannot be "known" by means of historical study, but only on the basis of faith. This is not because historians are required to adopt "unbelieving presup-positions" or "secular assumptions hostile to religion." It is purely the result of the nature of historical inquiry itself—whether un-dertaken by believers or unbelievers—as I will try to explain later in this chapter.

At the same time, historians are able to talk about events that are not miraculous and that do not require faith in order to know about them, including the fact that some of the followers of Jesus (most of them? all of them?) came to *believe* that Jesus was physically raised from the dead. That belief is a historical fact. But other aspects of the accounts of Jesus's death are historically problematic. In this chapter and the next I discuss both the facts we can know and the claims we cannot know, historically. We begin with what we are *not* able to say, either at all or with relative certainty, about the early Christian belief in the resurrection.

Why Historians Have Difficulty Discussing the Resurrection

I HAVE STRESSED THAT historians, in order to investigate the past, are necessarily restricted to doing so on the basis of surviving sources. There are sources that describe the events surrounding Jesus's resurrection, and the first step to take in exploring the rise of the Christians' early belief is to examine these sources. The most important ones are the Gospels of the New Testament, which are our earliest narratives of the discovery of Jesus's empty tomb and of his appearances, after his crucifixion, to his disciples as the living Lord of life. Also critical to our exploration are the writings of Paul, who affirms with real fervor his belief that Jesus was actually, physically, raised from the dead.

The Resurrection Narratives of the Gospels
We have already seen why the Gospels are so problematic for historians who want to know what really happened. This is especially true for the Gospel accounts of Jesus's resurrection. Are these the *sorts* of sources that historians would look for when examining a past event? Even apart from the fact that they were written forty to sixty-five years after the facts, by people who were not there to see these things happen, who were living in different parts of the world, at different times, and speaking different languages—apart from all this, they are filled with discrepancies, some of which cannot be reconciled. In fact, the Gospels disagree on nearly every detail in their resurrection narratives.

These narratives are found in Matthew 28, Mark 16, Luke 24, and John 20–21. Read through the accounts and ask yourself some basic questions: Who was the first person to go to the tomb? Was it Mary Magdalene by herself (John)? or Mary along with another Mary (Matthew)? or Mary along with another Mary and Salome (Mark)? or Mary, Mary, Joanna, and a number of other women (Luke)? Was the stone already rolled away when they arrived at the tomb (Mark, Luke, and John), or explicitly not (Matthew)? Whom did they see there? An angel (Matthew), a man (Mark), or two men (Luke)? Did they immediately go and tell some of the disciples what they had seen (John), or not (Matthew, Mark, and Luke)? What did the person or people at the tomb tell the women to do? To tell the disciples that Jesus would meet them in Galilee (Matthew and Mark)? Or to remember what Jesus had told them earlier when *he* had been in Galilee (Luke)? Did the women then go tell the disciples what they were told to tell them (Matthew and Luke), or not (Mark)? Did the disciples see Jesus (Matthew, Luke, and John), or not (Mark)?[1] Where did they see him?—only in Galilee (Matthew), or only in Jerusalem (Luke)?

There are other discrepancies, but this is enough to get the point across. I should stress that some of these differences can scarcely be reconciled unless you do a lot of interpretive gymnastics when reading the texts. For example, what does one do with the fact that the women apparently meet different people at the tomb? In Mark, they meet one man; in Luke, two men; and in Matthew, one angel. The way this discrepancy is sometimes reconciled, by readers who can't accept that there could be a genuine discrepancy in the text, is by saying that the women actually met two angels at the tomb. Matthew mentions only one of them but never denies there was a second one; moreover, the angels were in human guise, so Luke claims they were two men; Mark also mistakes the angels as men but mentions only one, not two, without denying there were two. And so the problem is easily solved! But it is solved in a very curious way indeed, for this solution is saying, in effect, that what really happened is what is not narrated by *any* of these Gospels: for none of them mentions two angels! This way of interpreting the texts does so by imagining a new text that is unlike any of the others, so as to reconcile the four to one another. Anyone is certainly free to construct their own Gospel if they want to, but that's probably not the best way to interpret the Gospels that we already have.

Or take a second example—one that is even more glaring. Matthew is explicit when he says that the disciples are told to go to Galilee since that is where they will meet Jesus (28:7). They do so (28:16), and that is where Jesus meets them and gives them his final commands (28:17–20). This is both clear-cut and completely at odds with what happens in Luke. There, the disciples are not told to go to Galilee. The women are informed at the empty tomb, by the two men, that when Jesus had earlier *been* in Galilee, he had announced that he would be raised. Since the disciples are not told to go to Galilee, they do not do so. They stay in Jerusalem, in the land of Judea. And it is there that Jesus meets them "that very day" (24:13). Jesus speaks with them and emphatically instructs them *not* to leave the city until they receive the power of the Spirit, which happens more than forty days later, according to Acts 1–2 (that is, they are *not* to go to Galilee; 24:49). He leads them right outside Jerusalem, to nearby Bethany, and gives them his last instructions and departs from them (24:50–51). And we learn they did as he commanded: they stayed in the city, worshiping in the temple (24:53). In the book of Acts, written by the same author as the book of Luke, we find out that they stayed in Jerusalem for more than a month, until the day of Pentecost (Acts 1–2).

There is clearly a discrepancy here. In one Gospel the disciples immediately go to Galilee, and in the other they never go there. As New Testament scholar Raymond Brown—himself a Roman

Catholic priest—has emphasized: "Thus we must reject the thesis that the Gospels can be harmonized through a rearrangement whereby Jesus appears several times to the Twelve, first in Jerusalem, then in Galilee. . . . The different Gospel accounts are narrativing, so far as substance is concerned, the *same* basic appearance to the Twelve, whether they locate it in Jerusalem or in Galilee."[2]

Later we will explore further how this discrepancy matters for reconstructing the actual course of events. For now it is enough to note that the earliest Gospels say that when Jesus was arrested, his disciples fled the scene (Mark 14; Matt. 24:46). And the earliest accounts also suggest that it was in Galilee that they had visions of Jesus alive after the crucifixion (intimated in Mark 14:28; stated in Matthew 24). The most plausible explanation is that when the disciples fled the scene for fear of arrest, they left Jerusalem and went home, to Galilee. And it was there that they—or at least one or more of them—claimed to see Jesus alive again.

Some people have argued that if Jesus really was raised from the dead, it would have been such a spectacular event that of course in their excitement the eyewitnesses would have gotten a few details muddled. But my points in the discussion so far are rather simple. First, we are not dealing with eyewitnesses. We are dealing with authors living decades later in different lands speaking different languages and basing their tales on stories that had been in oral circulation during all the intervening years. Second, these accounts do not simply have minor discrepancies in a couple of details; they are clearly at odds with one another on point after point. They are not the kinds of sources that historians would hope for in determining what actually happened in the past. What about the witness of Paul?

The Writings of the Apostle Paul
Paul speaks of the resurrection of Jesus constantly throughout the seven letters that scholars agree he actually wrote.[3] No passage

states Paul's views more clearly or forcefully than 1 Corinthians 15, the so-called resurrection chapter. In this chapter Paul is not intent on "proving" that Jesus was raised from the dead, as it is sometimes misread. Instead, he is assuming, with his readers, that Jesus really was raised; and he is using that assumption to make his bigger point, which is this: since Jesus was raised bodily from the dead, it is clear that his followers—despite what Paul's Christian opponents are saying—have not yet experienced the future resurrection. The resurrection for Paul is not a spiritual matter unrelated to the body, as it was for some of his opponents. It is precisely the body that will be raised immortal on the last day, when Jesus returns in triumph from heaven. The Christians in Corinth therefore are not experiencing, in the here and now, the glories of the resurrected life. That is yet to come, when their bodies will be raised.

Paul begins his discussion of the resurrection of Jesus, and the future resurrection of believers, by citing a standard Christian confession, or creed (i.e., a statement of faith), that was already known to his readers (as he himself indicates):

> *³For I handed over to you among the most important things what I also had received, that Christ died for our sins in accordance with the scriptures, ⁴and that he was buried; and that he was raised on the third day in accordance with the scriptures; ⁵and that he appeared to Cephas, then to the Twelve; ⁶then he appeared to more than five hundred brothers at one time, many of whom survive until now, though some have fallen asleep. ⁷Then he appeared to James, then to all the apostles; ⁸and last of all he appeared even to me, as to one untimely born. (1 Cor. 15:3–8)*

Paul's letters are the first Christian writings that we have from antiquity; he was writing, for the most part, in the 50s of the Common Era, so some ten or fifteen years *before* our earliest surviving Gospel, Mark. It is hard to know exactly when 1 Corinthians was written; if we place it in the middle of Paul's letter-writing period, we could put it around 55 CE or so—some twenty-five years after Jesus's death.

What is striking is that Paul indicates that this statement of faith is something he already had taught the Christians in Corinth, presumably when he converted them. And so it must go back to the founding of the community, possibly four or five years earlier. Moreover—and this is the important part—Paul indicates that he did not devise this statement himself but that he "received" it from others. Paul uses this kind of language elsewhere in 1 Corinthians (see 11:22–25), and it is believed far and wide among New Testament specialists that Paul is indicating that this is a tradition already widespread in the Christian church, handed over to him by Christian teachers, possibly even the earlier apostles themselves. In other words, this is what New Testament scholars call a *pre-Pauline tradition*—one that was in circulation before Paul wrote it and even before he gave it to the Corinthians when he first persuaded them to become followers of Jesus. So this is a very ancient tradition about Jesus. Does it go back even to before the time when Paul himself joined the movement around the year 33 CE, some three years after Jesus had died?[4] If so, it would be very ancient indeed!

There is evidence in the passage itself that it, or part of it, is pre-Pauline, and it is possible to determine just which parts were the original formulation. As we will see more fully in Chapter 6, there are a number of "preliterary" traditions in Paul's writings and in the book of Acts—that is, quotations of statements of faith, poems, possibly even hymns that were in circulation before being cited in our surviving literary texts. Scholars have devised a number of ways to detect these preliterary traditions. For one thing, they tend to be tightly constructed, with terse statements that contain words not otherwise attested by the author in question—in this case Paul—and to use grammatical formulations that are otherwise foreign to the author. This is what we find here in this passage. For example, the phrase "in accordance with the scriptures" is found nowhere else in Paul's writings; nor is the verb "he appeared"; nor is any reference to "the Twelve."

This passage almost certainly contains a pre-Pauline confession, or creed, of some kind. But is the entire thing, all of vv. 3–8, part of that creed? The second half of v. 6 ("many of whom survive . . . ") and all of v. 8 ("last of all he appeared even to me . . . ") are Paul's comments on the tradition, so they could not have originally been part of the creed. There are very good reasons, in fact, for thinking that the original form of the creed was simply vv. 3–5, to which Paul has added some comments of his own based on what he knew. One reason for restricting the original pre-Pauline creed to just these three verses is that doing so produces a very tightly formulated creedal statement that is brilliantly structured. It contains two major sections of four statements each that closely parallel one another (in other words, the first statement of section one corresponds to the first statement of section two, and so on). In its original form, then, the creed would have read like this:

> 1a *Christ died*
>> 2a *For our sins*
>>> 3a *In accordance with the scriptures*
>>>> 4a *And he was buried.*
> 1b *Christ was raised*
>> 2b *On the third day*
>>> 3b *In accordance with the scriptures*
>>>> 4b *And he appeared to Cephas.*

The first section is all about Jesus's death, and the second is all about his resurrection. The parallel statements work like this: first there is a statement of "fact" (1a: Christ died; 1b: Christ was raised); then there is a theological interpretation of the fact (2a: he died for our sins; 2b: he was raised on the third day), followed by a statement, in each section, that it was "in accordance with the scriptures" (3a and 3b, worded identically in the Greek); and finally a kind of proof is given by means of the physical evidence for the claim (4a: he was buried—showing that he really was dead; 4b: he appeared to Cephas [that is, the disciple Peter]— showing that he really was raised).

This then was the very ancient pre-Pauline tradition that Paul cites in 1 Corinthians 15 and that he expands, at the end, by giving even more "witnesses" to the resurrection—including himself, the last to see Jesus alive afterward (some two or three years after Jesus's death). Some scholars have argued that this terse statement of faith originated in Aramaic, meaning that it might go all the way back to the Aramaic-speaking followers of Jesus in Palestine during the early years after his death; other scholars are not so sure about this. In either case, it is a powerful, concise, and cleverly constructed creedal statement.

If this reconstruction of the original form of this statement is correct, several interesting and important observations can be made. First, if it is right that the second statement of each section is a "theological interpretation" of the statement of "fact" that precedes it, then the idea that Jesus was raised on the third day is not necessarily a historical recollection of when the resurrection happened, but a theological claim of its significance. I should point out that the Gospels do not indicate on which day Jesus was raised. The women go to the tomb on the third day, and they find it empty. But none of the Gospels indicates that Jesus arose that morning before the women showed up. He could just as well have arisen the day before or even the day before that—just an hour, say, after he had been buried. The Gospels simply don't say.

If Paul's statement is indeed a theological interpretation rather than a historical claim, one needs to figure out what it means. It is important to stress that this "third day" is said to have been in accordance with the testimony of scripture, which for any early Christian author would not have been the New Testament (which had not yet been written) but the Hebrew Bible. There is a widespread view among scholars that the author of this statement is indicating that in his resurrection on the third day Jesus is thought to have fulfilled the saying of the Hebrew prophet Hosea: "After two days he will revive us; on the third day he will raise us up, that we may live before him" (Hos. 6:2). Other scholars—a minority of them, although I find myself attracted to this view— think that the reference is to the book of Jonah, where Jonah was in the belly of the great fish for three days and three nights before being released and, in a kind of symbolic sense, brought back from the dead (see Jonah 2). Jesus himself is recorded in the Gospels as likening his upcoming death and resurrection to "the sign of Jonah" (Matt. 12:39–41). Whether the reference is to Hosea or Jonah, why would it be necessary to say that the resurrection happened on the third day? Because that is what was predicted in scripture. This is a theological claim that Jesus's death and resurrection happened according to plan. This will be an important point for us later when we consider what we can say about when the earliest followers of Jesus first came to think he was raised from the dead—and on what grounds.

Second, it is important to realize that all the statements of the two sections of the creed are tightly parallel to one another in every respect—except one. The second section contains a name as part of the tangible proof for the statement that Jesus was raised: "He appeared to [literally: "he was seen by"] Cephas." The fourth statement of the first section does not name any authorizing party. There we are told simply that "he was buried"— not that he was buried by anyone in particular. Given the effort that the author of this creed has taken to make every statement of the first section correspond to the parallel statement of the second section, and vice versa, this should give us pause. It would have been very easy indeed to make the parallel precise, simply by saying "he was buried by Joseph [of Arimathea]." Why didn't the author make this precise parallel? My hunch is that it is because he knew nothing about a burial of Jesus by Joseph of Arimathea. I should point out that nowhere else does Paul ever say anything about Joseph of Arimathea, or the way in which Jesus was buried—not in this creed, not in the rest of 1 Corinthians, and not in any of his other letters. The tradition that there was a specific, known person who buried Jesus appears to have been a later one. Below, I will show why there are reasons to doubt that the tradition is historically accurate.

One other frequently noted feature of this creed—and its expansion by Paul in vv. 5–8—is that Paul seems to be giving an exhaustive account of the people to whom Jesus appeared after being raised. The reason for thinking this is that after listing all the others who saw Jesus, Paul indicates that he was the "last of all." This is frequently understood, rightly I think, to mean that he is giving the fullest list he can. But then the list is striking indeed, in no small measure because Paul doesn't mention any women. In the Gospels it is women who discover the empty tomb, and in two of the Gospels—Matthew and John—it is women who first see Jesus alive afterward. But Paul never says anything about anyone discovering an empty tomb, and he doesn't mention any resurrection appearances to women—either here or in any other passage of his writings.

On the first point, for many years scholars have considered it highly significant that Paul, our earliest "witness" to the resurrection, says nothing about the discovery of an empty tomb. Our earliest account of Jesus's resurrection (1 Cor. 15:3–5) discusses the appearances without mentioning an empty tomb, while our earliest Gospel, Mark, narrates the discovery of the empty tomb without discussing any of the appearances (Mark 16:1–8). This has led some scholars, such as New Testament expert Daniel Smith, to suggest that these two sets of tradition—the empty tomb and the appearances of Jesus after his death—probably originated independently of one another and were put together as a single tradition only later—for example, in the Gospels of Matthew and Luke.[5] If this is the case, then the stories of Jesus's resurrection were indeed being expanded, embellished, modified, and possibly even invented in the long process of their being told and retold over the years.

But what lies at the foundation of these stories? What, if anything, can we say historically about the resurrection event? At this point I need to pause to explain why historians—insofar as and as long as they are working as historians—are unable to use knowledge derived from the historical disciplines to affirm that Jesus really was, physically, raised from the dead, even if they personally believe it happened. The view I stake out here is that if historians, or anyone else, do believe this, it is because of their faith, not because of their historical inquiry. I should stress that unbelievers (like me) cannot *disprove* the resurrection either, on historical grounds. This is because belief or unbelief in Jesus's resurrection is a matter of faith, not of historical knowledge.

The Resurrection and the Historian

The reason historians cannot prove or disprove whether God has performed a miracle in the past—such as raising Jesus from the dead—is *not* that historians are required to be secular humanists with an anti-supernaturalist bias. I want to stress this point because conservative Christian apologists, in order to score debating points, often claim that this is the case. In their view, if historians did not have anti-supernaturalist biases or assumptions, they would be able to affirm the historical "evidence" that Jesus was raised from the dead. I should point out that these Christian apologists almost never consider the "evidence" for other miracles from the past that have comparable—or even better—evidence to support them: for example, dozens of Roman senators claimed that King Romulus was snatched up into heaven from their midst; and many thousands of committed Roman Catholics can attest that the Blessed Virgin Mary has appeared to them, alive—a claim that fundamentalist and conservative evangelical Christians roundly discount, even though the "evidence" for it is very extensive. It's always easy to scream "anti-supernatural bias" when someone does not think that the miracles of one's own tradition can be historically established; it's much harder to admit that miracles of other traditions are just as readily demonstrated.

But the view I map out here is that none of these divine miracles, or any others, can be established historically. Conservative evangelical Christian apologists are right to say that this is because of the presuppositions of the investigators. But not for the reason they think or say.

The first thing to stress is that everyone has presuppositions, and it is impossible to live life, think deep thoughts, have religious experiences, or engage in historical inquiry *without* having presuppositions. The life of the mind cannot proceed without presuppositions. The question, though, is always this: What are the appropriate presuppositions for the task at hand? The presuppositions that the Roman Catholic believer brings to his experience of the mass will be different from the presuppositions that the scientist brings to her exploration of the Big Bang theory and different from the presuppositions that historians bring to their study of the Inquisition. So let me stress that historians, working as historians, do indeed have presuppositions. It is important, therefore, to know something about the *kind* of presuppositions historians have when they are engaged in the act of reconstructing what happened in the past.

Most historians would agree that they necessarily presuppose that the past did happen. We can't actually prove it, of course, the way we can prove a scientific experiment. We can repeat scientific experiments, and by doing so we can establish predictive probabilities that can show us what almost certainly *will* happen the next time we do the experiment. Historians can't do this with past events because they can't repeat the past. And so historians have different ways of proceeding. They don't use scientific "proofs" but look for other kinds of evidence for what has happened before now. The basic operating assumption though, which itself cannot be proved, is that something did in fact happen before now.

Moreover, historians presuppose that it is possible for us to establish, with some degree of probability, what has happened in the past. We can decide whether it is probably the case, or not, that the Holocaust happened (yes it did), that Julius Caesar crossed the Rubicon (yes he did), and that Jesus of Nazareth actually existed (yes he did). Historians maintain that some of the things in the past (almost) certainly happened, other things very probably happened, others somewhat probably happened, others possibly happened, others probably did not happen, others almost certainly did not happen, and so on. It is (virtually) certain that the University of North Carolina basketball team, the Tar Heels, won the national championship in 2009. It is also (virtually) certain that they got knocked out of the NCAA tournament in 2013 by Kansas. (It is *absolutely* certain that this was an enormous tragedy, but that's a value judgment, not a historical claim.)

Related to the presupposition that it is possible to establish with degrees of probability what has happened in the past (some things more probable than others) is the assumption that "evidence" for past events exists, so reconstructing the past is not a matter of pure guesswork. And historians presuppose that some evidence is better than other evidence. Eyewitness reports are, as a rule, superior to hearsay from years, decades, or centuries later. Extensive corroboration among multiple sources that show no evidence of collaborating with one another is far better than either collaboration or noncorroboration. A source who provides disinterested off-the-cuff comments about a person or event is better than a source who makes interested claims about a person or event in order to score an ideologically driven point. What historians want, in short, are lots of witnesses, close to the time of the events, who are not biased toward their subject matter and who corroborate one another's points without showing signs of collaboration. Would that we had such sources for all significant historical events!

These then are among the kinds of presuppositions that historians tend to share. On the other hand, some presuppositions are decidedly not at all appropriate for historians who want to establish what happened in the past. It is not appropriate, for example, for a historian to presuppose her conclusions and to try to locate only the evidence that supports those presupposed conclusions. The investigation needs to be conducted without prejudice as to its outcome, simply to see what really happened. Similarly, it is not appropriate for a historian to treat evidence as irrelevant when it does not happen to be convenient to his personal views.

Moreover—and here is where the rubber meets the road—it is not appropriate for a historian to presuppose a perspective or worldview that is not generally held. "Historians" who try to explain the founding of the United States or the outcome of the First World War by invoking the visitation of Martians as a major factor of causality will not get a wide hearing from other historians—and will not, in fact, be considered to be engaging in serious historiography. Such a view presupposes notions that are not generally held—that there are advanced life-forms outside our experience, that some of them live on another planet within our solar system, that these other beings have sometimes visited the earth, and that their visitation is what determined the outcome of significant historical events. All these presuppositions may in fact be true—there is no way for historians to know one way or the other, using the historical approach to establishing what happened in the past. But since they are presuppositions that the vast majority of us do not share, historical reconstruction cannot be based on them. Anyone who has these presuppositions has to silence them, sit on them, or otherwise squelch them when engaging in their historical investigations.

This is also true of all religious and theological beliefs that a historian happens to have: these beliefs cannot determine the outcome of a historical investigation, because they are not generally shared. This means that a historian cannot establish that the angel Moroni made revelations to Joseph Smith, as in the Mormon tradition. Such views presuppose that angels exist, that Moroni is one of them, and that Joseph Smith was particularly chosen to receive a revelation from on high. These are theological beliefs; they are not based on historical evidence. Maybe there is an angel Moroni and maybe he did reveal secret truths to Joseph Smith, but there is no way for historians to establish any of that: to do so would require accepting certain theological views that are not held by the majority of other historians—for example, those who are Roman Catholics, Reformed Jews, Buddhists, and nonreligious hard-core atheists. Historical evidence has to be open to examination by everyone of every religious belief.

The belief that a Christian miracle—any Christian miracle—happened in the past is rooted in a particular set of theological beliefs (the same is true of Jewish miracles, Muslim miracles, Hindu miracles, and so on). Without such beliefs, miracles cannot be established as having happened. Since historians cannot assume these beliefs, they cannot demonstrate historically that such miracles happened.

At the same time, in some cases in which a past miracle is narrated, *elements* of the episode may be subject to historical inquiry even if the overarching claim that God has done something miraculous cannot possibly be accepted on the basis of historical evidence (since historical evidence precludes any particular set of religious beliefs).

Let me illustrate. My grandmother firmly believed that the Pentecostal evangelist Oral Roberts could heal the sick, the diseased, and the disabled by praying over them and touching them. Now, in theory it would be possible for a historian to examine a case in which a person had symptoms of a disease before having an encounter with Oral Roberts and that they disappeared after the encounter. The historian could report that yes, apparently the person was sick before and was not sick afterward. But what the historian cannot report—if she is acting as a historian—is that Oral Roberts healed the person through the power of God. Other explanations are possible that are open to examination by scholars without any theological presuppositions required for the "divine solution"—for example, that it was a kind of psychosomatic healing (that is, the person believed so thoroughly that he would be healed that the mind healed the ailment); or that the person was only apparently healed (the next day he was again sick as a dog); or that he was not really sick in the first place; or that it was a hoax, or, well, lots of other explanations. These other "explanations" can explain the same data. The supernatural explanation, on the other hand, cannot be appealed to as a historical response because (1) historians have no access to the supernatural realm, and (2) it requires a set of theological beliefs that are not generally held by all historians doing this kind of investigation.

So too with the resurrection of Jesus. Historians can, in theory, examine aspects of the tradition. In theory, for example, a historian could look into the question of whether Jesus really was buried in a known tomb and whether three days later that same tomb was found to be empty, with no body in it. What the historian cannot conclude, as a historian, is that God therefore must have raised the body and taken it up to heaven. The historian has no access to information like that, and that conclusion requires a set of theological presuppositions that not all historians share. Moreover, it is possible to come up with perfectly sensible other solutions as to why a once-occupied tomb may have become empty: someone stole the body; someone innocently decided to move the body to another tomb; the whole story was in fact a legend, that is, the burial and discovery of an empty tomb were tales that later Christians invented to persuade others that the resurrection indeed happened.

So too the historian can look into the question of whether the disciples really had visions of Jesus after his death. People have visions all the time. Sometimes they see things that are there, and sometimes they see things that are not there. (I'll discuss this more fully in the next chapter.) What historians cannot conclude, however, as historians, is that the disciples had visions of Jesus after he was really, actually dead and that it was because Jesus really, actually appeared to them alive after God had raised him from the dead. This conclusion would be rooted in theological presuppositions not generally held by all historians.

To press the point further, it is in theory possible even to say that Jesus was crucified, and buried, and then he was seen alive, bodily, afterward. A historian could, in theory, argue this point without appealing to divine causality—that is, without saying that God raised Jesus from the dead. This is because we do have (numerous) instances within our own world of near-death experiences, when someone apparently (or really?) dies and then wakes up again to tell the tale. Recognizing that people have such experiences does not require a belief in the supernatural. Of course, it would be a different matter if a person was dead for ninety-five years and then came back. But that never happens in near-death experiences. Instead, a person is dead, or apparently dead (however we define "dead"), for a brief time and then somehow comes back to life. Did Jesus have that kind of experience? I doubt it, but it is at least a plausible historical conclusion.

What is not a plausible *historical* conclusion is that God raised Jesus into an immortal body and took him up to heaven where he sits on a throne at his right hand. That conclusion is rooted in all sorts of theological views that are not widely shared among historians, and so is a matter of faith, not historical knowledge.

At this stage it is important to stress a fundamental point. History, for historians, is not the same as "the past." The past is everything that has happened before; history is what we can establish as having happened before, using historical forms of evidence. Historical evidence is not and cannot be based on religious and theological assumptions that some, but not all, of us share. There are lots and lots of things from the past that we cannot establish as having happened. Sometimes, this is because our sources are so paltry. (And so, for example, it is impossible to establish what my grandfather had for lunch on May 15, 1954.) Other times, it is because history, as established by historians, is based only on *shared* presuppositions. And among these shared presuppositions are not the sorts of religious and theological views that make it possible to conclude that Jesus was exalted to heaven after he died and allowed to sit at God's right hand, never to die again. This is the traditional Christian belief, but people do not hold it on the basis of historical evidence but because they accept it by faith. For the same reason, historians cannot conclude that the thief crucified with Jesus was exalted and was the first human to enter heaven upon his death, as claimed by a Gospel known as the *Narrative of Joseph of Arimathea;* or that the Blessed Virgin Mary has appeared to thousands of her followers, as numerous eyewitnesses attest; or that Apollonius of Tyana came to one of his followers after he ascended to heaven, as we have on the basis of eyewitness testimony reported later. All of these claims presuppose religious beliefs that cannot be part of the arsenal of historical presuppositions.

With all this in mind, what can we say—historically—about the traditions of Jesus's resurrection? If we can't know, historically, whether God actually raised him from the dead, what can we know? And what else can we not know? As we will see, one thing we can know with relative certainty is that the belief that Jesus was raised from the dead is the key to understanding why Christians eventually began to think of him as God. But first, what we cannot know.

The Resurrection: What We Cannot Know

IN ADDITION TO THE resurrection itself—the act of God by which he raised Jesus from the dead—a number of other traditions are subject to historical doubt. The two I mention here will come as a surprise to many readers. In my judgment, we cannot know that Jesus received a decent burial and that his tomb was later discovered to be empty.

These two traditions obviously stand hand-in-hand, in that the second makes no sense unless the first is historically true. No one could have discovered that Jesus was no longer in his tomb if he had never been buried in a tomb in the first place (although the reverse does not necessarily follow: in theory Jesus could have been decently buried, and the tomb was never discovered empty). And so in many respects the second claim depends on the first. Therefore, I devote more discussion to it, explaining why we cannot know on historical grounds whether Joseph of Arimathea buried Jesus, as the Gospels claim he did.

Did Jesus Receive a Decent Burial?

According to our earliest account, the Gospel of Mark, Jesus was buried by a previous unnamed and unknown figure, Joseph of Arimathea, "a respected member of the council" (Mark 15:43)— that is, a Jewish aristocrat who belonged to the Sanhedrin, which was the ruling body made up of "chief priests, elders, and scribes" (14:53). According to Mark 15:43, Joseph summoned up his courage and asked Pilate for Jesus's body. Pilate granted Joseph his wish, and Joseph took the body from the cross, wrapped it in a linen shroud, "laid it in a tomb that had been hewn out of the rock," and then rolled a stone in front of it (15:44–47). Mary Magdalene and another woman named Mary saw where this happened (15:48).

Let me stress that all of this—or something very much like it—needs to happen within Mark's narrative in order for what happens next to make sense, namely, that on the day after the Sabbath, Mary Magdalene and two other women go to the tomb and find it empty. If there were no tomb for Jesus, or if no one knew where the tomb was, the bodily resurrection could not be proclaimed. You have to have a known tomb.

But was there one? Did Joseph of Arimathea really bury Jesus?

General Considerations

There are numerous reasons for doubting the tradition of Jesus's burial by Joseph. For one thing, it is hard to make historical sense of this tradition just within the context of Mark's narrative. Joseph's identification as a respected member of the Sanhedrin should immediately raise questions. Mark himself said that at Jesus's trial, which took place the previous evening, the "whole council" of the Sanhedrin (not just some or most of them—but *all* of them) tried to find evidence "against Jesus to put him to death" (14:55). At the end of this trial, because of Jesus's statement that he was the Son of God (14:62), "they all condemned him as deserving death" (14:64). In other words, according to Mark, this unknown person, Joseph, was one of the people who had called for Jesus's death just the night before he was crucified. Why, after Jesus is dead, is he suddenly risking himself (as implied by the fact that he had to gather up his courage) and seeking to do an act of mercy by arranging for a decent burial for Jesus's corpse? Mark gives us no clue.[6] My hunch is that the trial narrative and the burial narrative come from different sets of traditions inherited by Mark. Or did Mark simply invent one of the two traditions himself and overlook the apparent discrepancy?

In any event, a burial by Joseph is clearly a historical problem in light of other passages just within the New Testament. I pointed out earlier that Paul shows no evidence of knowing anything about a Joseph of Arimathea or Jesus's burial by a "respected member of the council." This datum was not included in the very early creed that Paul quotes in 1 Corinthians 15:3–5, and if the author of that creed *had* known such a thing, he surely would have included it, since without naming the person who buried Jesus, as we have seen, he created an imbalance with the second portion of the creed where he does name the person to whom Jesus appeared (Cephas). Thus, this early creed knows nothing about Joseph. And Paul also betrays no knowledge of him.

Moreover, another tradition of Jesus's burial says nothing about Joseph of Arimathea. As I pointed out earlier, the book of Acts was written by the same person who wrote the Gospel of Luke. When writing Luke, this unknown author (we obviously call him Luke, but we don't know who he really was) used a number of earlier written and oral sources for his stories, as he himself indicates (Luke 1:1–4). Scholars today are convinced that one of his sources was the Gospel of Mark, and so Luke includes the story of Joseph of Arimathea in his version of Jesus's death and resurrection. When Luke wrote his second volume, the book of Acts, he had yet other sources available to him. Acts is not about the life, death, and resurrection of Jesus but about the spread of the Christian church throughout the Roman empire afterward. About one-fourth of the book of Acts consists of speeches made by its main characters, mainly Peter and Paul—speeches, for example, to convert people to believe in Jesus or to instruct those who already believe. Scholars have long recognized that Luke himself wrote these speeches—they are not the speeches that these apostles really delivered at one time or another. Luke is writing decades after the events he narrates, and no one at the time was taking notes. Ancient historians as a whole made up the speeches of their main characters, as such a stalwart historian as the Greek Thucydides explicitly tells us (*Peloponnesian War* 1.22.1–2). They had little choice.

When Luke composed his speeches, however, it appears that he did so, in part, on the basis of earlier sources that had come down to him—just as his accounts of Jesus's teachings in the Gospel came from earlier sources (such as Mark). But if different traditions (speeches, for example) come from different sources, there is no guarantee that they will stand in complete harmony with one another. If they do not stand in harmony, it is almost always because someone is changing the stories or making something up.

That makes Paul's speech in Acts 13 very interesting. Paul is speaking in a synagogue service in Antioch of Pisidia, and he uses the occasion to tell the congregation that the Jewish leaders in Jerusalem had sinned severely against God by having Jesus killed: "Though they could charge him with nothing deserving death, yet they asked Pilate to have him killed. And when they had fulfilled all that was written of him, they took him down from the tree and laid him in a tomb" (Acts 13:28–29).

This may appear to harmonize generally with what the Gospels say about Jesus's death and burial—in that he died and was buried—but here it is not a single member of the Sanhedrin who buries Jesus, but the council as a whole. This is a different tradition. There is no word of Joseph here, any more than there is in Paul's letters. Does this pre-Lukan tradition represent an older tradition than what is found in Mark about Joseph of Arimathea? Is the oldest surviving burial tradition one that says Jesus was buried by a group of Jews?

It would make sense that this was the older tradition of the two. Any tradition that is going to lead up to an empty tomb simply has to show that Jesus was properly buried, in a tomb. But who could do the burial? According to all the traditions, Jesus did not have any family in Jerusalem, and so there was no possibility of a family tomb in which to lay him or family members to do the requisite work of burial. Moreover, the accounts consistently report that his followers had all fled the scene, so they could not do the job. The Romans were not about to do it, for reasons that will become clear below. That leaves only one choice. If the followers of Jesus knew that he "had" to be buried in a tomb—since otherwise there could be no story about the tomb being empty—and they had to invent a story that described this burial, then the only ones who could possibly do the deed were the Jewish authorities themselves. And so that is the oldest tradition we have, as in Acts 13:29. Possibly this is the tradition that lies behind 1 Corinthians 15:4 as well: "and he was buried."

As the burial tradition came to be told and retold, it possibly became embellished and made more concrete. Storytellers were apt to add details to stories that were vague, or to give names to people otherwise left nameless in a tradition, or to add named individuals to stories that originally mentioned only nameless individuals or undifferentiated groups of people. This is a tradition that lived on long after the New Testament period, as my own teacher Bruce Metzger showed so elegantly in his article "Names for the Nameless."[7] Here he showed all the traditions of people who were unnamed in New Testament stories receiving names later; for example, the wise men are named in later traditions, as are priests serving on the Sanhedrin when they condemned Jesus and the two robbers who were crucified with him. In the story of Joseph of Arimathea we may have an early instance of the phenomenon: what was originally a vague statement that the unnamed Jewish leaders buried Jesus becomes a story of one leader in particular, who is named, doing so.

In addition, we have clear evidence in the Gospel traditions that as time went on, and stories were embellished, there was a tendency to find "good guys" among the "bad guys" of the stories. For example, in Mark's Gospel both of the criminals being crucified with Jesus malign and mock him on the cross; in Luke's later Gospel only one of the two does so, and the other confesses faith in Jesus and asks him to remember him when he comes into his kingdom (Luke 23:39–43). In John's Gospel there is an additional good guy among the Sanhedrin bad guys who wants to help with Jesus's burial, as Nicodemus accompanies Joseph to do his duties to Jesus's corpse (John 19:38–42). Most notable is Pontius Pilate, who, as a thoroughly bad guy, condemned Jesus to death in our earliest Gospel Mark. But he does so only with great reluctance in Matthew and only after explicitly declaring Jesus innocent three times in both Luke and John. In later Gospels from outside the New Testament, Pilate is portrayed as an increasingly innocent good guy, to the point that he actually converts and becomes a believer in Jesus. In part, this ongoing and increasing exoneration of Pilate is enacted in order to show where the real guilt for Jesus's undeserved death lies. For these authors living long after the fact, the guilt lies with the recalcitrant Jews. But the pattern is also part of a process of trying to find someone good in the barrel of rotten opponents of Jesus. Naming Joseph of Arimathea as a kind of secret admirer or respecter or even follower of Jesus may be part of the same process.

In addition to the rather general considerations I have just given for questioning the idea that Joseph of Arimathea buried Jesus, there are three more specific reasons for doubting the tradition that Jesus received a decent burial at all, in a tomb that could later be recognized as empty.

Roman Practices of Crucifixion

Sometimes Christian apologists argue that Jesus had to be taken off the cross before sunset on Friday because the next day was the

Sabbath and it was against Jewish law, or at least Jewish sensitivities, to allow a person to remain on the cross during the Sabbath. Unfortunately, the historical record suggests just the opposite. It was not Jews who killed Jesus, and so they had no say about when he would be taken down from the cross. Moreover, the Romans who did crucify him had no concern to obey Jewish law and virtually no interest in Jewish sensitivities. Quite the contrary. When it came to crucified criminals—in this case, someone charged with crimes against the state—there was regularly no mercy and no concern for anyone's sensitivities. The point of crucifixion was to torture and humiliate a person as fully as possible, and to show any bystanders what happens to someone who is a troublemaker in the eyes of Rome. Part of the humiliation and degradation was the body being left on the cross after death to be subject to scavenging animals.

John Dominic Crossan has made the rather infamous suggestion that Jesus's body was not raised from the dead but was eaten by dogs.[8] When I first heard this suggestion, I was no longer a Christian and so was not religiously outraged, but I did think it was excessive and sensationalist. But that was before I did any real research on the matter. My view now is that we do not know, and cannot know, what actually happened to Jesus's body. But it is absolutely true that as far as we can tell from all the surviving evidence, what *normally* happened to a criminal's body is that it was left to decompose and serve as food for scavenging animals. Crucifixion was meant to be a public disincentive to engage in politically subversive activities, and the disincentive did not end with the pain and death—it continued on in the ravages worked on the corpse afterward.

Evidence for this comes from a wide range of sources. An ancient inscription found on the tombstone of a man who was murdered by his slave in the city of Caria tells us that the murderer was "hung . . . alive for the wild beasts and birds of prey."[9]

The Roman author Horace says in one of his letters that a slave was claiming to have done nothing wrong, to which his master replied, "You shall not therefore feed the carrion crows on the cross" (*Epistle* 1.16.46–48).[10] The Roman satirist Juvenal speaks of "the vulture [that] hurries from the dead cattle and dogs and corpses, to bring some of the carrion to her offspring" (*Satires* 14.77–78).[11] The most famous interpreter of dreams from the ancient world, a Greek Sigmund Freud named Artemidorus, writes that it is auspicious for a poor man in particular to have a dream about being crucified, since "a crucified man is raised high and his substance is sufficient to keep many birds" (*Dream Book* 2.53).[12] And there is a bit of gallows humor in the *Satyricon* of Petronius, a one-time advisor to the emperor Nero, about a crucified victim being left for days on the cross (chaps. 11–12).

It is unfortunate that we do not have from the ancient world any literary description of the process of crucifixion, so we are left guessing about the details of how it was carried out. But consistent references to the fate of the crucified show that part of the ordeal involved being left as fodder for the scavengers upon death. As the conservative Christian commentator Martin Hengel once observed: "Crucifixion was aggravated further by the fact that quite often its victims were never buried. It was a stereotyped picture that the crucified victim served as food for wild beasts and birds of prey. In this way his humiliation was made complete."[13]

I should point out that other conservative Christian commentators have claimed that there were exceptions to this rule, as indicated in the writings of Philo, and that Jews were sometimes allowed to bury people who had been crucified. In fact, however, this is a misreading of the evidence from Philo, as can be seen simply by quoting his words at length (emphasis is mine):

> Rulers who conduct their government as they should and do not
> pretend to honour but do really honour their benefactors make a

practice of not punishing any condemned person until those notable celebrations in honour of the birthdays of the illustrious Augustan house *are over. . . . I have known cases when on the eve of a holiday* of this kind, *people who have been crucified have been taken down and their bodies delivered to their kinsfolk, because it was thought well to give them burial and allow them the ordinary rites. For it was meet that the dead also should have the advantage of some kind treatment* upon the birthday of the emperor *and also that the sanctity of the festival should be maintained.*[14]

When the statement is read in toto, it is clearly seen to provide the exception that proves the rule. Philo is mentioning this kind of exceptional case precisely because it goes *against* established practice. Two things should be noted. The first, and less important, is that in the cases that Philo mentions, the bodies were taken down so that they could be given to the crucified person's family members for decent burial—that is, it was a favor done for certain families, and one might assume these were elite families with high connections. Jesus's family did not have high connections; they did not have the means of burying anyone in Jerusalem; they weren't even from Jerusalem; none of them knew any of the ruling authorities to ask for the body; and what is more, in our earliest accounts, none of them, even his mother, was actually at the event.

The bigger point has to do with when and why these exceptions Philo mentions were made: when a Roman governor chose to honor a Roman emperor's birthday—in other words, to honor a *Roman* leader on a Roman holiday. This has nothing to do with Jesus's crucifixion, which did not occur on an emperor's birthday. It happened during a Jewish Passover feast—a Jewish festival widely recognized as fostering *anti*-Roman sentiments. It is just the opposite kind of occasion from that mentioned in Philo. And

we have no record at all—none—of governors making exceptions in any case such as that.

In sum, the common Roman practice was to allow the bodies
of crucified people to decompose on the cross and be attacked by
scavengers as part of the disincentive for crime. I have not run
across any contrary indications in any ancient source. It is always
possible that an exception was made, of course. But it must be
remembered that the Christian storytellers who indicated that
Jesus was an exception to the rule had an extremely compelling
reason to do so. If Jesus had not been buried, his tomb could not
be declared empty.

Greek and Roman Practices of Using Common Graves for Criminals

My second reason for doubting that Jesus received a decent burial
is that at the time, criminals of all sorts were, as a rule, tossed
into common graves. Again, a range of evidence is available from
many times and places. The Greek historian of the first century
BCE Diodorus Siculus speaks of a war between Philip of Macedonia (the father of Alexander the Great) in which he lost twenty
men to the enemy, the Locrians. When Philip asked for their
bodies in order to bury them, the Locrians refused, indicating that
"it was the general law that temple-robbers should be cast forth
without burial" (*Library of History* 16.25.2).[15] From around 100
CE, the Greek author Dio Chrysostom indicates that in Athens,
anyone who suffered "at the hands of the state for a crime" was
"denied burial, so that in the future there may be no trace of a
wicked man" (*Discourses* 31.85).[16] Among the Romans, we learn
that after a battle fought by Octavian (the later Caesar Augustus,
emperor when Jesus was born), one of his captives begged for a
burial, to which Octavian replied, "The birds will soon settle
that question" (Suetonius, *Augustus* 13). And we are told by the
Roman historian Tacitus of a man who committed suicide to

avoid being executed by the state, since anyone who was legally condemned and executed "forfeited his estate and was debarred from burial" (*Annals* 6.29h).[17]

Again, it is possible that Jesus was an exception, but our evidence that this might have been the case must be judged to be rather thin. People who were crucified were usually left on their crosses as food for scavengers, and part of the punishment for ignominious crimes was being tossed into a common grave, where very soon one decomposed body could not be distinguished from another. In the traditions about Jesus, of course, his body had to be distinguished from all others; otherwise, it could not be demonstrated to have been raised physically from the dead.

The Policies of Pontius Pilate in Particular

My third reason for doubting the burial tradition has to do with the Roman rule of Judea at the time. One of the chief regrets of any historian of early Christianity is that we do not have more—lots more—information about Pontius Pilate, the governor of Judea from 26 to 36 CE, who, among many other things, condemned Jesus to be crucified. What we do know about him, however, all points in the same direction: he was a fierce, violent, mean-spirited ruler who displayed no interest at all in showing mercy and kindness to his subjects and showed no respect for Jewish sensitivities.

Pilate's governorship is lightly documented in the surviving material record, as we have some coins that were issued during his reign and an inscription, discovered in modern times at Caesarea, that mentions him. The New Testament record is somewhat mixed, for reasons already mentioned. As time wore on, Christian authors, including those of the Gospels, portrayed Pilate as more and more sympathetic toward Jesus and more and more opposed to the recalcitrant Jews who demand Jesus's death. As I have suggested, this progressive exoneration of Pilate serves clear anti-Jewish purposes, so the accounts of Jesus's trial in the later Gospels—Matthew, Luke, and John—must be taken with a pound of salt. In an earlier tradition of Luke we get a clearer picture of what the man was like, as we hear, very opaquely, of "the Galileans whose blood Pilate had mixed with their sacrifices" (Luke 13:1). This sounds as if Pilate had Jews murdered while they were performing their religious duties. It's an unsettling picture.

But it coincides well with what we know about Pilate from other literary sources, especially the first-century Jewish historian Josephus. Josephus tells of two episodes that transpired while Pilate was governor of Judea. The first occurred when he took office. Under veil of night, when Pilate first came into Jerusalem, he had stationed around town the Roman standards, which had an image of the emperor embellished on them. When the Jews of Jerusalem saw the standards in the morning, they were outraged: no images were allowed in the holy city, as suggested in the law of Moses, let alone images of a foreign ruler who was worshiped elsewhere as a god. A Jewish crowd appeared to Pilate at his palace in Caesarea and demanded that he remove the standards, leading to a standoff that lasted five days. Pilate had no interest at all in bowing to Jewish demands (contrast the stories of Jesus's trial in the Gospels!). On the contrary, at the end of the five days he directed his troops to surround the Jewish protestors, three rows deep, and cut them to shreds. Rather than backing down, the Jews to a person reached out their necks and told the soldiers to do their utmost. They would rather die than cave in. Pilate realized that he could not murder such masses in cold blood and, "surprised at their prodigious superstition," ordered the standards removed (*Antiquities of the Jews* 18.3.1).[18]

The second incident resulted in actual violence. Pilate wanted to build an aqueduct to provide freshwater to Jerusalem. That was well enough, but he financed the project by raiding the sacred

treasury of the temple. The authorities and the people were outraged and protested loudly. Pilate responded by having his soldiers mix in with the crowds, disguised, to attack the people, not
with swords but with clubs, at his command. They did so, and
"many" of the Jews were killed in the onslaught, and many others
were trampled to death in the tumult that followed (*Antiquities*
18.3.2).

Pilate was not a beneficent prefect who kindly listened to the
protests of the people he governed. Was Pilate the sort of ruler
who would break with tradition and policy when kindly asked by
a member of the Jewish council to provide a decent burial for a
crucified victim? Not from what we can tell. As Crossan dismis-
sively states: "[Pilate] was an ordinary second-rate Roman governor with no regard for Jewish religious sensitivities and with
brute force as his normal solution to even unarmed protesting or
resisting crowds."[19] Even more graphic is the complaint of Philo,
who lived during Pilate's time and indicated that his administra-
tion was characterized by "his venality, his violence, his thefts,
his assaults, his abusive behavior, his frequent executions of un-
tried prisoners, and his endless savage ferocity" (*Embassy to Gaius*
302).[20]

As I have said, there are some things that we just cannot know
about the traditions relating to Jesus's resurrection. One of those
traditions, which the resurrection narrative itself presupposes, is
that Jesus received a decent burial, either from members of the
Sanhedrin or from one of their prominent associates, Joseph of
Arimathea. As a historian, I do not think we can say definitively
that this tradition is false, although I think it is too much to say
definitively that Jesus was eaten by dogs. On the other hand, we
certainly do not know that the tradition is true, and there are, in
fact, some very compelling reasons to doubt it. I personally doubt
it. If the Romans followed their normal policies and customs, and
if Pilate was the man whom all our sources indicate he was, then

it is highly unlikely that Jesus was decently buried on the day of his execution in a tomb that anyone could later identify.

Was There an Empty Tomb?

The discovery of the empty tomb presupposes that there was a tomb in the first place, and that it was known, and of course that it was discovered. But if serious doubt is cast on whether there ever was a tomb, then the accounts of its discovery are similarly thrown into doubt. Christian apologists often argue that the discovery of the empty tomb is one of the most secure historical data from the history of the early Christian movement. I used to think so myself. But it simply isn't true. Given our suspicions about the burial tradition, there are plenty of reasons to doubt the discovery of an empty tomb.

Among other things, this means that historians who do not believe that Jesus was raised from the dead should not feel compelled to come up with an alternative explanation for why the tomb was empty. Apologists typically have a field day with such explanations. Anyone who says that the disciples stole the body is attacked for thinking that such moral men who firmly believed what they did could never have done such a thing. Anyone who says that the Romans moved the body is shouted down with claims that they would have had no reason to do so and would have produced the body if it had been theirs to produce. Anyone who says that the tomb was empty because the women went to the wrong tomb is maligned for not realizing that it might occur to someone else—for example, an unbeliever—to go to the right tomb and reveal the body. Anyone who claims that Jesus never really died but simply went into a coma and eventually awoke and left the tomb is mocked for thinking that a man who was tortured to within an inch of his life could roll away a stone and appear to his disciples as the Lord of life, when in fact he would have looked like death warmed over.

I don't subscribe to any of these alternative views because I don't think we know what happened to the body of Jesus. But simply looking at the matter from a historical point of view, any of these views is more plausible than the claim that God raised Jesus physically from the dead. A resurrection would be a miracle and as such would defy all "probability." Otherwise, it wouldn't be a miracle. To say that an event that defies probability is more probable than something that is simply improbable is to fly in the face of anything that involves probability. Of course, it's not likely that someone innocently moved the body, but there's nothing inherently improbable about it. Of course, it's unlikely that one of Jesus's followers stole the body and then lied about it, but, well, people do wrong things all the time and lie about it. Even religious people. Even people who become religious leaders. And no one should be put off by the claim, "No one would be willing to die for what he knew to be a lie." We don't know what happened to most of the disciples in the end. We certainly have no evidence that they were all martyred for their faith. On the contrary, almost certainly most of them were not. So there is no need for talk about anyone dying for a lie. (Moreover, we have lots of instances in history for people dying for lies when they think it will serve a greater good. But that's neither here nor there: we don't know how most of the disciples died.) My point is that one could think of dozens of plausible scenarios for why a tomb would be empty, and any one of these scenarios is, strictly speaking, more probable than an act of God.

But all of this is beside the point, which is that we don't know whether the tomb was discovered empty because we don't know whether there even was a tomb.

In this connection I should stress that the discovery of the empty tomb appears to be a late tradition. It occurs in Mark for the first time, some thirty-five or forty years after Jesus died. Our earliest witness, Paul, does not say anything about it.

Would Anyone Invent the Women at the Tomb?

Christian apologists often argue that no one would make up the story of the discovery of the empty tomb precisely because according to these stories, it was *women* who found the tomb. This line of reasoning believes that women were widely thought of as untrustworthy and, in fact, their testimony could not be allowed in courts of law. According to this view, if someone wanted to invent the notion of a discovered tomb, they would be sure to say that it was discovered by credible witnesses, namely, by the male disciples.[21]

I used to hold this view as well, and so I see its force. But now that I've gone more deeply into the matter, I see its real flaw. It suffers, in short, from a poverty of imagination. It does not take much mental effort to imagine who would come up with a story in which the female followers of Jesus, rather than the male followers, discovered the tomb.

The first thing to point out is that we are not talking about a Jewish court of law in which witnesses are being called to testify. We're talking about oral traditions about the man Jesus. But who would invent women as witnesses to the empty tomb? Well, for openers, maybe women would. We have good reasons for thinking that women were particularly well represented in early Christian communities. We know from the letters of Paul—from passages such as Romans 16—that women played crucial leadership roles in the churches: ministering as deacons, leading the services in their homes, engaging in missionary activities. Paul speaks of one woman in the Roman church as "foremost among the apostles" (Junia in Rom. 16:7). Women are also reputed to have figured prominently in Jesus's ministry, throughout the Gospels. This may well have been the case, historically. But in any event, there is nothing implausible in thinking that women who found their newfound Christian communities personally liberating told stories about Jesus in light of their own situations, so that women were portrayed as playing a greater part in the life and death of Jesus than they actually did, historically. It does not take a great deal of imagination to think that female storytellers indicated that women were the first to believe in the resurrection, after finding Jesus's tomb empty.

Moreover, this claim that women found the empty tomb makes the best sense of the realities of history. Preparing bodies for burial was commonly the work of women, not men. And so why wouldn't the stories tell of women who went to prepare the body? Moreover, if, in the stories, they are the ones who went to the tomb to anoint the body, naturally they would be the ones who found the tomb empty.

In addition, our earliest sources are quite clear that the male disciples fled the scene and were not present for Jesus's crucifixion. As I stated earlier, this may well be a historical fact—that the disciples feared for their own lives and went into hiding or fled town in order to avoid arrest. Where would they go? Presumably back home, to Galilee—which was more than one hundred miles away and would have taken at least a week on foot for them to reach. If the men had scattered, or returned home, who was left in the tradition to go to the tomb? It would have been the women who had come with the apostolic band to Jerusalem but who presumably did not need to fear arrest.

Moreover, one can imagine strictly literary reasons for "inventing" the women at the empty tomb. Let's suppose that Mark invented the story. I personally don't think he did; there is no way to know, of course, but my suspicion is that Mark inherited the story from his tradition. But suppose he did invent it. There would be plenty of reasons, just from his literary perspective, to do so. The more you know about Mark's Gospel, the easier it is to think of reasons. I'll give just one. Mark makes a special point throughout his narrative that the male disciples never understand who Jesus is. Despite all his miracles, despite all his teachings, despite everything they see him do and say, they never "get it." And so at the end of the Gospel, who learns that Jesus has not stayed dead but has been raised? The women. Not the male disciples. And the women never tell, so the male disciples never do come to an understanding of Jesus. This is all consistent with Mark's view and with what he is trying to do from a literary standpoint.

Again, I'm not saying that I think Mark invented the story. But if we can very easily imagine a reason for Mark to have invented it, it doesn't take much of a leap to think that one or more of his predecessors may also have had reasons for doing so. In the end, we simply cannot say that there would be "no reason" for someone to invent the story of women discovering the empty tomb.

The Need for an Empty Tomb

In short, there are lots of reasons for someone wanting to invent the story that Jesus was buried in a known tomb and that it was discovered empty (whoever would have discovered it). And the most important is that the discovery of the empty tomb is central to the claim that Jesus was resurrected. If there was no empty tomb, Jesus was not physically raised.

I want to stress that adjective. Without an empty tomb, there would be no ground for saying that Jesus was *physically* raised. As we will see more fully in the next chapter, some early Christians believed that Jesus was raised in spirit but that his body decomposed. Eventually, this view came to be prominent among different groups of Christian Gnostics. We can see evidence of its presence even in the communities of the authors who produced our canonical Gospels. The later the Gospel, the more the attempt to "prove" that Jesus was raised bodily, not simply spiritually. In our earliest Gospel, Mark, Jesus is clearly raised physically because the tomb is empty—the body is gone. Later, in Matthew, it is even more clear that Jesus is raised physically (not just in his spirit) because Jesus appears to his followers and some of them touch him (Matt. 28:9). In Luke it is even clearer because when Jesus appears to his disciples, he flat-out tells them that he has flesh and bones, unlike "a spirit," and he tells them to handle him to see for themselves (Luke 24:39–40). Then he eats some food in front of them to convince them (24:41–43). Later still in John, Jesus not only cooks a meal for the disciples (John 21:9–14), but when one of them doubts, he invites him to place his finger in his wounds to know for sure that it is he and that he has been raised physically from the dead, wounds and all (20:24–29).

Some Christians doubted that the resurrection was a physical affair. The Gospels that made it into the New Testament—as opposed to a number that did not—stress that the resurrection was indeed the resurrection of Jesus's physical body. These debates may have been raging in early Christian communities from the beginning. If so, then the empty tomb tradition not only worked to show unbelievers that Jesus was resurrected, it worked to show believers that the resurrection was not a matter just of the spirit but of the body as well.

CHAPTER 5

The Resurrection of Jesus

What We Can Know

I RECEIVE A LOT OF e-mails from people who are concerned that I lost my faith. Many of them tell me that I must never have had a personal relationship with Jesus; obviously my faith was all intellectual and I "reasoned" my way out of it. In their view, if I weren't a scholar and such an egghead but realized that faith in Jesus is a matter of relating to a person as one's Lord and Savior, I would still be within the believing community. I'm never quite sure why strangers are so concerned about me. And I wonder if the fact that I left the faith is somehow seen as threatening, at least among people who have a gnawing suspicion, which they never explicitly acknowledge to themselves, that their own faith may need to be reexamined. Whether that's the case or not, it simply is not true that I never had a personal relationship with Jesus. Quite the contrary: Jesus and I were very close, and for many years. He was my daily companion, comforter, guide, and teacher, as well as my Lord and Savior.

At the same time, it is true that conservative evangelical Christianity—the kind I converted into—is not entirely about a personal relationship with the divine. It has a strong intellectual component as well. This is one of the great ironies of modern religion: more than almost any other religious group on the planet, conservative evangelicals, and most especially fundamentalist Christians, are children of the Enlightenment.

The seventeenth- and eighteenth-century intellectual movement known as the Enlightenment arose during an age when reason, not revelation, came to be valued as the ultimate source of true knowledge. The natural sciences were on the rise, technologies were developing, and philosophies of the mind were in vogue. The Enlightenment caused the demise of traditional religion for many educated people and others whose views were shaped by them. Among other things, the Enlightenment encouraged reasoned skepticism of every religious tradition that was based on the miraculous, the supernatural, and revelation. By stressing the power of human thought, the Enlightenment dispelled the myths of the dominant religious traditions. It emphasized the importance of a person seeking objective verification for what he or she thinks and believes.

When I say that conservative evangelical Christians and fundamentalists are children of the Enlightenment, I mean that more than almost anyone else, thinkers among these groups are committed to "objective truth"—which was precisely the commitment that led to the demise of Christianity in the modern world in the first place, especially in Europe. And so this evangelical commitment is ironic. Or maybe it's a case of trying to fight fire with fire. But the reality is that modern Christian apologists stress the importance of objectivity and champion it more than anyone— much more than most other educated people in our world. University intellectuals almost never speak of "objectivity" any more, unless they happen to live on the margins of intellectual life.

But Christian apologists do, and when I was one of them, I did as well. That is why Christian apologists are so keen to "prove" that the resurrection happened. This is a standard weapon in the apologetic arsenal: you can look at all the evidence for the resurrection, objectively, and conclude, on the basis of overwhelming proof, that God really did raise Jesus from the dead. No other explanation can account for the objectively established historical data—for example, that Jesus's tomb was empty and that his disciples claimed to see him afterward. And so apologists proceed by taking these two data as "facts" and showing that no other explanation is plausible (that the disciples stole the body, that they went to the wrong tomb, that they were hallucinating, and so on).

If one wants to play the objectivity game (it is a game; there is nothing objectively that makes objectivity objectively true), it is relatively easy to poke holes in this apologetic ploy—a ploy that I myself used for years when I was a Christian trying to convert people to believe in the resurrection. For one thing, as I've already argued, there are very serious reasons to doubt that Jesus was buried decently and that his tomb was discovered to be empty. Moreover, as I've argued, any other scenario—no matter how unlikely—is more likely than the one in which a great miracle occurred, since the miracle defies *all* probability (or else we wouldn't call it a miracle).

But apart from whether it makes sense to wrangle over the "objectively" best explanation for the data, there is the bigger problem—namely, that faith in a miracle is a matter of faith, not of objectively established knowledge. That is why some historians believe that Jesus was raised and other equally good historians do not believe he was. Both sets of historians have the same historical data available to them, but it is not the historical data that make a person a believer. Faith is not historical knowledge, and historical knowledge is not faith.

At the same time, the historian can talk about certain aspects of the resurrection tradition without presupposing either belief or unbelief. This is not a matter of requiring historians to have anti-supernaturalist biases. It is a matter of suspending one's biases—whether they are supernaturalist or anti-supernaturalist—in order to do what historians do: reconstruct to the best of their ability what probably happened in the past on the basis of the surviving evidence, and admitting that there are lots of things that we not only do not know, but also cannot know, historically.

In the previous chapter I argued that there are some things, given our current evidence, that we cannot know about the resurrection traditions (in addition to the big issue itself—whether God raised Jesus from the dead): we cannot know whether Jesus was given a decent burial, and we cannot know, therefore, whether his tomb was discovered empty. But what can we know? We can know three very important things: (1) some of Jesus's followers believed that he had been raised from the dead; (2) they believed this because some of them had visions of him after his crucifixion; and (3) this belief led them to reevaluate who Jesus was, so that the Jewish apocalyptic preacher from rural Galilee came to be considered, in some sense, God.

The Belief of the Disciples

THERE CAN BE NO doubt, historically, that some of Jesus's followers came to believe he was raised from the dead—no doubt whatsoever. This is how Christianity started. If no one had thought Jesus had been raised, he would have been lost in the mists of Jewish antiquity and would be known today only as another failed Jewish prophet. But Jesus's followers—or at least some of them—came to believe that God had done a great miracle and restored Jesus to life. This was not a mere resuscitation, a kind of near-death experience. For Jesus's disciples, Jesus was raised into an immortal body and exalted to heaven where he currently lives and reigns with God Almighty.

I say "some" of his followers because it is not altogether certain that all of the disciples came to believe this, for reasons I explain below. Our records are simply not good enough to allow us to know exactly which among Jesus's closest followers came to accept this great miracle. Some obviously did, but our accounts were written many years after the fact, and we hear almost nothing about "the Twelve."

The other matter of uncertainty is *when* belief in Jesus's resurrection and exaltation began. The tradition, of course, states that it began on the third day after he died. But as I argued in the analysis of 1 Corinthians 15:3–5, the idea that Jesus rose on the "third day" was originally a theological construct, not a historical piece of information. Moreover, if it is true that the disciples fled from Jerusalem to Galilee when Jesus was arrested, and that it was there that some of them "saw" him, they could not have seen him on the first Sunday morning after his death. If they fled on Friday, they would not have been able to travel on Saturday, the Sabbath; and since it was about 120 miles from Jerusalem to Capernaum, their former home base, it would have taken a week at least for them to get there on foot.[1] Maybe some of them, or one of them, had a vision of Jesus in Galilee soon after he was crucified—possibly that following week? The week after that? The next month? We simply don't have sources of information that make this kind of judgment possible.[2]

It is striking, and frequently overlooked by casual observers of the early Christian tradition, that even though it was a universal belief among the first Christians that Jesus had been raised from the dead, there was not a uniformity of belief concerning what, exactly, "raised from the dead" meant. In particular, early Christians had long and heated debates about the nature of the resurrection—specifically, the nature of the resurrected body. Here I explore three options for what that resurrected body of Jesus actually was, as evidenced in writings from the early church.

The Raising of a Spiritual Body

I start with our earliest recorded source, the writings of Paul, and once again with his "resurrection chapter" (1 Cor. 15), so named because it is devoted to the question of Jesus's resurrection and the future resurrection of believers. Here Paul stresses that Jesus rose from the dead in a *spiritual body*. Both terms are important for understanding Paul's view of the resurrection of Jesus: Jesus was raised in the body; but it was a body that was spiritual.

Many readers of 1 Corinthians undervalue and misinterpret the first point. But Paul is emphatic: Jesus was *bodily* raised from the dead. Paul states this view vigorously in 1 Corinthians 15, and in some sense the entire chapter is written to make the point—precisely because Paul's opponents in Corinth had a different view. In their opposing view, Jesus was raised in the spirit, not in the body, such that Christians who enjoy the resurrection with him in their own lives are also spiritually raised—not in their bodies but in their inner beings. These opponents believed that they were already experiencing the full benefits of salvation in the present. Paul mocks this view in his letter by sarcastically reflecting their own views back to them: "Already you have all you want! Already you have become rich! Quite apart from us you have become kings!" (1 Cor. 4:8). That he is not stating this as fact, but sarcastically, is clear from the context: in the next breath he tells them that he wishes it were true. But alas, it is not. This current evil age is an age of weakness and powerlessness. It is only in the age to come, when Christ returns from heaven, that his followers will enjoy the full benefits of salvation when they are raised from these poor, lowly, weak, inferior, mortal bodies to be given amazing, spiritual, immortal bodies such as Jesus himself had at his resurrection.

And that is the point of 1 Corinthians 15. The fact—Paul takes it as a fact—that the resurrected bodies of believers will be like the resurrected body of Jesus shows that the resurrection has not yet taken place. It is a bodily (not purely spiritual) event, and since it is a bodily event, it obviously has not happened yet because we are still living in our pathetic mortal bodies.

But the body Jesus had when he was raised was not simply his resuscitated corpse brought back to life. It was an astoundingly immortal body, a "spiritual" body. A body, yes. A material body, yes. A body intimately connected to the body that died and was buried, yes. But a transformed body that could not experience pain, misery, or death.

Paul reports that some of his opponents mock his views that there is to be a future resurrection of bodies: "But someone will ask, 'How are the dead raised? With what kind of body do they come?'" His reply is forceful: "Fool! What you sow does not come to life unless it dies" (1 Cor. 15:35–36). He goes on to say that it is like a seed. It goes into the ground as a bare seed, but it grows into a live plant. The body is like that. It dies a paltry, bare, dead thing and is raised gloriously. For "there are both heavenly bodies and earthly bodies, but the glory of the heavenly is one thing, and that of the earthly is another" (15:40). Then he explains that it is this way "with the resurrection of the dead. What is sown is perishable, what is raised is imperishable. It is sown in dishonor, it is raised in glory. It is sown in weakness, it is raised in power. It is sown a physical body, it is raised a spiritual body" (15:42–44).

And so the body of the believer that is to be raised is still a body—and it is intimately connected with the present body—but it is a glorious, immortal, spiritual body, the present body transformed. And Paul knows this because that is the kind of body that Jesus had when he himself was raised.

Some modern readers have trouble understanding how there can be such a thing as a "spiritual body" that is still an actual body. The problem is that today we tend to think of "spirit" and "body" as two opposite things, with the spirit being invisible and non-material and the body being visible and material. For us, spirit is intangible and body is made of "stuff." Most ancient people, however, did not see spirit and body this way, which is why it is possible for Paul to speak of a spiritual body. It was widely believed in antiquity that the spirit we have within us was also made of "stuff." It was material. But it was very highly refined material that could not be seen with the eyes. (Kind of like what people think when they imagine they've seen a "ghost"—there's something there, made of stuff, since it can be seen, even though it's pure spirit.)[3] When Paul speaks of a spiritual body, then, he means a body not made of this heavy, clunky stuff that now makes up our bodies, but of the highly refined spiritual stuff that is superior in every way and is not subject to mortality. That's what the future bodies will be like, because that's what Jesus's resurrected body was like. His body did indeed come out of the grave. But when it did, it was a transformed body, made of spirit, and raised immortal.

Modern readers are not the only ones who find Paul's views confusing or who read Paul to mean something that he didn't say. We know that other Christians stressed either one or the other aspect of his spiritual body to an extreme. Some maintained that Jesus was not raised in the body at all but only in the spirit, and others insisted that his raised body was so closely connected to his corpse that it bore all the marks of its mortality still upon it.

The Raising of the Spirit

Some ancient Christians—taking a line very similar to that found among Paul's opponents in Corinth—maintained that Jesus was raised in the spirit, not in the body; that his body died and rotted in the grave, as bodies do; but that his spirit lived on and ascended to heaven. This view became prominent among various groups of Gnostic Christians.

There is no need for me to go into a lengthy discussion of early Christian Gnosticism in this context; there are numerous excellent studies.[4] For my purposes here it is enough to say that a variety of groups after the New Testament period—all of whom claimed, of course, to represent the "original" views of Jesus and his disciples—maintained that the material world we inhabit is a wicked, fallen place and that it stands at odds with the greater, purely spiritual realm to which ultimately we belong. The way to escape our entrapment in this world of matter is to acquire secret "knowledge" (= gnosis) from above of who we really are, how we came to be here, and how we can return to our heavenly, spiritual home. In this view, Jesus is the one who came down from the heavenly realm to provide us with this secret knowledge. These groups are called Gnostic because of their emphasis on gnosis/knowledge.

I will discuss this view of Christ more fully in Chapter 7. At this stage it is enough to stress that for many of these Gnostics, the figure we think of as Jesus Christ was not a single person, but was actually two persons—a divine being from above who had come temporarily to inhabit the material body of the man Jesus. In this view, the material body, belonging to the material world, and to the inferior God who created it, was transcended at Jesus's death and resurrection, such that the body was killed but the divine spirit, which was distinct from it, was not touched. The divine spirit returned to its heavenly home, while the body was left to corrupt here on earth. In this view, the physical body was not transformed into a spiritual body, as in Paul; it was abandoned to the grave. The spirit lived on past the crucifixion—so much so that it did not actually need to be "raised." It simply escaped the flesh at the crucifixion.

You can find this view in a book called the *Coptic Apocalypse of Peter,* which was discovered along with a cache of other Gnostic writings in 1945 near the Egyptian town of Nag Hammadi. This text gives a firsthand account of the crucifixion of Jesus as observed by Peter himself. What is striking—and very strange indeed—is that while Peter is actually talking to Jesus, he sees another Jesus being crucified. So there are apparently two Jesuses here, at the same time. And more than that, Peter sees yet a third figure hovering above the cross and laughing. This also is Jesus. In his completely understandable confusion, Peter asks Jesus (the one he is talking with) what it is he is seeing. The Savior tells Peter that they are crucifying not him, but only "his physical part." It is the laughing Jesus above the cross who is "the living Jesus." Peter is then told:

> He whom they crucified is the firstborn, and the home of demons, and the clay vessel in which they dwell, belonging to Elohim, and belonging to the cross that is under the law. But he who stands near him is the living Savior, the primal part in him whom they seized. And he has been released. He stands joyfully looking at those who persecuted him. . . . Therefore he laughs at their lack of perception. . . . Indeed, therefore, the suffering one must remain, since the body is the substitute. But that which was released was my incorporeal body. (Apoc. Pet. 82)[5]

And so, what is killed is merely the physical shell of Jesus, which belongs to the God of this world (Elohim—the Hebrew term for God in the Old Testament), rather than the true God. The real Jesus is the incorporeal spirit that inhabited that body for a time but then was released. This "living Jesus" is laughing because his enemies think they can kill him, but in fact they can't touch him. The divine Spirit of Jesus is raised, according to this view, not Jesus's body.[6]

The Raising of the Mortal Body
We don't know how early such full-blown Gnostic views came to expression in the Christian movement; they were certainly in place by the middle of the second century, and possibly earlier.

But there were *tendencies* toward such views already in the New Testament period. If my reconstruction of the events in Corinth stated above are correct, then already in the 50s some believers in Jesus would have been open to the view that Jesus's spirit, not his physical body, was raised from the dead. Further evidence that some Christians held this view can be found in the fact that some of the later Gospel traditions go to some lengths in order to counter it.

In Luke's Gospel, for example, written possibly around 80–85 CE, when Jesus is raised the disciples have trouble believing that it is really him, in the body—even when they see him. This is explicitly stated in Luke 24:36–37: "While they were saying these things, Jesus himself stood in their midst and said to them, 'Peace be with you.' They were startled and afraid, and thought that they were seeing a spirit" (sometimes translated "ghost"). Jesus rebukes them and tells them to feel his body so they can see it is real: "Look at my hands and my feet, to see it is I. Handle me and see—for a spirit does not have flesh and bones as you see that I have" (24:39). They still have trouble believing it, and so he asks them for something to eat. They give him a piece of broiled fish, and he eats it before their eyes.

The point of this story is that it really is Jesus, the same Jesus who had died, and he still is thoroughly a body, with flesh, bones, mouth, and, presumably, digestive system. Why such an emphasis on the bodily nature of the resurrected Jesus? Almost certainly because other Christians were denying that it was the body that was raised. If there had been a debate between Paul (from 1 Corinthians) and Gnostics (from the *Coptic Apocalypse of Peter*) about whether Jesus was raised in the body, Luke would land firmly in the Pauline camp.

But with a possible difference. When Paul speaks of Jesus's spiritual body, he is emphatic in 1 Corinthians that that body is transformed into an immortal being. That, for Paul, is necessary, because the flesh-and-blood body is not of the right "stuff" to enter the kingdom of God. As he states unequivocally in that context: "flesh and blood cannot inherit the kingdom of God, nor does the perishable inherit the imperishable" (1 Cor. 15:50). The mortal, perishable body will be transformed into something else—an immortal, imperishable, spiritual body. Only then will it inherit eternal life. And so that is the kind of body, for Paul, that Jesus also had at his resurrection.

But for Luke it appears that Jesus's resurrected body was simply his corpse that had been reanimated. It is true that he does not say that the body is still "flesh and blood" (to use Paul's term for what cannot enter the kingdom). But he explicitly does say it is "flesh and bones" (Luke 24:39). And unlike a spirit, it can eat a meal of broiled fish. It looks as if Luke is emphasizing that Jesus's resurrection was precisely in the *body* to counter those who wanted to argue that it was in the *spirit*. In doing so, he may have altered Paul's views by emphasizing even more the very real fleshly character of Jesus's body, not as transformed, but as in pure continuity with the body that died.

Later one finds a similar emphasis in John, in the scene of "doubting Thomas." According to John 20:24–28, Thomas was not with the other disciples when Jesus first appeared to them. He does not believe that they have seen the risen Lord and tells them, somewhat overemphatically, that he won't believe it until Jesus appears to him and he can feel the wounds in his hands and side. And sure enough, Jesus shows up and tells Thomas to do just that. Thomas instantly believes.

Here again, Jesus is in the very body that was crucified, wounds and all. Thus, both Luke and John want to emphasize the reality of Jesus's resurrected body and, correspondingly, its absolute continuity with the crucified body, so that it is not obviously "transformed" into something else, as it was in Paul. One could argue that it is no longer a normal body, because even in these

Gospels Jesus seems to be able to show up through locked doors, and so *some* kind of transformation appears to have occurred. But it needs to be remembered that even during Jesus's life his body allegedly had superhuman abilities—it was able to walk on water, for example, and to become "transfigured" in the presence of his disciples. And so the stress of Luke and John appears to be that it really was the same body, raised from the dead.

This was the view that ultimately became the dominant one throughout Christianity in later periods, in no small measure because, as we will see in Chapter 8, some Christians denied that Jesus ever had a body *at all*. A stress on the physicality of Jesus was meant to put any such view to rest. Jesus had a real body during his life and even after his resurrection. Paul's stress that it was a different kind of body—one made of spirit instead of flesh and blood—came to be deemphasized with the passing of time.

It is hard to know what the very earliest Christians, before Paul, thought about Jesus's body after the resurrection—whether they had a view more like that found in Paul, our earliest witness, or more like the one found Luke and John, who were writing later. What is certain is that the earliest followers of Jesus believed that Jesus had come back to life, in the body, and that this was a body that had real bodily characteristics: it could be seen and touched, and it had a voice that could be heard. Why did they come to think this, at the very beginning of the Christian tradition? What made them believe that Jesus had been bodily raised from the dead? Something did. And I think we know what it was. Some of Jesus's followers had visions of him after he had been crucified.

The Visions of Jesus

IT IS INDISPUTABLE THAT some of the followers of Jesus came to think that he had been raised from the dead, and something had to have happened to make them think so. Our earliest records are consistent on this point, and I think they provide us with historically reliable information in one key respect: the disciples' belief in the resurrection was based on visionary experiences.

The Importance of Visions to the Resurrection Faith

I should stress that it was visions, and nothing else, that led the first disciples to believe in the resurrection. Frequently it is stated that a combination of things led to this faith: the discovery of the empty tomb and the appearances of Jesus. My view is that an empty tomb had nothing to do with it. This is not only because the reports of an empty tomb are highly doubtful, as I have tried to show, but even more because an empty tomb would not produce faith, as I will try to demonstrate, and even more important because the earliest records indicate that the tomb did *not* produce faith.

I begin with our early records. The oldest tradition that we have of the resurrection faith is the pre-Pauline creed in 1 Corinthians 15:3–5, which we examined in Chapter 4. This creed says nothing about an empty tomb and indicates that the reason the disciples came to believe in the resurrection was that Jesus appeared to them. The same thing is true of Paul himself: he believed because of a vision, not because he saw an empty tomb (Gal. 1:15–16; 1 Cor. 15:8).

Several of the Gospel accounts, which were written later, present the same view. Our first Gospel is Mark; it records the "fact" that the tomb was empty, but strikingly, no one is said to come to believe that Jesus was raised because of it. Even more striking, in Luke's account the report that the tomb was discovered to be empty was dismissed as "an idle tale" and is explicitly said not to have led anyone to believe (24:11). Only when Jesus appears to the disciples do they come to faith (24:13–53). The same view is advanced in the Gospel of John. Mary Magdalene discovers the empty tomb and is confused, but she does not believe. She instead thinks someone has moved Jesus's body to a different location (20:1–13). Not until Jesus appears to her does she comes to believe (20:14–18).

These stories show what should have come as a logical surmise even without them: if someone was buried in a tomb and later the body was not there, this fact alone would not make anyone suspect that God had raised the person from the dead. Suppose you place a corpse in a rock-hewn tomb. Later the body is missing. What is your immediate thought? It is definitely *not* "resurrection." Instead, it is "grave robbers!" Or, "someone has moved the body." Or, "hey, I must have come to the wrong tomb." Or something else. You do *not* think, "Oh my! This person has been exalted to the right hand of God!"

I want to stress this point in contradistinction to the view set forth by Dale Allison in a book that is otherwise a fine discussion of the resurrection of Jesus.[7] But on one point (well, several others too) I disagree with him. Allison wants to maintain that if the disciples of Jesus had visions of him after his death—both Allison and I agree that they did—this would not lead them to think that Jesus was *bodily* raised from the dead unless they could examine the empty tomb to see that it was so. On the surface this view seems reasonable enough, but the problem is that it overlooks exactly who these followers of Jesus were and what they believed before the events leading up to Jesus's death and its aftermath.

Jesus, as we have seen (and Allison agrees with this), was a Jewish apocalypticist who, among other things, agreed with other Jewish apocalypticists that at the end of this current wicked age the dead would be judged and resurrected. In Jesus's view, the dead would be raised bodily to face judgment, either to be rewarded if they had sided with God or to be punished if they had aligned themselves with the forces of evil. This afterlife in the kingdom would entail a *bodily* resurrection.

And who were the disciples? They were followers of Jesus who, of course, accepted his apocalyptic message and themselves adopted such apocalyptic views.[8] If an apocalyptic Jew of this kind were to come to believe that the resurrection of the dead had begun—for example, with the raising of God's specially favored one, his messiah—what would that resurrection involve? It would naturally and automatically involve precisely a *bodily* resurrection. That's what "resurrection" meant to these people. It did not mean the ongoing life of the spirit without the body. It meant the reanimation and glorification of the body. If the disciples came to believe that Jesus was raised from the dead, they would have on the spot understood that this meant his body was no longer dead but had been brought back to life. They wouldn't need an empty tomb to prove it. Of course, for them, the tomb was empty. It goes without saying and without seeing. Jesus is alive again, which means his body has been raised.

The empty tomb narratives came later—after the creed in 1 Corinthians 15:3–5 and after the writings of Paul. In other words, they were not part of the early tradition. And even when they did come to be told and discussed, Christians realized that the empty tomb itself would not generate faith—as Mark, Luke, and John inform us. Something else did. Some of Jesus's followers had visions of him alive after he had been crucified.

Terminology: What Visions Are

Before we proceed, it is important to be clear about the terminology I am using. When I say that some of the disciples almost certainly had "visions" of Jesus after his death, what do I mean?

I am not using the term *vision* in any particularly technical sense. By "vision" I simply mean something that is "seen," whether it is really there or not. In other words, I am not taking a stand on the question of whether there was some kind of external reality behind what the disciples saw. Scholars who study visions speak of those that are *veridical*—meaning that a person sees something that is really there—and of those that are *nonveridical*—meaning that what a person sees is not really there. Sometimes you see a shadowy figure in your bedroom at night because someone is really there; other times you're "just seeing things."

When it comes to the visions of Jesus that his disciples experienced, Christian believers would typically say that there was indeed an external reality behind them. That is, Jesus really appeared to these people. Anyone with that view would probably call such veridical visions "appearances" of Jesus. Non-Christians would say that the visions were nonveridical, that there was nothing there and that the visions were, possibly, psychologically or neurophysiologically induced. Such people would probably call these visions "hallucinations." The *Diagnostic and Statistical Manual of Mental Disorders* of the American Psychiatric Association defines *hallucination* as "a sensory perception that has the compelling sense of reality of a true perception but that occurs without external stimulation of the relevant sensory organ."[9] It should be noted that "sensory perception" here is understood to refer to not only "seeing," but also to any of the other senses: hearing, feeling, smelling, and even tasting.

I am not going to take a stand on this issue of whether Jesus really appeared to people or whether their visions were hallucinations, so my case does not rise or fall depending on whether the visions were veridical or not. As an agnostic, I personally do not believe Jesus was raised from the dead and so I do not believe he "appeared" to anyone. But what I have to say about the disciples' visions are things I could have said just as easily back in the days when I was a firm believer.

Many discussions of the resurrection are focused on just this question of whether the visions were veridical or not. Most New Testament scholars are themselves Christian and they naturally tend to take the Christian view of the matter—that the visions were bona fide appearances of Jesus to his followers. You can find such views forcefully stated in any number of publications, including the recent, and very large, books by Christian apologist Mike Licona and by renowned New Testament scholar N. T. Wright.[10]

But some prominent New Testament scholars argue vociferously on the other side of the question as well. For example, the German scholar and skeptic Gerd Lüdemann argues that the visions of Jesus experienced by Peter, and then later by Paul, were psychologically induced. In his view, when Jesus died his body decomposed like any other body; thus, Lüdemann says, since Christianity is rooted in the physical resurrection but Jesus actually was not physically raised, "Christian faith is as dead as Jesus."[11]

And then there is the late British New Testament scholar and intellectual gadfly Michael Goulder, who argued that there are numerous occasions when people once provided supernatural explanations for things that now we can explain through science. But once a natural explanation exists for a phenomenon, we no longer need a supernatural one. For example, Goulder points out that in the Middle Ages the effects of what we now would call hysteria—paralysis, tremors, anesthesia, etc.—were attributed to demon possession. No doctor today would think she was grappling with demons when treating hysteria. Now we have a natural explanation for what once required a supernatural one. Another of his examples comes from 1588, when the English fired upon the Spanish Armada and the cannon balls at first did not penetrate the distant ships. An English captain declared that this was because of "our sins." But as the Spanish ships got within closer range, the balls did begin to penetrate. A natural explanation (relative proximity) thus superseded the religious one ("because of our sins"), making the religious one no longer required. In Goulder's view, the same can be said of the visions of the disciples. If we can come up with natural explanations—for example, psychologically induced hallucinations—there is no need for supernatural ones.[12]

I find these debates between believers and unbelievers fascinating, but for my purposes they are beside the point. Whether one believes the visions of Jesus's followers were veridical or non-veridical, the results I think will be the same. The visions led followers of Jesus to believe he had been raised from the dead. And so I incline toward the view of Dale Allison, who maintains the following:

> *The situation is such, I believe, that nothing would prohibit a conscientious historian from steering clear of both theological and anti-theological assumptions, or of both paranormal and anti-paranormal assumptions, and simply adopting a phenomenological approach to the data, which do not in and of themselves demand from historians any particular interpretation. Would it be an historical sin to content oneself with observing that the disciples' experiences, whether hallucinatory or not, were genuine experiences that they at least took to originate outside their subjectivity?*[13]

I do not think it would be a historical sin at all to leave the matter of external stimuli—were the visions veridical or not—undecided, so that believers and unbelievers can reach common ground on the *significance* of these experiences. That is my ultimate concern.

Who Had the Visions? Exploring the "Doubt Tradition"

In considering the significance of the visions of Jesus, a key question immediately comes to the fore that in my judgment has not been given its full due by most scholars investigating the issue. Why do we have such a strong and pervasive tradition that some of the disciples doubted the resurrection, even though Jesus appeared to them? If Jesus came to them, alive, after his death, and talked with them—what was there to doubt?

The reason this question is so pressing is that, as we will see, modern research on visions has shown that visions are almost always believed by the people who experience them. When people have a vision—of a lost loved one, for example—they really and deeply believe the person has been there. So why were the visions of Jesus not always believed? Or rather, why were they so consistently doubted?

Jesus does not appear to anyone in Mark's Gospel, but he does in Matthew, Luke, John, and the book of Acts. Most readers have never noticed this, but in every one of these accounts we have rather direct statements that the disciples doubted that Jesus was raised.

In Matthew 28:17 we are told that Jesus appeared to the eleven, but "some doubted." Why would they doubt if Jesus was right there, in front of them? We have already seen that in Luke 24, when the women report that Jesus has been raised, the disciples consider it an "idle tale" and do not believe it (24:10–11). Then, even when Jesus appears to them, he has to "prove" that he is not a spirit by having them handle him. And even that is not enough: he needs to eat a piece of broiled fish in order finally to convince them (24:37–43). So too in John's Gospel, at first Peter and the beloved disciple do not believe Mary Magdalene that the tomb is empty; they have to see for themselves (John 20:1–10). But what is more germane, the text clearly implies that even when the disciples see Jesus, they don't believe it is he: that is why he has to show them his hands and the wound in his side, to convince them (20:20). So too with doubting Thomas—he sees Jesus, but his doubts are overcome only when he is told to inspect the wounds physically (20:24–28).

And then comes one of the most puzzling verses in all of the

New Testament. In Acts 1:3 we are told that after his resurrection Jesus spent forty days with the disciples—forty days!—showing them that he was alive by "many proofs." Many proofs? How many proofs were needed exactly? And it took forty days to convince them?

Closely related to these doubt traditions are the scenes in the Gospels in which Jesus appears to his disciples after the resurrection and they don't recognize who he is. This is the leitmotif of the famous story of the two disciples on the road to Emmaus in Luke 24:13–31. These two do not realize they are talking to the person they have just been talking about, and they do not recognize Jesus until he breaks bread with them. Similarly, in John 20:14–16, Mary Magdalene is the first to see Jesus raised, but she does not immediately recognize him. She thinks she is talking with the gardener. So too in John 21:4–8, the disciples are fishing after the resurrection and Jesus appears to them on the shore and speaks with them. But they don't realize who it is until the beloved disciple does.

What is one to make of these stories? Some readers have suggested that if the disciples had merely had "visions," it would make sense that there was considerable doubt about what they had seen. This is an interesting point, but as I have already said, and as we will see more fully later, people who have visions tend *not* to doubt what they have seen. The most impressive thing about people who report visionary experiences in numerous different contexts is that they consistently insist, sometimes with some vehemence, that the visions were real—not made up in their heads. This applies across the board—to people who have seen loved ones after they have died (and sometimes talk to them, and hold them), to people who see great religious figures such as the Blessed Virgin Mary (whose sightings are reported and documented to an astonishing extent), to people who claim that they have been abducted by UFOs.[14] People who have visions really believe them. But a number of the disciples are reported not to have believed them, until they were given "proof."

My tentative suggestion is that three or four people—though possibly more—had visions of Jesus sometime after he died. One of these was almost certainly Peter, since reports about his seeing Jesus are found everywhere in our sources, including our earliest record of Paul in 1 Corinthians 15:5. And it needs to be remembered that Paul actually knew Peter. Paul too explicitly states that he had a vision of Jesus, and I think we can take him at his word that he believes Jesus appeared to him. It is also significant that Mary Magdalene enjoys such prominence in all the Gospel resurrection narratives, even though she is virtually absent everywhere else in the Gospels. She is mentioned in only one passage in the entire New Testament in connection with Jesus during his public ministry (Luke 8:1–3), and yet she is always the first to announce that Jesus has been raised. Why is this? One plausible explanation is that she too had a vision of Jesus after he died.

These three people—Peter, Paul, and Mary, as it turns out—must have told others about their visions. Possibly others had them as well—for example, James, Jesus's brother—but I think it is difficult to say. Most of their close associates believed them and came to think that Jesus was raised from the dead. But possibly some of the original disciples did not believe it. This would explain why there is such a strong doubt tradition in the Gospels, and why there is such an emphasis (in Luke, John, and especially Acts) on the fact that Jesus had to "prove" that he was raised, even when he was allegedly standing in front of the disciples. If historically only a few people had the visions, and not everyone believed them, this would explain many things. Mary didn't doubt what she had seen, nor did Peter or Paul. But others did. Still, as the stories of Jesus's "appearances" were told and retold, of course, they were embellished, magnified, and even made up; so soon, probably within a few years, it was said that all of the disciples had seen Jesus, along with other people.

Visions from a Broader Perspective

I have said that it is not important for my purposes whether the visions of Jesus were veridical or not. But in order to understand these visions more deeply, it is necessary to see what scholars who have studied such things have said about visionary experiences. Most serious research on visions is on those that are nonveridical, for an obvious reason. People who see something that is right before their eyes are simply seeing what is there. But why and how do people see things that are not right before their eyes? To appreciate more fully the early reports of visions by Jesus's disciples, we need to explore what other people have said about the visions they have had.

One authoritative account is given by the psychologist Richard Bentall in an article titled "Hallucinatory Experiences."[15] Bentall says that the first real attempt to see whether it was possible for people to have nonveridical visions without suffering from physical or mental illness came at the end of the nineteenth century. A man named H. A. Sidgewick interviewed 7,717 men and 7,599 women and found that 7.8 percent of the men and 12 percent of the women reported having had at least one vivid hallucinatory experience. The most common vision was of a living person who was not present at the time. A number of the visions involved religious or supernatural content. The most common visions were reported by people who were twenty to twenty-nine years old.

The first truly modern survey—using modern methods of analysis accepted today in the social sciences—was conducted by P. McKellar in 1968. One out of four "normal" people reported having had at least one hallucinatory experience. Fifteen years later a study by T. B. Posey and M. E. Losch considered auditory hallucinations—in which a person hears a voice without seeing anyone. Among 375 college students, fully 39 percent reported having had the experience.

The most comprehensive survey of the general population

was conducted by A. Y. Tien in 1991. This study involved 18,572 people. Remarkably, 13 percent of them claimed to have experienced at least one vivid hallucination—a statistic very close to what Sidgewick had found, using less scientific methods, nearly a century earlier. It is worth noting that the risk of schizophrenia in the general population is usually estimated as being 1 percent. This means that there are more than ten times as many people who have experienced hallucinations as who suffer from schizophrenia.

How does one explain these large numbers? Bentall argues that the ability to distinguish between self-generated events (that is, imaginary sensations originating in the mind) and externally generated ones (that is, those induced by causes exterior to the mind) is a real skill that humans acquire, and like all skills, it "is likely to fail under certain circumstances."[16] This skill is called *source monitoring*—since it is the skill of monitoring where the source of a sensation comes from, either inside or outside the mind. Bentall argues that source monitoring judgments are affected by the culture in which a person grows up. If a person's culture subscribes to the existence of ghosts or the reality of dead people appearing, the chance that what one "sees" will be assumed to be a ghost or a dead person is obviously heightened. Moreover, and this is a key point, stress and emotional arousal can have serious effects on a person's source monitoring skills. Someone who is under considerable stress, or experiencing deep grief, trauma, or personal anguish, is more likely to experience a failure of source monitoring.

This may be why two of the most frequently reported forms of visions involve the comforting presence of a deceased loved one or of a respected religious figure. Of course people have all sorts of other visions—some of them induced by mental imbalance or physiological stimulants, such as hallucinatory drugs, as so wonderfully documented in Oliver Sacks's book *Hallucinations*. But for people who are not suffering from mental disease and are not ingesting LSD, visions appear to occur with particular frequency among those who are experiencing bereavement or religious awe and expectation.

Bereavement Visions

A significant amount of research has been done on visions caused by bereavement. One of the most striking features of this research is that those who experience such visions almost always assume, and wholeheartedly believe, that they are veridical. The person who has died really has come back to visit. Outsiders tend to see these visions as hallucinations. As with the visions of the historical Jesus, I see no need to take a side on the debate on whether the dead really do visit those they have left behind.

Certain typical aspects of these visions are of some relevance for understanding the disciples' visions of Jesus—who was, after all, a beloved one who had died suddenly and tragically and was deeply mourned and grieved. As Dale Allison summarizes the research on bereavement visions, these usually entail a feeling that the lost loved one continues to be present, even in the same room, with the one mourning.[17] Such visions are more commonly experienced when a person has a sense of guilt over some aspect of his or her relationship with the one who has died (recall: the disciples had all betrayed, denied, or fled from Jesus during his hour of need). Often they are accompanied by anger at the circumstances or the people who caused the loved one's death (another obvious parallel to the disciples and Jesus). Strikingly, after the loved ones have died, the survivors idealize them, smoothing over the difficult aspects of their personalities or remembering only their good sides. And not infrequently, those suffering bereavement seek to form community with others who remember the loved ones and tell stories about them. All of these features relate closely with what we have in the case of Jesus, the beloved teacher and master who met an untimely death.

One particularly intriguing set of modern findings has to do with what Bill and Judy Guggenheim have called "After-Death Communications."[18] I should stress that the Guggenheims are not trained in psychology or in other fields relevant to the scientific study of visions; therefore, their analysis of their data is not useful for scholarly purposes. But the data themselves are significant, and by gathering it, the Guggenheims have performed a service of real value: they have interviewed more than thirty-three hundred people who have claimed they were contacted by a dead loved one, and they have presented numerous accounts of such contacts in their publications. Let me stress: these are pieces of anecdotal evidence. But they are fascinating anecdotes indeed and are valuable for giving insight into what people experience when they have visions of dead loved ones.

These interviews show that such visions happen both to people who are asleep and to people who are awake. Moreover, even when people have the vision in a dream, they almost always take it to mean not that they "were simply dreaming," but that the person they saw really has survived death and is still alive and communicating with them. These experiences often happen immediately after a person's death—but sometimes they happen a year later, three years later, ten years later, or more. They almost always bring a peaceful assurance that all is well with the person who has died. The person who is mourned is not always a family member—he or she can also be a friend or another loved one.

It appears that people who are physically or emotionally exhausted are more likely to have an After-Death Communication. In the Guggenheims' extensive experience the communications occur more frequently when someone has died unexpectedly or tragically. The key element seems to be that a person is deeply missed. That person then communicates with the one who is grieving. It is especially striking that many of the people interviewed by the Guggenheims did not know that such a thing as

After-Death Communication existed or had ever occurred—before experiencing it themselves. That was part of what made these experiences so convincing to the people who had them: they were sudden, unexpected, and vivid.

It is not the Guggenheims' mission to compare these modern experiences to those the disciples of Jesus had. But the similarities cannot be overlooked by someone who is interested in the beginnings of Christianity. The much beloved teacher of the disciples—the one for whom they had given up everything and to whom they had devoted their lives—was suddenly and brutally taken away from them, publicly humiliated, tortured, and crucified. According to our early records, the disciples had plenty of reasons for feeling guilt and shame over how they had failed Jesus both during his life and at his greatest time of need. Soon thereafter—and for some time to come?—some of them believed they had encountered him after his death. They were deeply comforted by his presence and felt his forgiveness. They had not expected to have these experiences, which had come upon them suddenly and with a vividness that made them believe that their beloved teacher was still alive.

But unlike the modern people interviewed by the Guggenheims, these followers of Jesus were ancient Jewish apocalypticists. Many modern people who believe a loved one lives on may think their souls have gone to heaven, since that's a common modern version of life after death. As apocalyptic Jews, the disciples believed that the afterlife entailed a resurrection of the dead. When they experienced Jesus after he had died, they naturally understood his new life in light of their own deeply held convictions. He had been bodily raised from the dead.

Visions of Esteemed Religious Figures

Of additional relevance to our reflections are visions of revered religious figures from the past, which are among the best documented kind of visionary experience. Here I briefly explore the "appearances" of the Blessed Virgin Mary and visions in the modern world of Jesus himself.

The Blessed Virgin Mary

René Laurentin is a modern-day Catholic theologian and expert on modern apparitions who has written many books on the topic.[19] He has a degree in philosophy from the Sorbonne in Paris and two doctorates, one in theology and one in literature. And he deeply and sincerely believes that Mary—the mother of Jesus who died two thousand years ago—has appeared to people in the modern world and that she continues to do so. Here I give just two examples from his writings.

In Betania, Venezuela, a woman named Maria Esperanza Medrano de Bianchini received peculiar spiritual powers: she could tell the future, levitate, and heal the sick. The Virgin Mary appeared to her several times, starting in March 1976. The most striking occurrence, on March 25, 1984, involved lots of other people. After the Catholic mass that morning, a number of people went to enjoy some time outdoors near the local waterfall, and the Virgin Mary appeared above it. This began a series of visions. Mary came and went, often visible for five minutes or so, the last time for half an hour. Among the observers were doctors, psychologists, psychiatrists, engineers, and lawyers. People over the weeks to come started picnicking there. At times, up to a thousand people observed Mary there, bathed in light and accompanied by the smell of roses. This continued until 1988. Later, a Jesuit priest, Monsignor Pio Bello Ricardo, who was a professor of psychology at the Central University of Caracas, interviewed 490 people who claimed to have seen Mary there. They convinced him that Mary had really been at the waterfall.

A second example comes from Cairo, Egypt, from 1986, at a Coptic church. Mary had appeared there a number of times between 1983 and 1986. Once, she appeared on the roof, and four Coptic bishops authenticated the vision. They did indeed see her. At other times, she was seen by Muslims (who were not Christians, obviously). In some instances, she was actually photographed. Laurentin says that he has a photograph of a similar apparition from another Coptic suburb from 1968.

My point is not that Mary really is appearing in these times and places, but that people deeply believe she is. And not just people whom we might "write off" as being particularly gullible—but people whom we might think should "know better." Anecdotal collections of Mary visions can be found in numerous books, such as Janice Connell's *Meetings with Mary: Visions of the Blessed Mother* (1995). Connell provides fourteen chapters detailing visions of Mary, from a believer's perspective, from the nineteenth and twentieth centuries, as these are documented from places such as Lourdes, France; Fatima, Portugal; Garabandal, Spain; and Medjugorje, Bosnia-Herzegovina. There is, for example, the "cosmic miracle of the sun" that took place at Fatima on October 13, 1917. We are told the sun was seen to spin wildly and to tumble down to earth before stopping and returning to its normal position, radiating indescribably beautiful colors. The miracle was seen and attested to by more than fifty thousand people.

Do such miracles happen? Believers say yes, unbelievers say no. But it is striking and worth noting that typically believers in *one* religious tradition often insist on the "evidence" for the miracles that support their views and completely discount the "evidence" for miracles attested in some other religious tradition, even though, at the end of the day, it is the same kind of evidence (for example, eyewitness testimony) and may be of even greater abundance. Protestant apologists interested in "proving" that Jesus was raised from the dead rarely show any interest in applying their finely honed historical talents to the exalted Blessed Virgin Mary.

Jesus's Appearances in the Modern World

Jesus also appears to people today, and some of these sightings are documented by Phillip H. Wiebe in his book *Visions of Jesus: Direct Encounters from the New Testament to Today* (1997).[20] Wiebe presents twenty-eight case studies, which he examines from psychological, neuropsychological, mentalist, and other perspectives. Included is a vision of Jesus experienced by Hugh Montefiore, a well-known New Testament scholar at Cambridge University and later bishop of the Church of England, who converted to Christianity from Judaism at age sixteen because he had a vision in which Jesus appeared to him and told him to "follow me"— words that, at the time, the young Montefiore did not know were drawn from the New Testament.

Of particular interest are instances in which Jesus is said to have appeared to entire groups of people, rather than just to an individual. No case is more intriguing than the last one Wiebe recounts, that of Kenneth Logie, a preacher in a Pentecostal Holiness Church in Oakland, California, in the 1950s. Two appearances are worth detailing. The first occurred in April 1954 when Logie was preaching at an evening service. In the middle of his sermon, around 9:15 P.M., the door to the church opened, and Jesus walked in and came down the aisle smiling to people on the right and the left. He then walked *through* (not around) the pulpit and placed his hand on Logie's shoulder. Logie, understandably, collapsed. Jesus spoke to him in an unknown foreign tongue, and Logie revived enough to reply to him in English, having understood what he said. Wiebe tells us that fifty people witnessed the event.

Strange things happen. But what happened five years later was even stranger. And two hundred people saw and confirmed they had seen it. And remarkably, it was captured on film. The reason it was filmed, Logie later said, was that very strange things had been happening in the church and they wanted to document them. Wiebe himself saw the film in 1965. A woman from the congregation was giving her testimony when suddenly she disappeared and was replaced by a male figure who was obviously Jesus. He was wearing sandals and a glistening white robe, and he had nail marks in his hand. His hands were dripping with oil. After several minutes, during which he apparently said nothing, he disappeared and the woman reappeared.

Unfortunately, by the time Wiebe had decided to write his book, some twenty-six years after first seeing the film of the event, the film had disappeared. Logie claimed it had been stolen. Still, Wiebe was able to find, and interview, five people who had been there and agreed that they had seen the event. Moreover, there still were surviving photographs of the other odd occurrences in the church back in 1959: images of hands, hearts, and crosses had started to appear on the church walls, with liquid like oil flowing from them and a fragrance being emitted from them. The walls were checked by a skeptic, who had no natural explanation for these appearances (no hidden windows or the like). Wiebe has seen the photographs.

Skeptics may point out that the time between when these events allegedly happened in the 1950s and Wiebe's written account of them amounts to several decades, so one may be justified in suspecting the accuracy of the witnesses' memories. But Wiebe points out that about the same amount of time fell between the life of Jesus and the accounts of the earliest Gospels.

The Disciples' Visions of Jesus

Let us return to the visions that Jesus's disciples apparently had. Christian apologists sometimes claim that the most sensible historical explanation for these visions is that Jesus really appeared to the disciples. Let me bracket for a second the question of whether a historian can conclude that a miracle probably happened in the past (the historian definitely cannot, as I've argued; but I'll bracket

the question for a moment). Often one hears from these apologists that the visions must be veridical because "mass hallucinations" cannot happen—so if Paul says "five hundred brothers"
all saw Jesus at one time, it defies belief that this could have been
imagined by all five hundred at once. There is a certain force to
this argument, but it does need to be pointed out that Paul is the
only one who mentions this event, and if it really happened—or
even if it was widely believed to have happened—it is hard to
explain why it never made its way into the Gospels, especially
those later Gospels such as Luke and John that were so intent on
"proving" that Jesus was physically raised from the dead.[21] Apart
from that, most people at the end of the day believe that mass hallucinations are not only possible, but that they really can happen.
Precisely those conservative evangelical scholars who claim that
mass hallucinations don't happen are the ones who deny that the
Blessed Virgin Mary has appeared to hundreds or thousands of
people at once, even though we have modern, verified eyewitness
testimony that she has.

Sometimes such apologists claim that a hallucination could
not possibly produce the result that Jesus's appearances did: causing a complete moral and personal transformation of the disciples.
This view, too, cannot be sustained after more than a moment's
thought. In order for a vision to have its effect—to relieve guilt,
to remove shame, to provide a sense of comfort, to make a person
want to live again, or any other effect—it does not have to be
veridical. It has to be *believed*. Some of the disciples wholeheartedly believed that they had seen Jesus after he had died. They
concluded that he had been raised from the dead. That changed
everything, as we will see. Whether Jesus was really there or not
has no bearing on the fact that the disciples *believed* he was.

Finally, in a more scholarly vein, some people have argued
that a vision of Jesus would not lead the disciples to believe that
he had been raised from the dead because Judaism at the time

did not have a sense that an individual would be resurrected before the "general resurrection" at the end of time, when all people would be brought back to life. This too is an interesting argument, but it also is not convincing to someone who knows something about ancient beliefs of life and the afterlife. The New Testament itself reports that Herod Antipas believed that Jesus was actually John the Baptist "raised from the dead"; therefore, some such belief was not implausible. Moreover, a belief was attested in non-Christian Jewish circles that the emperor Nero would return from the dead to wreak more havoc on the earth, as reported in a group of Jewish texts known as the *Sibylline Oracles*.[22] It was not unthinkable that someone would come back from the dead (as, for example, Lazarus did). But anyone who was an apocalyptic Jew like Jesus's closest follower Peter, or Jesus's own brother James, or his later apostle Paul, who thought that Jesus had come back to life, would naturally interpret it in light of his particular apocalyptic worldview—a worldview that informed everything that he thought about God, humans, the world, the future, and the afterlife. In that view, a person who was alive after having died would have been bodily raised from the dead, by God himself, so as to enter into the coming kingdom. That's how the disciples interpreted Jesus's resurrection. Moreover, that is why Jesus was understood to be the "first fruits" of those who had died (e.g., 1 Cor. 15:20): because he was the first to be raised, and all others were to be raised soon as well. In that sense his resurrection *was* the beginning of the general resurrection.

At the end of the day, belief in Jesus's resurrection "works" whether the visions were veridical or not. If they were veridical, it was because Jesus was raised from the dead.[23] If they were not veridical, they are easily explained on other grounds. The disciples were bereaved and deeply grieving for their dearest loved one, who had experienced a sudden, unexpected, and particularly violent death. They may have felt guilt about how they had behaved toward him, especially in the tense hours immediately before his death. It is not at all unheard of for such people to have an "encounter" with the lost loved one afterward. In fact, such people are more inclined to have just such an encounter. My view is that historians can't "prove" it either way.

The Outcome of Faith

EVEN THOUGH HISTORIANS CANNOT prove or disprove the historicity of Jesus's resurrection, it is certain that some of the followers of Jesus came to *believe* in his resurrection. This is the turning point in Christology. *Christology,* as I have said, is a term that literally means *the understanding of Christ.* My point in this chapter—indeed, in this book—is that belief in the resurrection changed everything Christologically. Before the followers of Jesus believed in his resurrection, they thought he was a great teacher, an apocalyptic preacher, and, probably, the one chosen to be king in the coming kingdom of God. Since they followed him wholeheartedly, they must have subscribed to his teaching wholeheartedly. Like him, they thought the age they were living in was controlled by the forces of evil, but that God would soon intervene to make right all that was wrong. In the very near future, God was going to send a cosmic judge over the earth, the Son of Man, to destroy the wicked powers that were making life so miserable in this world and to set up a good kingdom, a utopian place where good would prevail and God would rule through his messiah. The disciples would sit on thrones as rulers in the coming kingdom, and Jesus would be seated on the greatest throne of all, as the messiah of God.

But he was purely human. He was a great teacher, yes. A charismatic preacher, yes. And even the son of David who would rule in the future kingdom, yes. But he was a man. Born like other humans, raised like other humans, in nature no different from others, only wiser, more spiritual, more insightful, more righteous, more godly. But not God—certainly not God, in any of the ancient senses of the term.

That all changed with the belief in the resurrection. When the disciples came to believe that God had raised Jesus from the dead, they did not think it was a resuscitation such as you can find elsewhere among the Jewish and Christian traditions. In the Hebrew Bible, Elijah was said to have brought a young man back from the dead (1 Kgs. 17:17–24). But that young man went on to live his life here on earth and then he died. Later there were stories about Jesus raising the daughter of Jairus from the dead (Mark 5:21–43). She did not ascend to heaven and become immortal: she grew up, grew old, and died. Jesus allegedly raised his friend Lazarus from the dead (John 11:1–44). He too eventually died. These were all instances of resuscitation, when the body came back from the dead in order to live and then die again. They were the ancient equivalents of near-death experiences.

But that is not what the disciples believed about Jesus. The reason is clear. They believed Jesus had come back from the dead—but he was not still living among them as one of them. He was nowhere to be found. He did not resume his teaching activities in the hills of Galilee. He did not return to Capernaum to continue his proclamation of the coming Son of Man. He did not come back to engage in yet more heated controversies with the Pharisees. Jesus in a very palpable and obvious sense was no longer here. But he had come back from the dead. So where was he?

This is the key. The disciples, knowing both that Jesus was raised and that he was no longer among them, concluded that he had been exalted to heaven. When Jesus came back to life, it was not merely that his body had been reanimated. God had taken Jesus up to himself in the heavenly realm, to be with him. God had exalted him to a position of virtually unheard-of status and authority. The expectation that Jesus would be the future king in the kingdom, a human messiah, was just a foretaste of what was really in store for him. God had done something far beyond what anyone could have thought or imagined. God had taken him into the heavenly sphere and bestowed divine favor upon him such as had never, in the disciples' opinion, been bestowed on a human before. Jesus no longer belonged to this earthly realm. He was now with God in heaven.

This is why the disciples told the stories of Jesus's post-resurrection appearances the way they did. Jesus did not resume his earthly body. He had a heavenly body. When he appeared to his disciples, in the earliest traditions, he appeared from heaven. And his heavenly body could do things no earthly body could do. In Matthew's Gospel, when the women arrived at the tomb on the third day, the stone was not yet rolled away. It rolled away as they arrived. But the tomb was empty. That meant that Jesus's body had been taken through solid rock. Later, when he appeared to the disciples, he walked through locked doors. Jesus had a heavenly body, not just an earthly body.

Let me return to a comment I made earlier: that even in the Gospels Jesus appears to have a heavenly body during his earthly life—one that can walk on water, for example, or be transfigured into a radiating glow in the presence of some of his disciples. But it is important to remember: these Gospels were written by believers in Jesus decades later who already "knew" that Jesus had been exalted to heaven. As storytellers told the stories of Jesus's earthly career, year after year and decade after decade, they did not separate who Jesus was after his death—the one who had been exalted to heaven—from who he was during his life. And so their belief in the exalted Jesus affected the ways they told their stories about him. They recounted miracles that he had done as a divine human—healing the sick, casting out demons, walking on water, multiplying the loaves, raising the dead. Why could Jesus do these things?

They were attributed to him by his later followers who already "knew" that he wasn't a mere mortal because God had exalted him to heaven. As a heavenly being, Jesus was in some sense divine. The storytellers told their tales fully believing that he was uniquely divine, with that belief affecting how they told their stories.

Before these storytellers began their work of recounting the words and deeds of this divine man, the earliest believers—as soon as they had visions of Jesus and came to believe he had been raised from the dead—thought he had been exalted to heaven. His appearances to them were appearances from heaven. That was where he lived now and would live for all eternity, with God Almighty.

In some later traditions this belief came to be modified in an important way. Today, most Christians think that Jesus died; that he was raised from the dead on the third day; that he then appeared, while still on earth, to his disciples; and that only after that he went up to heaven, in his "ascension." As it turns out, the ascension is mentioned in only one book of the New Testament, the book of Acts.[24] The author of Acts—let's call him Luke— presents an innovation here in his story of Jesus. If you will recall, Luke is especially committed to showing that Jesus's resurrected body was a real, honest-to-goodness body. It had flesh and bones. It could be felt. It could eat broiled fish. Luke stresses this point because other Christians were saying that Jesus, at least in his resurrected form, was a spirit, not a body. For Luke, he was a body. And to make that point even more emphatic, Luke tells the story of the ascension. Possibly Luke himself came up with this story. As we have seen, according to the book of Acts, Jesus spent forty days with his disciples, showing them "with many proofs" that he really was alive again (1:3). And then, after the forty days, he physically went up to heaven—and the disciples watched him go. This account is meant to emphasize yet further the real bodily nature of Jesus after his resurrection.

But it stands in tension with the views found elsewhere in the Gospels, which say nothing about a physical ascension of a real, bony, fish-eating body. The earliest tradition was different from what is in Acts. In that earlier tradition, Jesus's resurrection was not simply a reanimation of a body that was then to be taken up into heaven. The resurrection itself was an exaltation into the heavenly realm. "God raised Jesus from the dead" was taken to mean that God had exalted Jesus from this earthly realm of life and death into the heavenly sphere. In this older understanding, Jesus appeared to his disciples by coming down briefly from heaven. This certainly is the understanding of our earliest witness, Paul, who speaks about his own vision of Jesus in exactly the same terms as the visions of the others two or three years before him—Cephas, James, the Twelve, and so on. There was nothing categorically different about any of these appearances. They were all appearances from heaven.

If the first believers in Jesus's resurrection understood it to mean that Jesus had been taken into heaven, how exactly did that lead them to change what they thought about Jesus? How did it mark the beginning of Christology? How did it cause his followers to believe that Jesus was God?

This is the subject of the next chapter, but for now, here's a brief foreshadowing. The followers of Jesus, during his life, believed that he would be the king of the future kingdom, the messiah. Now that they believed he had been exalted to the heavenly realm, they realized they had been right. He was the future king; but he would come from heaven to reign. In some traditions of the Jewish king in the Hebrew Bible, as we have seen, the king—even the earthly son of David—was thought to be in some sense God. Jesus now had been exalted to heaven and is the heavenly messiah to come to earth. In an even more real sense, he was God. Not God Almighty, of course, but he was a heavenly being, a superhuman, a divine king who would rule the nations.

Before Jesus's death the disciples believed he would sit on the future throne. If God has taken him up into heaven, he is already sitting on a throne. In fact, he is at the right hand of God. On earth the disciples considered him their master and "lord." Now he really is their Lord. The disciples recalled the scripture that said, "The LORD says to my Lord, 'Sit at my right hand until I make your enemies your footstool'" (Ps. 110:1). God had taken Jesus, exalted him to his right hand in a position of authority and power, made him the Lord of all, who would rule over all things. As one who ruled from beside God's throne, Jesus was in that sense also God.

The king in Israel was also known as the "Son of God." Jesus clearly was that—both by virtue of his being the future king and by the fact that God had elevated him to the heavenly realm. God had showered his special favor upon Jesus and made him in a unique sense the Son of God—far above the status enjoyed by the descendants of David. God had adopted Jesus to be his Son, his unique Son. Just as the emperors were sons of both God (since their adopted fathers were "God") and gods, so too Jesus, as the Son of God, was in that sense God.

Jesus, then, was coming to rule from heaven. In his own teaching he had proclaimed that the Son of Man was to appear as the cosmic judge over the earth. But now it was obviously Jesus himself who was coming from heaven to rule. The disciples very soon—probably right away—concluded that Jesus was the coming Son of Man. So when they told stories about him later, they had him speak of himself as the Son of Man—so much so that it became one of his favorite titles for himself in the Gospels. As we have seen, the Son of Man was sometimes understood to be a divine figure. In that sense also, then, Jesus was God.

It should be noted that all four of these exalted roles—Jesus as messiah, as Lord, as Son of God, as Son of Man—imply, in one sense or another, that Jesus is God. In no sense, in this early period, is Jesus understood to be God the Father. He is not the One Almighty God. He is the one who has been elevated to a divine position and is God in a variety of senses. As I have been arguing and will argue extensively in the next chapter, whenever someone claims that Jesus is God, it is important to ask: God *in what sense*? It took a long time indeed for Jesus to be God in the complete, full, and perfect sense, the second member of the Trinity, equal with God from eternity and "of the same essence" as the Father.

CHAPTER 6

The Beginning of Christology

Christ as Exalted to Heaven

WHEN I BECAME SERIOUS about my Christian faith in high school, my social life was rather profoundly affected. Not right away, but eventually. My first serious relationship was with a girl named Lynn, whom I started to date as a sophomore, the year before I became born again. Lynn was a wonderful human being: intelligent, attractive, funny, caring. She was also Jewish. I'm not sure I had ever known a Jewish person before, and I don't recall that our respective religions had much, if any, bearing on our relationship. I was an altar boy at the Episcopal church every Sunday, and she went to synagogue on Saturday. Or at least I assume she did; looking back, I don't remember whether her family was religious in any traditional sense of the word—attending services or even keeping Jewish holidays. I suppose they were rather secular Jews. Frankly, at the time, when it came to a girlfriend, I had other things on my mind than alternative worship practices.

Lynn was one of three daughters living with a single mom. They were like my family, somewhere in the middle to upper middle class, with many of the same values and outlooks on life as mine. Lynn and I had terrifically good chemistry and ended up spending a lot of time together, as we got increasingly serious throughout that sophomore year. But then disaster struck. (I had a very limited understanding of the possibilities of disaster at the time.) Lynn's mom was offered a better job in Topeka, Kansas, and they were going to move there from Lawrence. Her mom and I had always gotten along extremely well, but she was firm: even though the towns were only about twenty-five miles apart, this move should mark the end of our "going together" (as we called it back then). We should meet other people and have normal social lives. And so we did. I was heartbroken, but life must go on.

Soon after that, I was born again. Lynn and I still talked on the phone—and even saw each other on occasion. I vividly remember one conversation we had after I had "received Christ." I was trying to persuade her that she too should ask Jesus into her heart. She was understandably confused—in no small part because I myself had no clue what I was talking about. After a long talk in which I tried to explain it all in my amateurish way, she finally asked, "But if I already have God in my life, why do I need Jesus?" It was a stunner of a question for me. I was completely flummoxed. I was clearly not a good bet for a career in theology.

Lynn's question would not have flummoxed the earliest Christians. Quite the contrary, the first followers of Jesus had very clear ideas about who Jesus was and why he mattered. A look at the historical record shows that they not only talked about him all the time, they came up with increasingly exalted things to say about him and magnified his importance more and more with the passing of time. Eventually, they came to claim that he was God come to earth.

But what did the earliest Christians say about him right after they came to believe that he had been raised from the dead? In this chapter I explore the earliest Christologies—understandings of Christ—of the earliest Christians.

The Beliefs of the Earliest Christians

FOR THE PURPOSES OF this discussion, I am using the term *Christian* in its most basic sense, as referring to anyone who, after Jesus's life, came to believe that he was the Christ of God and was determined both to accept the salvation he brought and to follow him. I do not think that "Christian" is an appropriate term for Jesus's followers before his death; but used in the way I've just described makes good sense for those who came to believe that he had been raised from the dead and thought of him as one who was specially chosen by God to bring about salvation.

The first who came to this belief were his own remaining disciples—or at least some of them—and possibly others of his followers from Galilee, including Mary Magdalene and some other women. As it turns out, it is extremely difficult to know what these people believed as soon as they accepted the idea that Jesus had been raised from the dead, in no small measure because we have no writings from them, or writings of any kind, in fact, from the first two decades of the Christian movement.

Our Oldest Surviving Christian Sources

The first Christian author we have is the Apostle Paul, whose earliest surviving writing is probably 1 Thessalonians, written possibly around 49 or 50 CE—fully twenty years after Jesus had been crucified. Paul started out as an outsider to the apostolic band and originally opposed rather than supported their movement. Two years or so after Jesus's death, say 32 or 33 CE, when Paul first heard of Jews who believed Jesus to be the messiah—a crucified man!—he rejected their views with vehemence and set about persecuting them. But then in one of the great turnarounds in religious history—arguably the most significant conversion on record—Paul changed from being an aggressive persecutor of the Christians to being one of their strongest proponents. He eventually became a leading spokesperson, missionary, and theologian for the fledgling Christian movement. He later claimed that this was because he had had a vision of Jesus alive, long after his death, and concluded that God must have raised him from the dead.

Paul believed he was personally called by God to engage in missionary activities among the gentiles, persuading these "pagans" that their own gods were dead, lifeless, and of no use, but that the God of Jesus was the one who had created the world and entered history in order to redeem it. Only belief in the messiah could put a person into a right standing before God, because the messiah had died for the sins of others, and God, in order to show that this death did indeed bring atonement, had raised him from the dead. Arguably, Paul's greatest contribution to the theology of his day was his hard-fought view that this salvation in Christ applied to all people, Jew and gentile alike, on the same grounds: faith in the death and resurrection of Jesus. Being Jewish had nothing to do with it. To be sure, Jews were the "chosen people," and the Jewish scriptures were a revelation from God. But a gentile did not have to become a Jew in order to have salvation through the death and resurrection of the messiah. For Paul, salvation certainly had come "from the Jews," since Jesus was, after all, the Jewish messiah; but once this salvation had come to the world, it was good for the entire world, not just for Jews. It was the means of salvation that God had planned from eternity for all people.

As a Christian missionary Paul traveled from one urban center to another preaching this message, and he established churches in various parts of the Mediterranean, especially in Asia Minor (modern Turkey), Macedonia, and Achaia (modern Greece). After he started a Christian community and got it on its feet, he would head to another city and start a community there as well, and then move on again. As he heard news from one community or another of the problems they were having, he wrote back to them to instruct them further about what they should believe and how they should behave. The letters of Paul that we have in the New Testament are some of these communications. As I have indicated, 1 Thessalonians was probably the first. The others were all written over the course of the next decade, in the 50s. Of the thirteen letters that are under Paul's name in the New Testament, critical scholars are reasonably sure that Paul actually wrote seven of them—Romans, 1 and 2 Corinthians, Galatians, Philippians, 1 Thessalonians, and Philemon (the others were written by later followers of Paul in different contexts); these are called the *undisputed Pauline letters,* since almost no one disputes that Paul was their author.[1] These are our earliest surviving writings from an early Christian.

The Pauline letters are extremely valuable for knowing what Paul thought and for seeing what was happening in the Christianity of his day. But what if we want to know not simply what was happening in Paul's churches in, say, 55 CE, twenty-five years after Jesus's death, or how Matthew's community was understanding Jesus around 85 CE, some fifty-five years after Jesus's death? What if we want to know what the very earliest Christians believed, say, in the year 31 or 32, a year or two after Jesus died?

This is obviously a big problem, since, as I have said, we don't have any writings from that time. And the one New Testament writing that allegedly records what was happening at the earliest period in Christian history—the book of Acts—was written around 80–85 CE, again, fifty or fifty-five years after the time we are for now most interested in. Moreover, the author of Acts, whom we continue to call Luke, did what all historians of his day did: he told his story in light of his own beliefs, understandings, and perspectives, and these affected how he recounted his material, much of which he no doubt inherited from storytellers among the Christians who had long been recounting—and therefore changing and embellishing—the stories of the early years of the faith.

Given this state of affairs with our sources, how can we get to the earliest forms of Christian belief, before the time of our oldest surviving writings? As it turns out, there is a way. And it involves passages of a sort I mentioned earlier: preliterary traditions.

Detecting Sources "Behind" Our Sources: Preliterary Traditions

The first Ph.D. seminar I took in my graduate program was called "Creeds and Hymns in the New Testament." The professor was named Paul Meyer. He was an erudite and deeply learned New Testament scholar, respected by all the leading scholars of the day for the astonishing care he took when engaging in exegesis and, as a result, for his unusually penetrating insights into the text of the New Testament.

The idea behind the course was that some passages in the New Testament—especially in some of the epistles and in Acts—are remnants of much older traditions from the early decades of the Christian movement. For the sake of this class, we called these preliterary traditions *hymns* and *creeds* (recall: *preliterary* means that the traditions were formulated and transmitted orally before they were written down by the authors whose works we still have). Scholars had long supposed that some of these traditions had been sung during very early Christian worship services (hymns) and others of them were statements of faith (creeds) that had been recited in liturgical settings—for example, at a person's baptism or during a weekly worship service.

The value of being able to isolate preliterary traditions is that they give us access to what Christians were believing and how they were extolling God and Christ *before* our earliest surviving writings. Some of these preliterary traditions can plausibly be located to a time within a decade or less after Jesus's followers first came to believe he had been raised from the dead.

It is not easy to detect places where preliterary traditions survive in the New Testament writings, but as a rule there are several indicators. Not every creed or hymn (or poem) has all of these features, but the clearest such traditions have most of them. First, these traditions tend to be self-contained units—meaning that you can remove them from the literary context we now find them in and they still make sense, standing by themselves. These traditions are often highly structured in a literary sense; for example, they may have poetic-like stanzas and various lines that correspond in meaning to other lines. In other words, these traditions can be highly stylized. Moreover, one often finds that the words and phrases of these traditions are not favored, or used at all, by the author within whose works they are embedded (showing that he probably did not compose them). Even more striking, these preliterary traditions not infrequently express theological views that differ in lesser or greater ways from those found in the rest of an author's writing. You can see how these features suggest that the tradition did not originate in the writings of the author: the style, vocabulary, and ideas are different from what you find elsewhere in his work. Moreover, in some cases the unit that has been identified in these ways does not fit very well in the literary context where it is now found—it looks like it has been transplanted there. Often, if you take the unit out of its context and then read the context without it, the piece of writing makes sense and flows perfectly well, as if nothing were missing.

In Chapter 4 we examined one piece of preliterary tradition: 1 Corinthians 15:3–5. These verses meet several of the criteria I have laid out, as we have seen: they form a tightly structured creed in two parts, each part containing four lines that correspond in meaning with one another (between the first and second parts), and they contain certain key words not found elsewhere in Paul's letters. Paul is almost certainly quoting an earlier creed.

There are other such preliterary traditions in Paul's writings and in the book of Acts. What is striking is that a number of them embody Christological views that are not exactly those of

Paul himself, or of the author of Acts. In the judgment of a wide range of biblical scholars, these views are quite ancient.[2] In fact, they may represent the oldest views of the very earliest Christians, views first reached when the followers of Jesus came to believe he had been raised from the dead. These particular pre-literary traditions are consistent in their view: Christ is said to have been exalted to heaven at his resurrection and to have been made the Son of God at that stage of his existence. In this view, Jesus was not the Son of God who was sent from heaven to earth; he was the human who was exalted at the end of his earthly life to become the Son of God and was made, then and there, into a divine being.

The Exaltation of Jesus

WE FIND THIS VIEW of Christ in what is arguably the oldest fragment of a creed in all of Paul's letters, as well as in several of the speeches of Acts.

Romans 1:3–4

Romans 1:3–4 appears to contain a pre-Pauline creed at the beginning of what is Paul's longest and perhaps most important letter. I have said that Paul's letters are, as a rule, written to churches he had established in order to help them deal with the various problems that had arisen in his absence. The one exception is the letter to the Romans. In this letter Paul indicates not only that he was not the founder of this Christian community, but that he has never yet even visited Rome. His plan is to visit it now. Paul wants to engage in a Christian mission farther to the west—all the way to Spain, which for most people living in the Mediterranean world was the "end of the earth." Paul was one ambitious fellow. He believed God had called him to spread the gospel to all lands, and so naturally he had to go as far as was humanly possible. And that was Spain.

But he needed support for his mission, and the church in Rome was an obvious place to get it. This was a large church, located in the capital city of the empire. It could serve as a gateway to the West. We don't know who started the church or when. Later tradition said that it was founded by the disciple Peter (allegedly the first bishop there, hence the first "pope"), but this seems unlikely: Paul's letter provides us with the first surviving evidence for the fact that a church existed in Rome at all, and in it he greets the various people he knows there. But he never mentions Peter. This is hard to imagine if Peter was there—especially if he was the leader of that church.

Paul is writing the letter to the Romans in order to drum up support for his mission. The reason he needs to write such a long communication to accomplish this end becomes clear in the course of the letter itself. The Christians in Rome do not know fully, or accurately, what Paul's mission is all about. In fact, they seem to have heard some rather unsettling things about Paul's views. Paul is writing the letter to set the matter straight. So his purpose is to explain as fully and clearly as he can what it is that he preaches as his gospel. This is why the letter is so valuable to us today. It is not simply addressing this or that problem that had arisen in one of Paul's churches. It is meant to be a clear expression of the fundamental elements of Paul's gospel message, in his attempt to clear up any misunderstandings among Christians who were somewhat distrustful of his views.

In any situation like that, it is important for a lengthy communication to get off on the right foot. And so the beginning of Paul's letter is significant:

> ¹*Paul, a slave of Christ Jesus, called as an apostle and set apart*
> *for the gospel of God, ²which he announced in advance through*
> *his prophets in the holy scriptures, ³concerning his Son, who was*
> *descended from the seed of David according to the flesh, ⁴who was*

appointed Son of God in power according to the Spirit of holiness
by his resurrection from the dead, Jesus Christ our Lord.

As in all of Paul's letters, he begins by introducing himself by name and saying something about who he is: the slave and apostle of Christ who is committed to the gospel. Paul may be saying this because he had opponents who charged him with being a self-centered, self-aggrandizing, false apostle. But in fact, he is enslaved to Christ and is completely committed to spreading his gospel. This gospel, he tells us, is a fulfillment of what was proclaimed in the Jewish scriptures. As will be seen through the rest of this letter, this is a key claim precisely because Paul's opponents had charged him with preaching an anti-Jewish gospel. Paul insisted that gentiles could be made right with God without being Jews. But doesn't that undercut the privileges of the Jews as God's chosen people and deprive the gospel of its Jewish roots? Not for Paul. The gospel is precisely the good news proclaimed by the Jewish prophets in the Jewish scriptures. And then Paul indicates what the gospel is all about. It is here, in vv. 3–4 of this letter opening, that we have a statement of faith which scholars have long recognized as a preliterary creed that Paul is quoting.

Unlike the rest of the first chapter of Romans, these two verses are highly structured and well balanced into two thought units, in which the three statements of the first unit correspond to the three statements of the second—similar to what we saw with the creed from 1 Corinthians. Immediately before the creed Paul tells us that it is about God's Son, and immediately afterward he says it is about "Jesus Christ our Lord." If we set the verses between these two statements in poetic lines, they look like this:

> *A1 Who was descended*
> *A2 from the seed of David*
> *A3 according to the flesh,*

B1 *who was appointed*

   B2 *Son of God in power*

      B3 *according to the Spirit of holiness by his resurrection*
      from the dead.

The first statement of what I have labeled unit A corresponds to the first statement of unit B: Jesus descended (from David), and Jesus was appointed (Son of God). So too the second statements of each unit: seed of David (= the human messiah), and Son of God in power (= exalted divine Son). And the third: according to the flesh, and according to the Holy Spirit. This final statement in unit B is longer than the corresponding statement in unit A because "the flesh" involves both the realm in which Jesus existed and the means by which he came to exist in it: he existed in the fleshly, earthly realm because he was born as a human. All of this is conveyed by "according to the flesh." To make the contrast complete the author of the creed—whoever he was—needed again to address both the contrasting realm and the contrasting means by which Jesus entered it: it is the realm of the Holy Spirit, and it was entered when he was raised from the dead. Thus A3 speaks of his being made alive in this world where he was the messiah, and B3 speaks of his being brought back to life in the spiritual realm where he was made the powerful Son of God. The only phrase that does not seem needed for this correspondence of the two parts is "in power," and scholars have widely argued that Paul added these words to the creed.[3]

From this creed one can see that Jesus is not simply the human messiah, and he is not simply the Son of Almighty God. He is both things, in two phases: first he is the Davidic messiah predicted in scripture, and second he is the exalted divine Son.

That this is a pre-Pauline creed that Paul is quoting has seemed clear to scholars for a long time. For one thing, as we have just seen, it is highly structured, without a word wasted, quite unlike how normal prose is typically written and unlike the other statements Paul makes in the context. Moreover, even though the passage is very short, it contains a number of words and ideas that are not found anywhere else in Paul. Nowhere else in the seven undisputed Pauline letters does Paul use the phrase "seed of David"; in fact, nowhere else does he mention that Jesus was a descendant of David (which was requisite, of course, for the earthly messiah). Nowhere else does he use the phrase "Spirit of holiness" (for the Holy Spirit). And nowhere else does he ever talk about Jesus becoming the Son of God at the resurrection. For a short two verses, those are a lot of terms and ideas that differ from Paul. This can best be explained if he is quoting an earlier tradition.

Moreover, this earlier tradition has a different view of Christ than the one that Paul explicates elsewhere in his surviving writings. Here, unlike in Paul's writings, Jesus's earthly messiahship as a descendant of King David is stressed. Even more striking—as I will emphasize in a moment—the idea that Jesus was made the Son of God precisely at his resurrection is also stressed. It is interesting as well to note—for purposes of showing that this is an existing creed that Paul is quoting—that one can remove it from its context and the context flows extremely well, as if nothing is missing (showing that it has been inserted): "Paul, a slave of Christ Jesus, called as an apostle and set apart for the gospel of God, which he announced in advance through his prophets in the holy scriptures, concerning his son . . . Jesus Christ our Lord."

So, Paul appears to be quoting an earlier tradition here. How early was it, and why is Paul quoting it?

In fact, the tradition appears to be one of the oldest statements of faith that survives in our earliest Christian writings. Several features of this creed make it look very ancient indeed. The first is its emphasis on the human messiahship of Jesus as the descendant of David, a view not otherwise mentioned in the writings of

Paul, our earliest Christian author. As we saw in Chapter 3, there are good reasons for thinking that this was a view of Jesus that was circulating among his followers already during his lifetime: Jesus was thought to be the one who was predicted to come in fulfillment of the messianic prophecies of scripture. The earliest followers of Jesus continued to think this of him even after his death. His resurrection confirmed for them that even though he had not conquered his political enemies—the way the messiah was supposed to do—God had showered his special favor on him by raising him from the dead. So he really was the messiah. This view is stressed in the first part of the creed, as the first of the two most important things to say about him.

The second key feature is that the creed states that Christ was exalted at his resurrection. It is striking that Paul indicates this happened through the "Spirit of holiness." Not only is this phrase never found elsewhere in Paul, it is what scholars call a *Semitism*. In Semitic languages, such as Hebrew and Aramaic, the language of Jesus and his followers, the way an adjective-noun construction is made is different from the way it is made in other languages such as English. In these Semitic languages, this kind of construction is made by linking two nouns with the word "of." For example, if you want to say "the right way" in a Semitic language, you say "the way of righteousness." And instead of "Holy Spirit," you say "Spirit of holiness." This creed contains a clear Semitism, which makes it highly likely that it was originally formulated among Aramaic-speaking followers of Jesus in Palestine. And this means it could represent early tradition indeed, from the early years in Palestine after Jesus's first followers came to believe that he had been raised from the dead.

In that connection, it is particularly striking how this ancient creed understands Jesus to be the Son of God. As I have repeatedly emphasized, if someone says that Jesus is God, or that he is the Son of God, or that he is divine, one needs to ask, "*in what sense?"* The view here is clear. Jesus was "appointed" (or "designated") the "Son of God" when he was raised from the dead. It was at the resurrection that Jesus was made the Son of God. I pointed out that Paul himself probably added the phrase "in power" to the creed, so that now Jesus is made the Son of God "in power" at the resurrection. Paul may have wanted to add this phrase because according to his own theology, Jesus was the Son of God before the resurrection, but he was exalted to an even higher state at the resurrection (as we will see more fully in the next chapter). For the original framer of this creed, however, it may not have worked this way. For him, Jesus was the messiah from the house of David during his earthly life, but at the resurrection he was made something much more than that. The resurrection was Jesus's exaltation into divinity.

I have already asked why Paul might have felt compelled to quote this small creed at the beginning of his letter to the Romans. It is important to remember that he is writing to clarify any misunderstandings about himself or his gospel message and to introduce his views to Roman Christians who may have harbored suspicions concerning them. If this reading of the situation is right, it would make sense that Paul would quote this creed. It may have been a very old creed that was widely known in Christian circles throughout the Mediterranean. It may have been long accepted as expressing the standard belief of who Jesus is: both the earthly messiah descended from David and the heavenly Son of God exalted at his resurrection. Paul would be quoting the creed, then, precisely because it was well known and because it encapsulated so accurately the common faith Paul shared with the Christians in Rome. As it turns out, Paul's own views were somewhat different and more sophisticated than that, but as a good Christian, he could certainly subscribe to the basic message of this creed, which affirmed that at the resurrection something significant happened to Jesus. He was exalted to a position of grandeur and power, made not just the earthly messiah, but the heavenly Son of God.

This message may have resonated particularly with the Christians living in Rome. It is important to remember that the emperor of Rome, who also lived in the city, was understood by many people throughout the empire to be the son of God—that is, the son of the divinized Caesar who preceded him. As we have seen, in the entire empire, only two known people were specifically called the "son of God." The emperor was one of them, and Jesus was the other. This creed shows why Jesus was the one who deserved this exalted title. At his resurrection, God had made him his Son. He, not the emperor, was the one who had received divine status and so was worthy of the honor of being one raised to the side of God.

The Speeches in Acts

Several passages in the book of Acts appear to contain old, pre-literary elements with Christological views very similar to the one set forth in Romans 1:3–4. Now that we know how such elements are detected, I will not analyze them as fully.

Acts 13:32–33

In Chapter 4 I pointed out that the speeches in Acts were written by the author, "Luke," himself but that he incorporated within them earlier traditions, such as the one in 13:29 which indicated that members of the Jewish Sanhedrin had buried Jesus (rather than just one of their number, Joseph of Arimathea). One of the most remarkable of all the preliterary traditions of Acts, which records Paul explaining the significance of Jesus's resurrection from the dead, comes in the same chapter just a few verses later: "We preach the good news to you, that what God promised to the fathers, this he has fulfilled for us their children by raising Jesus; as also it is written in the second psalm, 'You are my Son, today I have begotten you'" (Acts 13:32–33).

I am not sure there is another statement about the resurrection in the entire New Testament that is quite so astounding. Let me stress at the outset that in Luke's personal view, Jesus did not become the Son of God at the resurrection. We know this because of what he says elsewhere in his two-volume work, including a statement that I will analyze later in this chapter in which even before Jesus's birth, at the "annunciation," Mary, Jesus's mother, is told that since she will be made pregnant by the Holy Spirit, "therefore" the one born of her will be called "the Son of God." Luke himself believed that Jesus was the Son of God from his birth—or rather, his conception. But this is decidedly not what the preliterary tradition in Acts 13:32–33 says. The speaker, Paul, indicates that God had made a promise to the Jewish ancestors and that this promise has been fulfilled now to their descendants by Jesus's resurrection from the dead. He then quotes Psalm 2:7 to clarify what he means: "You are my Son, today I have begotten you." If you recall, in the Hebrew Bible, this verse was originally taken to refer to the coronation day of the Jewish king, when he was anointed and therefore shown to stand under God's special favor.[4] "Paul," in this speech, takes the verse not to indicate what had already happened to the king as the Son of God, but as a prophecy of what would happen to the real king, Jesus, when he was made the Son of God. The fulfillment of the psalm, Paul declares, has happened "today." And when is that "today"? It is the day of Jesus's resurrection. That is when God declares that he has "begotten" Jesus as his Son.

In this pre-Lukan tradition, Jesus was made the Son of God at the resurrection. This is a view Luke inherited from his tradition, and it is one that coincides closely with what we already saw in Romans 1:3–4. It appears to be the earliest form of Christian belief: that God exalted Jesus to be his Son by raising him from the dead.

Acts 2:36

We find a similar point of view expressed in an earlier speech of Acts. I might point out at this stage that one of the reasons we know that it was Luke who wrote the speeches of his main characters is that the speeches all sound very much alike: the lower-class, uneducated, illiterate, Aramaic-speaking peasant Peter gives a speech that sounds almost exactly like a speech by the culturally refined, highly educated, literate, Greek-speaking Paul. Why do two such different people sound so much alike? Because neither one of them is actually speaking: Luke is. To make up his speeches, he used some older materials, with preliterary traditions embedded in the speeches.

In Acts 2, on the day of Pentecost when a great miracle has happened and Peter is explaining its significance to the crowd that has gathered, he speaks of Jesus's death and resurrection, stressing that "God raised this Jesus, of whom all of us are witnesses, as he was exalted to the right hand of God." He goes on to say that this exaltation of Jesus was a fulfillment of the psalms, but this time, rather than quoting Psalm 2:7, he quotes Psalm 110:1, another verse we examined previously as referring to the divine character of the king of Israel: "The LORD says to my Lord, 'Sit at my right hand until I make your enemies your footstool.'" Here the Lord God is speaking to his anointed one, who is also called the "Lord." Peter in this speech is indicating that God was speaking the words to Jesus, whom he made the Lord—and the conqueror of all his enemies—by raising him from the dead.

Then he says something even more clearly about the resurrection of Jesus: "Let the entire house of Israel know with assurance that God has made him both Lord and Christ, this Jesus whom you crucified" (Acts 2:36). The earliest followers of Jesus believed that the resurrection showed that God had exalted him to a position of grandeur and power. This verse is one piece of evidence. Here, in a preliterary tradition, we learn that it was precisely by raising Jesus from the dead that God had made him the messiah and the Lord. During his lifetime Jesus's followers had thought he would be the future messiah who would reign as king in the coming kingdom of God to be brought by the Son of Man, as Jesus himself had taught them. But when they came to believe he was raised from the dead, as Acts 2:36 so clearly indicates, they concluded that he had been made the messiah already. He was already ruling as the king, in heaven, elevated to the side of God. As one who sits beside God on a throne in the heavenly realm, Jesus already is the Christ.

More than that, he is the Lord. During his lifetime Jesus's disciples had called him "lord"—a term that could be used by a slave of a master, or by an employee of a boss, or by a student of a teacher. As it turns out, in Greek the term *lord* in each of these senses was the very same term as *Lord* used of God, as the "Lord of all." Just as the term *Christ* came to take on new significance once Jesus's followers believed he had been raised from the dead, so too did the term *lord*. Jesus was no longer simply the disciples' master-teacher. He actually was ruling as Lord of the earth, because he had been exalted to this new status by God. And it happened at the resurrection. The man Jesus had been made the Lord Christ.

Acts 5:31

A similar view is set forth in yet another speech of Acts, which again incorporates a very early view of Christ as one who was exalted to a divine status at his resurrection. In Acts 5, Jewish authorities arrest Peter and the other apostles as troublemakers for their preaching in Jerusalem. But an angel miraculously allows them to escape, to the consternation of the authorities, who bring them in for further questioning. The high priest forbids them to teach in Jesus's name any more, and Peter and the others reply that they will obey God rather than humans—meaning they will go on preaching. The apostles point out that the Jewish authorities were responsible for Jesus's death, but "the God of our fathers raised Jesus . . . This one God exalted to his right hand as Leader and Savior" (Acts 5:30–31).

Once more, then, in an early tradition we find that Jesus's resurrection was an "exaltation" specifically to "the right hand of God." In other words, God had elevated Jesus to his own status and given him a prominent position as the one who would "lead" and "save" those on earth.

Luke and His Earlier Traditions

One might wonder why the author of these speeches, "Luke," would use preliterary traditions that stood at odds with how he understood Jesus himself. As I've pointed out, nowhere else does Luke portray the resurrection as the time when Jesus came to be exalted to be the Son of God. Yet that's what these verses found in the speeches in Acts indicate. One might be tempted to say that these views are found in the speeches because the speeches faithfully represent what the apostles actually said on these occasions. But, as I have already pointed out, we know from ancient historians that the normal practice of an author was to write the speeches of the main characters himself, and the similarity among all the speeches in Acts suggests that they were written by the same person—Luke.

In fact there is a good explanation for why Luke would want to use these preliterary traditions in his speeches: because they encapsulate so well his emphasis in these addresses to "unbelievers" that God has drastically and dramatically reversed what humans did to Jesus, showing thereby that he had a radically different evaluation of who Jesus was. Humans abused and killed Jesus; God reversed that execution by raising him from the dead. Humans mocked Jesus and held him to be the lowest of the low, an inferior human being; God exalted Jesus and raised him to his right hand, making him a glorified divine figure.

These preliterary fragments provided Luke with just the material he needed to make this point, and so he used them throughout his speeches in order to stress his powerful message. The Almighty God had reversed what lowly humans had done, and Jesus, far from being a failed prophet or a false messiah, was shown to be the ruler of all. By raising Jesus from the dead, God had made him his own Son, the Messiah-King, the Lord.

Evaluating the Earliest Views of Christ

SO FAR I HAVE not given a descriptive name to this very early form of Christological belief in which God raised Jesus from the dead—not in order to give him a longer life here on earth, but in order to exalt him as his own Son up to the heavenly realm, where he could sit beside God at his right hand, ruling together with the Lord God Almighty himself. Traditionally in discussions of theology this understanding of Christ has been called a *low Christology* because it understands that Jesus started off as a human being who was like other humans. He may have been more righteous than others; he may have earned God's special favor more than others. But he started out as a human and nothing more. You will notice that in the preliterary traditions I have discussed there is no talk about Jesus being born of a virgin and certainly no talk of him being divine during his lifetime. He is a human figure, possibly a messiah. But then at a critical point of his existence, he is elevated from his previous lowly existence down here with us, the other mere mortals, to sit at God's right hand in a position of honor, power, and authority. In a moment I will register an objection to calling this a "low" Christology— but for now it is enough say that it does make sense that some theologians have called it that. In it, Jesus begins at a low point, down here with us.

Sometimes this view is also referred to as an *adoptionist* Christology, because in it Christ is not thought to be a divine being "by nature." That is, he did not preexist before he was born in the world, he was not a divine being who came to earth, he was not of the same kind of "essence" as God himself. He was instead a human being who has been "adopted" by God to a divine status. Thus he was not God by virtue of who he was, but by virtue of the fact that the Creator and Lord of all things chose to elevate him to a position of prominence, even though he began as a lowly human.

The problem with this adoptionist nomenclature—as with the term low Christology—is that it speaks of this view of Christ in a rather condescending way, as if it were an inadequate understanding (Jesus was originally "just" a man; he was "only" an adopted son). It is true that the view that Jesus began as a human but was exalted to a divine status was indeed superseded by another perspective—the one that I deal with in the next chapter. That other view indicates that Jesus was a preexistent divine being before he came into the world. That view is sometimes referred to as a *high Christology*—since in it Christ is understood to have started out "up there" with God in the heavenly realm. In that view Christ was not adopted to be the Son of God; he already was the Son of God by virtue of who he was, not by virtue of what God did to him in order to make him something other than what he was by nature.

All the same, even though later theologians came to consider a "low" or "adoptionist" Christology to be inadequate, I do not think we should overlook just how amazing this view was for the people who first held it. For them, Jesus was not "merely" adopted to be God's son. That's the wrong emphasis altogether. They believed that Jesus had been exalted to the highest status that anyone could possibly imagine. He was elevated to an *impossibly* exalted state. This was the most fantastic thing anyone could say about Christ: he had actually been elevated to a position next to God Almighty who had made all things and would be the judge of all people. Jesus was THE Son of God. This was not a low, inferior understanding of Christ; it was an amazing, breathtaking view.

For this reason, I usually prefer not to speak of it as a "low Christology" or even as an "adoptionist Christology," but as an *exaltation Christology*. In it, the man Jesus is showered with divine favors beyond anyone's wildest dreams, honored by God to an unbelievable extent, elevated to a divine status on a level with God himself, sitting at his right hand.

Part of what has convinced me that this understanding of Christ should not be shunted aside as an inferior view involves new research on what it meant to be adopted as a son in the Roman empire, which was the context, of course, within which these views of Christ were formulated. Today we may think that an adopted child is not a parent's "real" child, and in some circles, unfortunately, this is taken to mean that the child does not "really" belong to the parent. Many of us do not think this is a useful, loving, or helpful view, but there it is: some people have it. So too when thinking about God and his Son. If Jesus is "only" adopted, then he's not "really" the Son of God, but he just happens to have been granted a more exalted status than the rest of us.

A study of adoption in Roman society shows that this view is highly problematic and, in fact, probably wrong. A significant book by New Testament specialist Michael Peppard, *The Son of God in the Roman World,* deals with just this issue, to show what it meant at that time and place to be an adopted son.[5] Peppard persuasively argues that scholars (and other readers) have gotten it wrong when they have maintained that an adopted son had lower social status than a "natural" son (that is, as a son actually born of a parent). In fact, just the opposite was the case. In elite Roman families, it was the adopted son who really mattered, not the sons born of the physical union of a married couple. As one very obvious example, Julius Caesar had a natural son with Cleopatra who was named Caesarion. And he had one adopted son, a nephew whom we've already met and whom he made his son by adoption in his will. Which was the more important? Caesarion is a mere footnote in history; you've probably never heard of him. And Octavian? Because he was the adopted son of Caesar, he inherited his property, status, and power. You know him better as Caesar Augustus—the first emperor of the Roman empire. That happened because Julius Caesar had adopted him.

It was in fact often the case that a person who was a son by adoption in the Roman world was given a greater, higher status than a child who was a son by birth. The natural son was who he was more or less by accident; his virtues and fine qualities had nothing to do with the fact that he was born as the child of two parents. The adopted son on the other hand—who was normally adopted as an adult—was adopted precisely because of his fine qualities and excellent potential. He was made great because he had demonstrated the potential for greatness, not because of the accident of his birth. This can be seen in the praise showered upon the emperor Trajan by one of his subjects, the famous author Pliny the Younger, who stated that "your merits did indeed call for your adoption as successor long ago."[6]

This is why it was often the case that adopted sons were already adults when made the legal heir of a powerful figure or aristocrat. And what did it mean to be made the legal heir? It meant inheriting all of the adoptive father's wealth, property, status, dependents, and clients—in other words, all of the adopted father's power and prestige. As Roman historian Christiane Kunst has put it: "The adopted son . . . exchanged his own [status] and took over the status of the adoptive father."[7]

When the earliest Christians talked about Jesus becoming the Son of God at his resurrection, they were saying something truly remarkable about him. He was made the heir of all that was

God's. He exchanged his status for the status possessed by the Creator and ruler of all things. He received all of God's power and privileges. He could defy death. He could forgive sins. He could be the future judge of the earth. He could rule with divine authority. He was for all intents and purposes God.

These various aspects of his exalted state are closely connected with the various honorific titles Christians bestowed upon Jesus in his exalted state. He was the Son of God. By no stretch of the imagination did that mean that he was "merely" the "adopted" Son of God. It entailed the most fantastic claims about Jesus that these people could imagine: as the Son of God he was the heir to all that was God's. He was also the Son of Man, the one whom God had entrusted to be the future judge of the entire world. He was the heavenly messiah who was ruling—now—over the kingdom of his Father, the King of kings. And in that capacity as the heavenly ruler, he was the Lord, the master and sovereign over all the earth.

We may see why someone would call this a low Christology, but it certainly is not saying anything "lowly." This is an exaltation Christology that is affirming stunning things about the teacher from rural Galilee who was exalted to the right hand of God, who had raised him from the dead.

It is also important to stress that precisely when the Christians were starting to say such things about Jesus is when the emperors were beginning to be worshiped with increased frequency throughout the Roman world. The emperor was the son of God (because he was adopted by the preceding emperor who had been divinized at his death); Jesus was the Son of God. The emperor was regarded as divine; Jesus was divine. The emperor was the great ruler; Jesus was the great Ruler. The emperor was lord and sovereign; Jesus was Lord and Sovereign. This lower-class peasant from Galilee who had gotten on the wrong side of the law and had been crucified was in fact the most powerful being in the universe. The emperor, according to this Christian view, was in reality no competition. Jesus's adoptive father was not simply a preceding emperor; he was the Lord God Almighty.

It is because of this exalted status that Jesus was deemed worthy of worship. If the earliest Christians held such elevated views of Jesus as the exalted Son of God soon after his resurrection, it is probably already at this early stage that they began to show veneration to him in ways previously shown to God himself. In two important books, New Testament scholar Larry Hurtado has tried to solve the dilemma of how Jesus could be worshiped as a divine being so early in the history of the Christian religion—virtually right away—if in fact the Christians considered themselves monotheists, not ditheists (worshipers of two gods).[8] Hurtado argues that both things were simultaneously true: Christians maintained there was only one God, and they worshiped Jesus as God alongside God. How was this possible? Hurtado sees Christianity as developing a *binitary worship*—in which Jesus was worshiped as the Lord, alongside God, without sacrificing the idea that there is only one God. In his view, Christians maintained that since God had exalted Jesus to a divine status, he had not merely permitted but even required the veneration of Jesus. Hurtado sees this as a unique development within the history of ancient religion—the worship of two divine beings within a theology that claims there is only one. In later chapters we will see how theologians eventually came to grips with this problem of how Jesus could be revered as God without sacrificing a commitment to monotheism. For now it is enough to stress that this was indeed the case: Christians insisted that they believed in only one God, and yet they revered Jesus as divine and worshiped their "Lord Jesus" along with God.

The Backward Movement of Christology

THE VIEW THAT THE earliest Christians understood Jesus to have become the Son of God at his resurrection is not revolutionary among scholars of the New Testament. One of the greatest scholars of the second half of the twentieth century was Raymond Brown, a Roman Catholic priest who spent a large chunk of his career teaching students at the (Protestant) Union Theological Seminary in New York City. Brown wrote books that were challenging and insightful for fellow biblical scholars and books that were accessible and enlightening for the layperson.

Among his most famous contributions was a way of sketching the development of early Christian views of Jesus. Brown agreed with the view I have mapped out here: the earliest Christians held that God had exalted Jesus to a divine status at his resurrection. (This shows, among other things, that this is not simply a "skeptical" view or a "secular" view of early Christology; it is one held by believing scholars as well.) Brown pointed out that you can trace a kind of chronological development of this view through the Gospels.[9] This oldest Christology of all may be found in the preliterary traditions in Paul and the book of Acts, but it is not the view presented in any of the Gospels. Instead, as we will see at greater length, the oldest Gospel, Mark, seems to assume that it was at his baptism that Jesus became the Son of God; the next Gospels, Matthew and Luke, indicate that Jesus became the Son of God when he was born; and the last Gospel, John, presents Jesus as the Son of God from before creation. In Brown's view this chronological sequencing of the Gospels may well indeed be how Christians developed their views. Originally, Jesus was thought to have been exalted only at the resurrection; as Christians thought more about the matter, they came to think that he must have been the Son of God during his entire ministry, so that he became the Son of God at its outset, at baptism; as they thought even more about it, they came to think he must have been the Son of God for his entire life, and so he was born of a virgin and in that sense was the (literal) Son of God; and as they thought about it more again, they came to think that he must have been the Son of God even before he came into the world, and so they said he was a preexistent divine being.

The problem with this chronological sequencing of the Gospels is that it does not reflect the actual chronological development of early Christian views of Jesus. That is to say, even though it is true that these are the views as they develop through the Gospels (from the earliest to the latest), some Christians were saying that Jesus was a preexistent being (a "later" view) even *before* Paul began to write in the 50s—well before our earliest Gospel was written.[10] The reality is—and Brown would not have disagreed with this—views of Jesus did not develop along a straight line in every part of early Christianity and at the same rate. Different Christians in different churches in different regions had different views of Jesus, almost from the get-go. I argue that there were two fundamentally different Christological views: one that saw Jesus as a being from "down below" who came to be "exalted" (the view I'm exploring in this chapter), and the other that saw Jesus as a being originally from "up above" who came to earth from the heavenly realm (the view I'll explore in the next chapter). But even within these two fundamentally different types of Christology, there were significant variations.

Jesus as Son of God at His Baptism

Brown does appear to be right that at some times and places, after the initial belief that God had exalted Jesus at his resurrection, some Christians came to think that the exaltation had happened before his public ministry. That is why he could do spectacular deeds such as healing the sick, casting out demons, and raising the dead; that is why he could forgive sins as God's representative on earth; that is why he could occasionally reveal his glory—he was already adopted to be God's Son at the very outset of his ministry, when John the Baptist baptized him.

The Baptism in Mark

This appears to be the view of the Gospel of Mark, in which there is no word of Jesus's preexistence or of his birth to a virgin. Surely if this author believed in either view, he would have mentioned it; they are, after all, rather important ideas. But no, this Gospel begins by describing the baptism ministry of John the Baptist and indicates that like other Jews, Jesus was baptized by him. But when Jesus comes up out of the water, he sees the heavens split open, the Spirit of God descends upon him as a dove, and a voice from heaven says, "You are my beloved Son, in you I am well pleased" (Mark 1:9–11).

This voice does not appear to be stating a preexisting fact. It appears to be making a declaration. It is at this time that Jesus becomes the Son of God for Mark's Gospel.[11] Immediately after this, Jesus begins his spectacular ministry, not only proclaiming the imminent arrival of God's kingdom, but also healing all who are sick, showing that he is more powerful than the demonic spirits in the world—so that he is no mere mortal—and even raising the dead. He is the Lord of life, already during his ministry. He demonstrates that he has been given authority to forgive sins committed not against himself, but either against others or against God. His opponents declare that "no one can forgive sins but God alone." Jesus tells them that he, the Son of Man, has the authority on earth to forgive sins.

Jesus's glory can also be seen in his great miracles—multiplying loaves and fishes for the multitudes, commanding the storm to be still, walking on water. Halfway through the Gospel, Jesus reveals his true identity to three of his disciples, as he goes on a mountain in the presence of Peter, James, and John and is transfigured into a radiant being while Moses and Elijah appear in order to speak with him (symbolizing the fact that he is the one predicted in the law [= Moses] and the prophets [= Elijah]). Jesus is no mere mortal. He is the glorious Son of God who has come in fulfillment of God's plan.

If one always has to ask "in what sense" is Jesus divine, for Mark, Jesus is divine in the sense that he is the one who has been adopted to be the Son of God at his baptism, not later at his resurrection.

The Baptism in Luke

A remnant of this view can be found in the later Gospel of Luke. As we will see, Luke has a different understanding of when Jesus became the Son of God. But as we have already noticed, he will occasionally include a tradition that both predates and differs from his own views. This happens in the scene of Jesus's baptism. Here the matter is a little bit difficult to explain. In one of my earlier books, *Misquoting Jesus,* I discuss the fact that we do not have the original copy of Luke, or Mark, or Paul's writings, or any of the early Christian texts that make up the New Testament. What we have are later copies—in most instances, copies that were made many centuries later. These various copies all differ from one another, often in small ways, but sometimes in rather significant ways. One of the passages that has been changed in a significant way by later scribes involves the story of Jesus's baptism in Luke.

Scholars have long debated what the voice actually said at Jesus's baptism in this Gospel. This is because most manuscripts indicate that the voice said the same thing that it says in Mark, "You are my beloved son, in you I am well pleased." But in several of our old witnesses to the text, the voice says something else. It quotes Psalm 2:7: "You are my Son, today I have begotten you." There are good reasons for thinking that this is what Luke originally wrote in this passage (Luke 3:22).[12] It is a very stark saying, since it is when Jesus was baptized that he was "begotten"—that is, born—as the Son of God. The reason later scribes may have wanted to change the verse should be obvious: when scribes were copying their texts of Luke in later centuries, the view that Jesus was made the Son at the baptism was considered not just inadequate, but heretical. For later scribes, Jesus was the preexistent Son of God, not one who became the Son at the baptism.

Luke himself—whoever he was—does not think Jesus was a preexistent Son of God. As it turns out, he does not think Jesus became the Son at the baptism either, as we will see. Then why does he have the voice say this? Again, Luke is fond of incorporating a variety of preliterary traditions that he had heard, even if they differ from his own views. And so in a speech of Acts he can include a tradition that says Jesus became the Son of God at his resurrection (13:33); in his Gospel he can include one that says Jesus became the Son of God at his baptism (3:22); and he incorporates another tradition that says he became the Son of God at his birth (1:35). Maybe Luke simply wanted to stress that Jesus was the Son of God at all the significant points of his existence: birth, baptism, and resurrection.

Jesus as Son of God at His Birth

In the final form of Luke's Gospel, it appears that Jesus is to be thought of as becoming the Son of God, for the first time, at the moment of birth. Or, to be more precise, at the moment of his conception. We saw in Chapter 1 that in the pagan world there were a variety of ways that a human could be thought of as having become divine. Some humans were made divine at their deaths, when they were taken up to the heavenly realm to live with the gods (e.g., Romulus). This would be comparable to Christian traditions that Jesus was exalted to God's right hand as his Son at the resurrection. In other pagan traditions a divine human was born that way, after a god such as the lusty Zeus had sex with a beautiful woman he could not resist. The offspring was literally the son of Zeus (e.g., Heracles [Roman: Hercules]). There are no Christian traditions in which this happens. The God of the Christians was not like the philanderer Zeus, filled with lust and full of imaginative ways to satisfy it. For the Christians, God was transcendent, remote, "up there"—not one to have sex with beautiful girls. At the same time, something *somewhat* like the pagan myths appears to lie behind the birth narrative found in the Gospel of Luke.

The Birth of Jesus in Luke

In this Gospel, Jesus was born of Mary, who had never had human sex. She had never had divine sex either, exactly, but it was God, not a human who made her pregnant. In the famous "annunciation" scene, the angel Gabriel comes to Mary, who is betrothed to be married but has not yet gone through the ceremony or had any physical contact with her espoused, Joseph. Gabriel tells her that she is specially favored by God and will conceive and bear a son. She is taken aback—she has never had sex: How can she conceive? The angel tells her in graphic terms: "The Holy Spirit will come upon you and the Power of the Most High will overshadow you; therefore the one who is born will be called holy, the Son of God" (Luke 1:35). I call this description "graphic" because there is nothing in it to make the reader think that the angel is speaking in metaphors. In a very physical sense the Holy Spirit of God is to "come upon" Mary and "therefore"—an important word here—the child she bears will be called the Son of God. He will be *called* the Son of God because he will in fact *be* the Son of God. It is God, not Joseph, who will make Mary pregnant, so the child she bears will be God's offspring. Here, Jesus becomes the Son of God not at his resurrection or his baptism, but already at his conception.

The Birth of Jesus in Matthew

It is interesting to observe that the Gospel of Matthew also has an account of Jesus's birth in which his mother is a virgin. One might infer from this account as well that Jesus is the Son of God because of the circumstances of his unusual birth. But in the case of Matthew, this conclusion would indeed need to be made by inference: Matthew says nothing of the sort. There is no verse in Matthew similar to what Luke says in Luke 1:35. Instead, according to Matthew, the reason Jesus's mother was a virgin was so that his birth could fulfill what had been said by a spokesperson of God many centuries earlier, when the prophet Isaiah in the Jewish scriptures wrote, "A virgin shall conceive and bear a son, and his name shall be called Immanuel" (Isa. 7:14). Matthew quotes this verse and gives it as the reason for Jesus's unusual conception—it was to fulfill prophecy (Matt. 1:23).

It has frequently been noted that Isaiah actually does not prophesy that the coming messiah will be born of a virgin. If you read Isaiah 7 in its own literary context, it is clear that the author is not speaking about the messiah at all. The situation is quite different. It takes place in the eighth century BCE, during a calamitous time. Isaiah is talking to the king of Judah, Ahaz, who is very upset, and for good reason. The two kingdoms to the north of Judah—Israel and Syria—have attacked his capital city of Jerusalem to force him to join them in an alliance against the rising world power of Assyria. He is afraid that these two northern opponents will lay his kingdom to waste. Isaiah, the prophet, tells him that it is not so. There is a young woman (not a virgin) who has conceived a child, and she will give birth to a son, who will be called Immanuel, which means "God is with us." That God is "with" the Judeans will become clear, because before the child is old enough to know the difference between good and evil, the two kingdoms that are attacking Jerusalem will be dispersed, and good times will return to Ahaz and his people. That's what Isaiah was referring to.

As a Christian living centuries later, Matthew read the book of Isaiah not in the original Hebrew language, but in his own tongue, Greek. When the Greek translators before his day rendered the passage, they translated the Hebrew for word *young woman* (*alma*) using a Greek word (*parthenos*) that can indeed mean just that but that eventually took on the connotation of a "young woman who has never had sex." Matthew took the passage to be a messianic tradition and so indicated that Jesus fulfilled it, just as he fulfilled all the other prophecies of scripture, by being born of a "virgin." It does not take too much thought to realize, though, that Matthew may have been giving "scriptural justification" for a tradition he inherited that originally had a different import: like Luke's tradition, the one that came to Matthew may originally have spoken of Jesus as the unique Son of God because he was born of a virgin, with God as his father.

Whether this is the case or not, I should stress that these virginal conception narratives of Matthew and Luke are by no stretch of the imagination embracing the view that later became the orthodox teaching of Christianity. According to this later view, Christ was a preexistent divine being who "became incarnate [i.e., "human"] through the Virgin Mary." But not according to Matthew and Luke. If you read their accounts closely, you will see that they have nothing to do with the idea that Christ existed before he was conceived. In these two Gospels, Jesus comes into existence at the moment of his conception. He did not exist before.

Whether or not Matthew's tradition originally coincided with Luke's view that Jesus was conceived by a virgin without sexual intercourse so that he was literally the Son of God, this view, as most pronounced in Luke, is a kind of "exaltation" Christology that has been pushed back just about as far as such a view can go. If an exaltation Christology maintains that a human has been elevated to a divine status, then there is no point for that to happen earlier than the moment of conception itself. Jesus is now the Son of God for his entire life, beginning with . . . his beginning. One could argue, in fact, that this has pushed the moment of exaltation so far back that here we no longer even have an exaltation Christology, a Christology from "down below." For here, Jesus is not portrayed in any sense as beginning life as a normal human who because of his great virtue or deep obedience to the will of God is exalted to a divine status. He starts out as divine, from the point of his conception.

Jesus as the Exalted Son of God

THOSE OF US WHO are deeply invested in the early Christian traditions would give a great deal to discover a Gospel written by one of the first followers of Jesus a year or so after his resurrection. Unfortunately, we almost certainly never will. Jesus's disciples were lower-class, illiterate peasants from remote rural areas of Galilee, where very few people could read, let alone write, and let alone create full-scale compositions. We don't know of a single author from that time and place, Jewish or Christian, who was capable of producing a Gospel even had she or he thought of doing so. The first followers of Jesus probably never thought of doing so. They, like Jesus, anticipated that the end of the age was imminent, that the Son of Man—now thought to be Jesus himself—was soon to come from heaven in judgment on the earth and to usher in God's good kingdom. These people had no thought of recording the events of Jesus's life for posterity because in a very real sense, there was not going to be a posterity.

But even if the original apostles had been forward-looking and concerned about the needs of posterity (or at least the longings of twenty-first-century historians), they would not have been able to write a Gospel. The only way they could pass on the story of Jesus was by word of mouth. And so they told the stories to one another, to their converts, and to their converts'

converts. This happened year after year, until some decades later, in different parts of the world, highly educated Greek-speaking Christians wrote down the traditions they had heard, thereby producing the Gospels we still have.

Even so, historians can at least dream, and even if it is an idle dream, it is worth considering what a Gospel written in the year 31 CE by one of the surviving disciples might have looked like. If the views I have presented in this chapter are anywhere near correct, this imagined Gospel would look very different from the ones we have now inherited—and its view of Jesus would not at all be the view that came to be dominant among later theologians when Christianity became the official religion of the Roman world.

This nonexistent Gospel would be filled with the teachings of Jesus as he went from village to town proclaiming that the kingdom of God was soon to arrive with the coming of the Son of Man. The day of judgment was imminent, and people needed to prepare for it. My guess is that this Gospel would not be filled with the miraculous things that Jesus had done. He would not spend his days healing the sick, calming the storm, feeding the multitudes, casting out demons, and raising the dead. Those stories were to come later, as Jesus's followers described his early life in light of his later exaltation. Instead, this Gospel would tell in detail, probably from eyewitness reports, what happened during the last week of Jesus's life, when he made a pilgrimage with some of his followers to Jerusalem and enraged the local authorities with his outburst in the temple and his incendiary preaching of the imminent coming of judgment—a cataclysmic destruction that would be directed not only against the Roman oppressors, but also against the ruling authorities among the Jews, the elite priests and their followers.

The great highlight of the Gospel, though, would come at the end. Jesus had been rejected by the scribes and elders of the people and handed over to Pontius Pilate, who found him guilty for insurrection against the state. To put a decisive end to his troublemaking, rabble-rousing nonsense, Pilate had ordered him crucified. But even though Jesus had been unceremoniously executed by the power of Rome, his story was not yet over. For he had appeared to his disciples, alive again. How could he still be alive? It was not because he survived crucifixion. No, God had raised him, bodily, from the dead. And why is he still not among us? Because God not only brought him back to life, he exalted him up to heaven as his own Son, to sit on a throne at God's right hand, to rule as the messiah of Israel and the Lord of all, until he comes back as the cosmic judge of the earth, very soon.

In this Gospel Jesus would not have become the Son of God for his entire ministry, starting with his baptism, as in the Gospel of Mark and in a tradition retained in the Gospel of Luke. And he would not have been the Son of God for the whole of his life, beginning with his conception by a virgin who was overshadowed by the Holy Spirit so that her son would be God's own offspring, as in Luke and in traditions preserved by Matthew. Nor would he be a divine being who preexisted his coming into the world, as attested by such authors as Paul and John. No, he became the Son of God when God worked his greatest miracle on him, raising him from the dead and adopting him as his Son by exalting him to his right hand and bestowing upon him his very own power, prestige, and status.

CHAPTER 7

Jesus as God on Earth

Early Incarnation Christologies

I HAVE TAUGHT AT TWO major research universities since beginning my career. For four years, in the mid-1980s, I taught at Rutgers University in New Jersey, and since 1988 I have been at the University of North Carolina at Chapel Hill. I have taught a wide range of students in every respect, including with respect to religion: Christians, Jews, Muslims, Buddhists, Hindus, pagans, atheists. My Christian students have been internally diverse as well, from hard-core fundamentalists to liberal Protestants to Greek Orthodox to Roman Catholic to . . . name your denomination. Over the years it has struck me that even though my Christian students come from such a range of backgrounds, when it comes to their views of Christ, they are remarkably constant. The majority of them think that Jesus is God.

In traditional theology, as we will see in later chapters, Christ came to be regarded as both fully God and fully human. He was not half of each—part God and part human. He was God in every respect and human in every respect. My students tend to "get" the God part, but not so much the "human" part. For many of them, Jesus really was God walking the earth; and because he was God, he was not "really" human but was only in some sort of human guise. As God, Jesus could have done anything he wanted to do. If he had chosen, he could have spoken Swahili as an infant. Why not? He was God!

But being human means having human weaknesses, limitations, desires, passions, and shortcomings. Did Jesus have these? Was he "fully" human? Did he ever treat someone unfairly? Did he ever say something nasty about someone? Did he ever get angry without good reason? Was he ever jealous or covetous? Did he ever lust after a woman or a man? If not—in what sense, really, was he "fully" human?

I obviously don't expect my students to be advanced theologians—and my classes are not about theology. They are about the history of early Christianity and, especially, about historical approaches to the New Testament. But it is interesting, even in the class context, to see that my students' Christological views tend to be drawn more from the Gospel of John than from the other three, earlier Gospels. It is in the Gospel of John, and only in John, that Jesus says such things as "before Abraham was, I am" (8:58) and "I and the Father are one" (10:30). In this Gospel Jesus says, "Whoever has seen me has seen the Father" (14:9). And in this Gospel Jesus talks about existing in a glorious state with God the Father before he became human (17:5). That's what many of my students believe. But as they study the New Testament more, they come to see that such self-claims are not made by Jesus in Matthew, Mark, or Luke. So who is right?

Scholars have long held that the view of Christ in the Gospel of John was a later development in the Christian tradition. It was not something that Jesus himself actually taught, and it is not something that can be found in the other Gospels. In John, Jesus is a preexistent divine being who is equal with God. The earliest Christians—Jesus's disciples, for example—did not believe this.

And there are clear historical reasons for thinking they did not. The earliest Christians held exaltation Christologies in which the human being Jesus was made the Son of God—for example, at his resurrection or at his baptism—as we examined in the previous chapter. John has a different Christology. In his view, Christ was a divine being who became human. I call this an *incarnation Christology.*

Exaltation and Incarnation Christologies

WE HAVE ALREADY SEEN that early Christians had views corresponding to two of the common Greek, Roman, and Jewish notions of how a human being could also be divine: by being exalted to the divine realm or by being born to a divine parent. What I am now calling incarnation Christologies are related to the third model of a divine human, in which a divine being—a god—comes from heaven to take on human flesh temporarily, before returning to his original heavenly home. The word *incarnation* means something like *coming in the flesh* or *being made flesh.* An incarnation Christology, then, maintains that Christ was a preexistent divine being who became human before returning to God in heaven. Here, Jesus is not understood to be a human who is elevated to a divine status; instead, he is a heavenly being who condescends to become temporarily human.

I have already made the case that followers of Jesus were not calling him God during his lifetime and that he did not refer to himself as a divine being who had come from heaven. If they had done so, surely there would be a heavy dose of such views in our earliest records of his words—in the Synoptic Gospels and their sources (Mark, Q, M, and L). Instead, it was the resurrection that provided the turning point in understanding who Jesus was, as an exalted being. I contend that the earliest exaltation Christologies very quickly morphed into an incarnation Christology, as early Christians developed their views about Jesus during the early years after his death. The stimulus for the transformation of Christology was probably provided by a theological view that I have already discussed. One needs to ask: What did Jews think that a person became if he was taken up to heaven? As we have seen in the case of Moses and others, such a person was thought to have become an angel, or an angel-like being.[1]

In the most thorough investigation of Christological views that portray Jesus as an angel or an angel-like being, New Testament scholar Charles Gieschen, helpfully defines the Jewish notion of an angel as "a spirit or heavenly being who mediates between the human and divine realms."[2] Once Jesus was thought to be exalted to heaven, he was quickly seen, by some of his followers, to be this kind of heavenly mediator, one who obediently did God's will while he was here on earth. From there, it was a very small step to thinking that Jesus was this kind of being *by nature,* not simply because of his exaltation. Jesus was not only the Son of God, the Lord, the Son of Man, the coming messiah; he was the one who mediates God's will on earth as a heavenly, angelic being. In fact, it came to be thought that he had always been that kind of being.

If Jesus was the one who represented God on earth in human form, he quite likely had always been that one. He was, in other words, the chief angel of God, known in the Bible as the Angel of the Lord. This is the figure who appeared to Hagar, and Abraham, and Moses, who is sometimes actually called "God" in the Hebrew Bible. If Jesus is in fact this one, then he is a preexistent divine being who came to earth for a longer period of time, during his life; he fully represented God on earth; he in fact can be called God. Exaltation Christologies became transformed into incarnation Christologies as soon as believers in Jesus came to see him as an angelic being who performed God's work here on earth.[3]

To call Jesus the Angel of the Lord is to make a startlingly exalted claim about him. In the Hebrew Bible, this figure appears to God's people as God's representative, and he is in fact called God. And as it turns out, as recent research has shown, there are clear indications in the New Testament that the early followers of Jesus understood him in this fashion. Jesus was thought of as an angel, or an angel-like being, or even the Angel of the Lord—in any event, a superhuman divine being who existed before his birth and became human for the salvation of the human race. This, in a nutshell, is the incarnation Christology of several New Testament authors. Later authors went even further and maintained that Jesus was not merely an angel—even the chief angel—but was a superior being: he was God himself come to earth.

Incarnation Christology in Paul

I HAVE READ, PONDERED, researched, taught, and written about the writings of Paul for forty years, but until recently there was one key aspect of his theology I could never quite get my mind around. I had the hardest time understanding how, exactly, Paul viewed Christ. Some aspects of Paul's Christological teaching have been clear to me for decades—especially his teaching that it was Jesus's death and resurrection that makes a person right with God, rather than following the dictates of the Jewish law. But who did Paul think Christ was?

One reason for my perplexity was that Paul is highly allusive in what he says. He does not spell out in systematic detail his views of Christ. Another reason was that in some passages Paul seems to affirm a view of Christ that, until recently, I thought could not possibly exist as early as Paul's letters, which are our first Christian writings to survive. How could Paul embrace "higher" views of Christ than those found in later writings such as Matthew, Mark, and Luke? Didn't Christology develop from a "low" Christology to a "high" Christology over time? And if so, shouldn't the views of the Synoptic Gospels be "higher" than the views of Paul? But they're not! They are "lower." And I simply did not get it, for the longest time.

But now I do. It is not a question of "higher" or "lower." The Synoptics simply accept a Christological view that is *different* from Paul's. They hold to exaltation Christologies, and Paul holds to an incarnation Christology. That, in no small measure, is because Paul understood Christ to be an angel who became a human.

Christ as an Angel in Paul

Many people no doubt have the same experience I do on occasion, of reading something over and over and not having it register. I have read Paul's letter to the Galatians hundreds of times in both English and Greek. But the clear import of what he says in Galatians 4:14 simply never registered with me, until, frankly, a few months ago. In this verse Paul calls Christ an angel. The reason it never registered with me is that the statement is a bit obscure, and I had always interpreted it in an alternative way. Thanks to the work of other scholars, I now see the error of my ways.[4]

In the context of the verse, Paul is reminding the Galatians of how they first received him when he was ill in their midst and they helped restore him to health. Paul writes: "Even though my bodily condition was a test for you, you did not mock or despise me, but you received me as an angel of God, as Jesus Christ."

I had always read the verse to say that the Galatians had received Paul in his infirm state the way they would have received an angelic visitor, *or* even Christ himself. In fact, however, the grammar of the Greek suggests something quite different. As Charles Gieschen has argued, and has now been affirmed in a book on Christ as an angel by New Testament specialist Susan Garrett, the verse is not saying that the Galatians received Paul as an angel *or* as Christ; it is saying that they received him as they would an angel, *such as* Christ.[5] By clear implication, then, Christ is an angel.

The reason for reading the verse this way has to do with the Greek grammar. When Paul uses the construction "but as . . . as," he is not contrasting two things; he is stating that the two things are the same thing. We know this because Paul uses this grammatical construction in a couple of other places in his writings, and the meaning in those cases is unambiguous. For example, in 1 Corinthians 3:1 Paul says: "Brothers, I was not able to speak to you as spiritual people, but as fleshly people, as infants in Christ." The last bit "but as . . . as" indicates two identifying features of the recipients of Paul's letter: they are fleshly people and they are infants in Christ. These are not two contrasting statements; they modify each other. The same can be said of Paul's comments in 2 Corinthians 2:17, which also has this grammatical feature.

But this means that in Galatians 4:14 Paul is not contrasting Christ with an angel; he is equating him with an angel. Garrett goes a step further and argues that Galatians 4:14 indicates that Paul "identifies [Jesus Christ] with God's chief angel."[6]

If this is the case, then virtually everything Paul says about Christ throughout his letters makes perfect sense. As the Angel of the Lord, Christ is a preexistent being who is divine; he can be called God; and he is God's manifestation on earth in human flesh. Paul says all these things about Christ, and in no passage more strikingly than in Philippians 2:6–11, a passage that scholars often call the "Philippians Hymn" or the "Christ Hymn of Philippians," since it is widely thought to embody an early hymn or poem devoted to celebrating Christ and his incarnation.

My friend Charles Cosgrove, a lifelong scholar of Paul who is also one of the world's experts on music in the early Christian world, has convinced me that the passage could not have been an actual hymn that was sung, since it does not scan properly, as a musical piece—that is, it does not have a rhythmic and metrical structure—in the Greek. And so it may be a poem or even a kind of exalted prose composition. But what is clear is that it is an elevated reflection on Christ coming into the world (from heaven) for the sake of others and being glorified by God as a result. And it appears to be a passage Paul is quoting, one with which the Philippians may well have already been familiar. In other words, it is another pre-Pauline tradition.[7]

The Christ Poem of Philippians 2

I start my discussion of the Christ poem, as I call it, by quoting it at length in poetic lines (the lines work differently in Greek than in English, but the basic idea is the same).[8] Paul introduces the poem by telling the Philippians that they should "have the same mind" in themselves that was also in "Christ Jesus" (2:5). And then comes the poem:

> *Who, although he was in the form of God*
>> *Did not regard being equal with God*
>> *Something to be grasped after.*
> *But he emptied himself*
>> *Taking on the form of a slave,*
>> *And coming in the likeness of humans.*
> *And being found in appearance as a human*
>> *He humbled himself*
>> *Becoming obedient unto death—even death on a cross.*

> *Therefore God highly exalted him*
>> *And bestowed on him the name*
>> *That is above every name,*
> *That at the name of Jesus*
>> *Every knee should bow*
>> *Of those in heaven, and on earth, and under the earth.*

And every tongue confess
That Jesus Christ is Lord
To the glory of God the Father.

It is difficult to do justice to this theologically rich poem in just a few pages; scholars have written entire books on it.[9] But several points are particularly germane for my purposes.

The Philippians Poem as a Pre-Pauline Tradition

The first thing to stress is that the passage does indeed appear to be poetic. Scholars have set out the poetic lines in different ways. In the original Greek, of course, poetry was not indented on the page or indicated in any particular way—the Greek manuscripts of the book of Philippians simply give the passage like every other passage, one line and one word at a time. But the lines do make sense—even better sense—when set out poetically. The structure I have adopted here is common among scholarly analyses of the passage: the poem has two halves; each half has three stanzas; and each stanza has three lines. The first half begins by identifying the subject of the poem, "Who" (in reference back to Christ Jesus), and the second half begins with the word *therefore.* In terms of its overall meaning, the first half talks about the "condescension" of Christ, that is, how he came down from the heavenly realm to become human in order to die in obedience to God; and the second half talks about his "exaltation," that is, how God then raised him to an even higher level and status than he had before, as a reward for his humble obedience.

As I have said, scholars have long considered the passage to be a pre-Pauline tradition that Paul includes here in his letter to the Philippians. It is not simply something Paul composed on the spot, while writing his letter. There are several reasons for thinking this. For one thing, the passage does appear to be a self-contained unit that is poetic rather than proselike in its composition. Moreover, a number of words—including some of the key words—occur in this passage but nowhere else in Paul's letters. This includes the word *form* (used twice: *form of God* and *form of a slave*) and the phrase *grasped after*. The absence of such important words in Paul's writings suggests that he is quoting a passage that someone else wrote, earlier.

Confirmation for this view comes from the related fact that several of the key concepts in the passage cannot be found elsewhere in Paul's writings. Again, this includes some of the central concepts of the passage: that Jesus was in God's form before he became a human; that he had open to him the possibility of grasping after divine equality before coming to be human; and that he became human by "emptying himself." This last idea is usually interpreted to mean that Christ gave up the exalted prerogatives that were his as a divine being in order to become a human.

One final argument that Paul is here quoting a preexisting tradition that had been in circulation for a while is a little trickier to explain. It is the fact that part of the poem does not seem to fit its context in the letter to the Philippians very well. At this point in the letter, Paul is telling his Philippian Christian converts that they are to act unselfishly by treating other people better than they treat themselves. In the verse before this, he has said that they should not look out only for their own interests, but even more for the interests of others. Then he quotes this passage in order to show that this is in fact what Christ did, giving up what was rightfully his (the "form of God") in order to serve others (taking the "form of a slave") and being obedient to God to the point of dying for others.

The problem is that the second half of the Christ poem (vv. 9–11) does not at all convey this lesson, and if taken seriously, it may seem to run counter to it. For according to these three stanzas, God rewarded Jesus abundantly for his temporary condescension to become a human and to die. God exalted him even higher than he was before (that's what the Greek verb "highly exalted" seems to imply, as do the verses that follow), making him the Lord of all, to whom all living beings would offer confession and worship.

But the idea of Christ's eventual exaltation does not fit the purpose behind Paul's quotation of the poem, since if someone is humbly obedient because of what he or she will eventually get out of it, that is simply another way of doing things out of self-interest. And the whole point of the passage is that people should not act out of self-interest, but selflessly, for the sake of others.

Since the second half of the poem does not "work" very well in the context, it is almost certainly the case that this was indeed a preexistent poem that was familiar to Paul and, probably, to the Philippians as well. Paul quotes the entire poem because it is familiar to his readers and conveys the point that he wants to convey—that they should imitate Christ's example in giving themselves up for others—even though the second half could be interpreted to undercut this point.

These, then, are some of the reasons that scholars have thought that Paul probably did not compose this poem himself while writing to the Philippians. It is a pre-Pauline tradition. You may have noticed that one line is longer than the others in the poem: "obedient unto death—even death on a cross." It is even longer in the Greek. Scholars frequently think that Paul added the words "even death on a cross," since for him it was precisely the *crucifixion* of Jesus that was so important.

In his first letter to the Corinthians, Paul reminds his readers that when he was first with them—trying to convert them from worshiping idols to become followers of the God of Israel and his messiah, Jesus—his message was all about the cross of Jesus: "For I decided not to know anything among you except Jesus Christ, and this one as crucified" (1 Cor. 2:2). In his letter to the Galatians, he stresses that it was specifically a death by crucifixion that mattered for salvation. If Jesus had been stoned to death, for example, or strangled, that would have been one thing. But because he was crucified, in particular, he was able to bear the "curse" of sin that other people deserved. And that is because the scriptures indicate that anyone who "hangs on a tree" is cursed by God (Gal. 3:10–13). This is a reference to the law of Moses, Deuteronomy 21:23, which states: "cursed is everyone who hangs on a tree." In its original context the verse meant that anyone who had been executed and left to rot on a tree obviously stood under God's curse. For Paul, since Jesus died by being nailed to a "tree"—that is, crucified on a stake of wood—he bore God's curse. Since he did not deserve this curse, he must have borne the curse that was owed to others. So it was of utmost importance to Paul not just that Jesus died, but that he died by being crucified.

The lines of the Christ poem in Philippians 2 "work" somewhat better without the words "even death on a cross," suggesting that Paul added these words to the poem in order to make them conform even more closely to his own theological understanding of Jesus's death. If this is the case, it also suggests that Paul was not the original author of the poem but that he inherited it from tradition and quoted it here because it suited his purposes.

By quoting the poem Paul obviously is indicating that he agrees with its teaching about Christ. But what is that teaching exactly? I argue below that this poem presents an incarnational understanding of Christ—that he was a preexistent divine being, an angel of God, who came to earth out of humble obedience and whom God rewarded by exalting him to an even higher level of divinity as a result. But before embarking on this interpretation I should point out that some scholars have not seen this poem as embracing an incarnational theology at all.

The Christ Poem and Adam

Some scholars have had real difficulty imagining that a poem existing before Paul's letter to the Philippians—a poem whose composition must therefore date as early as the 40s CE—could already celebrate an incarnational understanding of Christ. That seems rather early for such a "high" Christology. As a way of partly resolving this problem, an alternative explanation has been proposed. In this alternative interpretation, the beginning of the poem does not represent Christ as a preexistent divine being. It presents him as a fully human being. In fact, it presents him as a human who was a kind of "second Adam," a second appearance, in a sense, of the father of the human race.[10]

According to this interpretation, when the poem indicates that Christ was in the "form of God," it is not suggesting some kind of preexistent state in heaven. He was instead like Adam, who was made in the "image of God." In this understanding, the words *image* and *form* are synonyms. When God made Adam and Eve, he made them in his own "image" (Gen. 1:27). But even though Adam and Eve were in God's image, they obviously were not equal with God—they were his creations. And God gave them one commandment about what they were not to do: they were not to eat "of the tree of the knowledge of good and evil." If they ate *that* fruit (it is not called an apple, by the way), they would die (Gen. 2:16–17).

And what happened? The serpent—which is not called Satan in Genesis; instead it is an actual snake (which originally walked on legs, apparently)—tempted Eve by telling her that eating the forbidden fruit would not cause them to die but would make them "be like God, knowing good and evil" (Gen. 3:5). And so Eve ate the fruit, gave some to her husband, Adam, and he too ate. Their eyes were then "opened," and they realized they were naked. They were no longer innocent but could and did make moral judgments. And they eventually died, as did all of their children and descendants (with two exceptions: Enoch and Elijah).

In Paul's letters he sometimes speaks of Christ as a "second Adam." Unlike the first sinful Adam, Christ was the "perfect man," who reversed the course of human affairs brought about by the first Adam. The first Adam brought sin into the world, and Christ removed the curse of sin; just as Adam brought death to all his descendants, so too Christ brought life to all who believed in him. As Paul says in Romans 5: "For just as the transgression through one man came as judgment for all people, so also the righteousness that came from one man leads to justification and life for everyone; for just as the many were made sinners through the disobedience of the one person, so also the many were made righteous by the obedience of one" (vv. 18–19).

Paul, then, saw Christ as a kind of second Adam who reversed the sin, condemnation, and death brought about by the first Adam. Could this understanding be applied to the Christ poem of Philippians? Some scholars have argued so. In their view, as I indicated, just as Adam was in the "image of God," so too was Christ in the "form of God." But Adam reacted to that state by sinning. Christ reacted by humble obedience. Adam sinned because he wanted to be "like God." Christ on the other hand "did not regard being equal with God / Something to be grasped after." And so, just as Adam brought death into the world by his disobedience, Christ brought the possibility of life into the world by his obedience. This is shown above all by the fact that God "highly exalted" Jesus and made him the Lord of all.

In short, according to this interpretation, Christ is not portrayed as a preexistent divine being in the Philippians poem. He is human, like other humans. He is in the image of Adam, who is in the image of God. But he reverses Adam's sin by his obedience, and only then is he exalted to a divine level.

I have long thought that this was an intriguing interpretation of the passage, and for many years I wished it were correct. That would help solve the problem I had in understanding Paul's Christology. But I'm afraid I've never been convinced by it—even when I wanted to be—for three reasons. First, if Paul (or the author of the poem) really wanted his reader to make the connection between Jesus and Adam, he surely would have done so more explicitly. Even if he chose not to call Adam by name, or to call Jesus the second Adam, he could have made verbal allusions to the story of Adam (and Eve) more obvious. In particular, rather than saying that Christ was "in the form of God," he would have said that Christ was "in the image of God." That is the word used in Genesis, and it would have been quite simple for the author to use it here in the poem if he wanted his reader to think of Genesis.

Second, in the Adam and Eve story in Genesis, it is not Adam who wants "to be like God"—it is Eve. Adam eats the fruit only when she gives it to him, and we are not told why he does so. But this means in his desire *not* to be equal with God, Christ would be the counter not to Adam, but to Eve. Nowhere in his writings does Paul make a connection between Christ and Eve.

Third, and possibly most important, from other passages in Paul it does indeed appear that he understands Christ to have been a preexistent divine being. One example comes from a very peculiar passage in 1 Corinthians, in which Paul is talking about how the children of Israel, after they escaped from Egypt under Moses, were fed while they spent so many years in the wilderness (as recounted in the books of Exodus and Numbers in the Hebrew Bible). According to Paul, the Israelites had enough to drink because the rock that Moses struck in order miraculously to bring forth water (Num. 20:11) followed them around in the wilderness. Wherever they went, the water-providing rock went. In fact, Paul says, "the rock was Christ" (1 Cor. 10:4). Just as Christ provides life to people today when they believe in him, so too he provided life to the Israelites in the wilderness. That would not have been possible, of course, unless he existed at the time. And so for Paul, Christ was a preexistent being who was occasionally manifest on earth.

Or take another passage, one in which Paul actually does speak of Christ as a second Adam. In 1 Corinthians, Paul contrasts Christ's place of origin with that of Adam: "The first man was from the earth, and was made of dust; the second man is from heaven" (15:47). What matters here is precisely the difference between Adam and Christ. Adam came into being in this world; Christ existed before he came into this world. He was from heaven.

And so, the interpretation of the Philippians poem that takes it as an indication that Christ was a kind of "perfect Adam" does not work, on one hand, because the passage has features that do not make sense given this interpretation. And on the other hand, this interpretation is completely unnecessary. It does not solve the problem of an incarnational Christology—because Paul clearly says in other passages that Jesus was indeed a preexistent divine being who came into the world. That's what this poem teaches as well.

The Christ Poem and Incarnational Christology

Lots of other things can be said about this amazing passage. Among scholars it is one of the most discussed, argued over, and commented upon passages in the New Testament. If the majority of scholars are correct in their opinion that it embodies an incarnational Christology, then the basic perspective on Christ that it paints is clear: Christ was a preexistent being who chose to come in the "likeness" of human flesh, who, because he humbled himself to the point of death, was elevated to an even higher status than he had before and was made the Lord of all. This view of Christ makes sense if we think of him as existing before his birth as an angelic being who abandoned his heavenly existence to come to earth to fulfill God's will by dying for others.

I want to stress that Christ appears to be portrayed here, in his preexistent state, as a divine being, an angel—but not as God Almighty. He is not the Father himself, since it is the Father who exalts him. And he is not—most definitely not—"equal" with God before he becomes human.

There are several reasons for thinking that he was not yet God's equal in his preexistent state. The first comes in the first part of the poem, where it says that Christ did not regard being equal with God "something to be grasped after." Interpreters of this passage have long debated the precise nuance of these words. Do they mean that he already had equality with God and that he did not clutch on to this equality as something to retain, but instead became human? Or do they mean that he did not already have equality with God and chose not to grasp for that kind of equality, but instead became human? It makes a big difference.

Part of the problem is that the key Greek word here—the verb for *grasped*—is rare and could in theory be used in both senses. But in reality, the word (and words related to it in Greek) is almost always used to refer to something a person doesn't have but grasps for—like a thief who snatches someone's purse. The German scholar Samuel Vollenweider has shown that the word is used this way widely in a range of Jewish authors; moreover, it is the word used of human rulers who become arrogant and so try to make themselves more high and mighty (divine) than they really are.[11] This seems to be, then, what is meant here in the Philippians poem.

A second reason for thinking that Jesus was not yet God's equal is that only this interpretation makes sense of the second half of the poem, in which God "exalts" Christ even more "highly" than he was before (which is the probable meaning of the verb I translated as "highly exalted" in the poem). If Christ were already equal with God, then it would not have been possible for him to be exalted even higher than that after his act of obedience. What could be higher than equality with God? Moreover, it was only after this higher exaltation that Christ is given "the name that is above every name" and is to become the object of worship for all living beings. Christ must have been a lower divine being before he humbled himself by becoming human and dying. When it says, then, that he was "in the form of God," it does not mean that he was the equal of God the Father. It means he was "Godlike," or divine—like the chief angel, the Angel of the Lord, as referred to in passages of the Hebrew Bible.

It seems strange to many people today that Christ could be a divine being yet not be fully equal with God. But it is important to remember what we found in Chapter 1. Our notion that there is an inseparable chasm between the divine and human realms, and that the divine realm has only one level or layer to it, is not the view held among Greeks, Romans, and Jews in the ancient world—or by Christians. Recall the inscription that I cited on page 39, about how Caesar Augustus was declared "divine," and if he provided even further benefits for the people during his reign, they could deem him even "more divine." How can someone become "more" divine? In the ancient world, they could—because divinity was a continuum. So too in Jewish and Christian circles. For the Philippians poem, Christ started out as divine, but at his exaltation he was made even "more divine." In fact, he was made equal with God.

This is a point that is widely agreed upon by interpreters, and it is because of the wording of the final two stanzas of the poem, vv. 10–11. There, we are told that God "hyperexalted" Jesus, so that "At the name of Jesus / Every knee should bow / Of those in heaven, and on earth, and under the earth. / And every tongue confess / That Jesus Christ is Lord / To the glory of God the Father." The casual reader may not realize this, but these lines allude to a passage in the Hebrew Bible. And a striking passage it is. According to the original passage as found in Isaiah 45:22–23, it is to Yahweh alone, the God of Israel, that "every knee shall bow, and every tongue confess":

> *Turn to me and be saved*
>> *All the ends of the earth!*
>> *For I am God, and there is no other.*
> *By myself I have sworn,*
>> *From my mouth has gone forth in righteousness*
>> *A word that shall not return:*
> *"To me every knee shall bow,*
>> *Every tongue confess."*

The prophet Isaiah is quite explicit. There is only one God, no other. That God is Yahweh.[12] That God has sworn that to no other shall every knee bow and every tongue make confession. Yet in the Philippians poem, it is not to God the Father—apart from whom, according to Isaiah, "there is no other"—but to the exalted Jesus that all knees will bow and tongues confess. Jesus has been granted the status and honor and glory of the One Almighty God himself.

This interpretation of the Christ poem in Philippians shows that very early in the Christian movement the followers of Jesus were making audacious claims about him. He had been exalted to equality with God, even though God himself had said that there was "no other" apart from him. Somehow, Christians were imagining that there was indeed "another." And this other one was equal with God. But it was not because he was God "by nature"—to use the later philosophical/theological term that came to be applied to discussions of Christ's deity. He was God because God had made him so. But how could he be God, if God was God, and there was only one God? This became the key question of the Christological debates in later times, as we will see. At this stage, all we can say is that early Christians were not bothered enough by this dilemma, or this paradox, to have written anything about it, so we don't know exactly *how* they dealt with it.

One final point to make about the Philippians poem may have occurred to you already. I have been calling the Christology that it embraces "incarnational," since it portrays Jesus as a preexistent divine being who becomes human. But there is obviously an "exaltation" element in the poem as well, since at Jesus's resurrection God exalted him to an even higher state than he had before. In a sense, then, this poem provides us with a transitional Christology that combines an incarnation view with an exaltation view. Later authors will move even further away from an exaltation Christology, such that Christ will come to be portrayed as being equal with God even before his appearance in the world—in fact, as equal with God for all time. But this is not the view of the Philippians poem. For this beautiful passage, as quoted by and presumably believed by Paul, Christ was indeed a preexistent divine being. But he was an angel or an angel-like being, who only after his act of obedience to the point of death was made God's equal.

Other Passages in Paul

The incarnational Christology that lies behind the Philippians hymn can be seen in other passages of Paul's letters as well. I have already said that Paul understood Christ to be the "rock" that provided life-giving water to the Israelites in the wilderness (1 Cor. 10:4) and pointed out that Paul stated that Christ, unlike the first Adam, came from "heaven" (1 Cor. 15:47). When Paul talks about God "sending" his son, he appears not to be speaking only metaphorically (like John the Baptist is said to have been "sent" from God in John 1:6, for example); instead, God actually sent Christ from the heavenly realm. As he put it in the letter to the Romans, "For what the law could not do, God did, sending his own Son in the likeness of sinful flesh" (8:3). It is interesting that Paul uses this term *likeness*—just as the Philippians poem did when it spoke of Christ coming in the "appearance" of humans. It is the same Greek word in both places. Did Paul want to avoid saying that Christ actually *became* human, but that he came only in a human "likeness"? It is hard to say.

But it is clear that Paul does not believe Christ just appeared out of nowhere, the way angels seem to do in the Hebrew Bible. One of the verses in Paul that long puzzled me was Galatians 4:4, in which Paul writes, "When the fullness of time came, God sent his son, born from a woman, born under the law." I always wondered why Paul would indicate that Christ had been born from a woman. What other option is there, exactly? But the statement makes sense if Paul believed that Christ was a preexistent angelic being. In that case, it is important to point out that Jesus was born in a human way: he did not simply appear as the Angel of the Lord did to Hagar, Abraham, and Moses. Here in the last days he actually was born in the likeness of human flesh, as a child.

Paul says even more exalted things about Christ. In Chapter 2, we saw that some Jewish texts understood God's Wisdom to be a hypostasis of God—an aspect or characteristic of God that took on its own form of existence. Wisdom was the agent through which God created all things (as in Proverbs 8), and since it was God's Wisdom in particular, it was both God and a kind of image of God. As the Wisdom of Solomon expressed it, Wisdom is "a pure emanation of the glory of the Almighty . . . for she is a reflection of eternal light, a spotless mirror of the working of God, and an image of his goodness" (7:25–26). Moreover, we saw that Wisdom could be seen as the Angel of the Lord.

Jesus, for Paul, was the Angel of the Lord. And so he too was God's Wisdom, before coming into this world. Thus Paul can speak of "the glory of Christ, who is the likeness of God" (2 Cor. 4:4). Even more striking, Christ can be described as the agent of creation:

> For us there is one God, the Father,
>   from whom are all things and for whom we exist,
> and one Lord, Jesus Christ,
>   through whom are all things and through whom we exist.
>   (1 Cor. 8:6)

This verse may well incorporate another pre-Pauline creed of some kind, as it divides itself neatly, as can be seen, into two parts, with two lines each. The first part is a confession of God the Father, and the second a confession of Jesus Christ. It is "through" Christ that all things come into being and that believers themselves exist. This sounds very much like what non-Christian Jewish texts occasionally say about God's Wisdom. And God's Wisdom was itself understood to be God, as we have seen.

So too Jesus in Paul. One of the most debated verses in the Pauline letters is Romans 9:5. Scholars dispute how the verse is to be translated. What is clear is that Paul is talking about the advantages given to the Israelites, and he indicates that the "fathers" (that is, the Jewish patriarchs) belong to the Israelites, and "from them is the Christ according to the flesh, the one who is God over all, blessed forever, amen." Here, Christ is "God over all." This is a very exalted view.

But some translators prefer not to take the passage as indicating that Christ is God and do so by claiming that it should be translated differently, to say first something about Christ and then, second, to give a blessing to God. They translate the verse like this: "from them is the Christ according to the flesh. May the God who is over all be blessed forever, amen." The issues of translation are highly complex, and different scholars have different opinions. The matter is crucial. If the first version is correct, then it is the one place in all of Paul's letters where he explicitly calls Jesus God.

But is it correct? My view for many years was that the second translation was the right one and that the passage does not call Jesus God. My main reason for thinking so, though, was that I did not think that Paul ever called Jesus God anywhere else, so he probably wouldn't do so here. But that, of course, is circular reasoning, and I think the first translation makes the best sense of the Greek, as other scholars have vigorously argued.[13] It is worth stressing that Paul does indeed speak about Jesus as God, as we have seen. This does not mean that Christ is God the Father Almighty. Paul clearly thought Jesus was God in a certain sense—but he does not think that he was the Father. He was an angelic, divine being before coming into the world; he was the Angel of the Lord; he was eventually exalted to be equal with God and worthy of all of God's honor and worship. And so I now have no trouble recognizing that in fact Paul could indeed flat-out call Jesus God, as he appears to do in Romans 9:5.

If someone as early in the Christian tradition as Paul can see Christ as an incarnate divine being, it is no surprise that the same view emerges later in the tradition. Nowhere does it emerge more clearly or forcefully than in the Gospel of John.

Incarnation Christology in John

I WAS IN GRADUATE school when I first came to realize just how different John is from the other Gospels. Before that, when I was in college, I read the Gospels as if they were all saying basically the same thing. Sure, there may have been different emphases here or there, but on the whole, I thought, they had the same basic views about most everything.

In my master's degree program I decided to do a kind of

thought experiment by reading only Matthew, Mark, and Luke (not John). I did this for three years. At the end of my third year, to complete the experiment, I sat down to read John. In Greek. In one sitting. It was a revelation. Having grown accustomed to the language, style, themes, stories, and perspectives of the Synoptic Gospels, I simply couldn't believe how different John was. In every respect. With John we are dealing not just with a different author, but with an entirely different world. Among other things, in this Gospel there are not simply allusions to Jesus's divine power and authority. There are bald statements that equate Jesus with God and say that he was a preexistent divine being who came into the world. This view is not simply like Paul's, in which Jesus was some kind of angel who then came to be exalted to a higher position of deity. For John, Jesus was equal with God and even shared his name and his glory in his preincarnate state. To use the older terminology (which I favored back then), this was an extremely high Christology.

Already at that early point in my research career, I had reasons to doubt that this Christology was the earliest one known among Jesus's followers. On one hand, it was not the Christology of the earlier Gospels—and that itself was obviously highly significant. If Jesus really were equal with God from "the beginning," before he came to earth, and he knew it, then surely the Synoptic Gospels would have mentioned this at *some* point. Wouldn't that be the most important thing about him? But no, in Matthew, Mark, and Luke he does not talk about himself in this way—nor does he do so in their sources (Q, M, and L).

On the other hand, I was taken aback when I realized that all the perspectives in John's Gospel are shared by Jesus himself and the author. Let me explain. Whoever wrote the Gospel of John (we'll continue to call him John, though we don't know who he really was) must have been a Christian living sixty years or so after Jesus, in a different part of the world, in a different cultural context, speaking a different language—Greek rather than Aramaic—and with a completely different level of education. Yet there are passages in John in which the narrator sounds just like Jesus, so much so that you cannot tell, in places, who is doing the talking.[14] Jesus sounds just like the narrator and the narrator sounds just like Jesus. But how can that be, if Jesus was from a different time and place, living in a different culture, speaking a different language, and without having the advantages of what we today would call a higher education? And so I realized with breathtaking suddenness what the answer was. It is because in John's Gospel we are not hearing two voices—the voice of Jesus and the voice of the narrator. We are hearing one voice. The author is speaking for himself *and* he is speaking for Jesus. These are not Jesus's words; they are John's words placed on Jesus's lips.

Elevated Teachings About Jesus in John

One of the most striking features of John's Gospel is its elevated claims about Jesus. Here, Jesus is decidedly God and is in fact equal with God the Father—before coming into the world, while in the world, and after he leaves the world. Consider the following passages, which are found only in John among the four Gospels:

- In the beginning was the Word, and the Word was with God, and the Word was God . . . And the Word became flesh and dwelt among us, and we have beheld his glory, glory as of the unique one before the Father, full of grace and truth. (1:1, 14; later this Word made flesh is named as "Jesus Christ," v. 17)
- But Jesus answered them, "My Father is working still, and I also am working." This was why the Jews sought all the more to kill him, because not only was he breaking the Sabbath, but he was also calling God his own

Father, thereby making himself equal to God. (5:17–18)

- [Jesus said:] "Very truly, I tell you, before Abraham was, I am." (8:58)
- [Jesus said:] "I and the Father are one." (10:30)
- Philip said to him, "Lord, show us the Father, and we will be satisfied." Jesus said to him, "Have I been with you all this time, Philip, and you still do not know me? Whoever has seen me has seen the Father." (14:8–9)
- [Jesus prayed to God:] "I glorified you on earth by finishing the work that you gave me to do. So now, Father, glorify me in your own presence with the glory that I had in your presence before the world existed." (17:4–5)
- [Jesus prayed:] "Father, I desire that those also, whom you have given me, may be with me where I am, to see my glory, which you have given me because you loved me before the foundation of the world." (17:24).
- Thomas answered him, "My Lord and my God!" (20:28)

I need to be clear: Jesus is not God the Father in this Gospel. He spends all of chapter 17 praying to his Father, and, as I pointed out earlier, he is not talking to himself. But he has been given glory equal to that of God the Father. And he had that glory before he came into the world. When he leaves this world, he returns to the glory that was his before. To be sure, Jesus comes to be "exalted" here—he several times talks about his crucifixion as being "lifted up"—a play on words in reference to being "lifted onto the cross" and being "exalted" up to heaven as a result. But the exaltation is not to a higher state than the one he previously possessed, as in Paul. For John, he was already both "God" and "with God" in his preincarnate state as a divine being. Nowhere can this view be seen more clearly than in the first eighteen verses of the Gospel, frequently called the Prologue of John.

The Prologue of John

In the Prologue we find the clearest expression in the New Testament of Christ as a preexistent divine being—the Word—who has become a human. We have already seen in Chapter 2 that God's Word—or *Logos* in Greek—was sometimes understood to be a divine hypostasis, an aspect of God that came to be thought of as its own distinct being. Since it was the Word of God, it was an entity that could be imagined as being separate and distinct from God (just as the words that I am typing come from inside my head but then take on their own existence). At the same time, since this Word was the Word of "God," it perfectly manifested the divine being of the Father and for that reason was itself rightly called "God." The idea of the divine Logos could be found not only in Jewish literature, but also in Greek philosophical circles connected with both Stoicism and Middle Platonism. All of these may have affected the most poetic and powerful expression of the Word to come down to us from early Christian literature—the first eighteen verses of John.

The Prologue as a Preliterary Poem

It is widely held among scholars that the Prologue is a preexisting poem that the author of John has incorporated into his work—possibly in a second edition.[15] This is because it has the earmarks of a preliterary tradition as a self-contained, poetic piece and because its key term—the *Word,* or *Logos*—occurs nowhere else in reference to Christ in the entire Gospel. If it is a preexisting piece, then the author of the Gospel—or its later editor—found its Christological views highly compatible with his own, even if the terms used in expressing those views were different from the ones he customarily used. And so he began his Gospel narrative with it.[16]

The poetic character of the passage can be seen in its use, in places, of what is called *staircase parallelism,* in which the final word of one line is also the beginning word of the next line. And so, for example, we have the following (key words are in italics):

In the beginning was *the Word*
And *the Word* was with *God*.
And *God* was the Word. (John 1:1)

In him was *life*,
And the *life* was the *light* of humans.
And the *light* shines in the *darkness*.
And the *darkness* did not overcome it. (1:4–5)

Inserted into the poetic passage of vv. 1–18 are two prose additions, which do not seem to fit with the flow of the poem, which is otherwise all about the Logos; both additions deal not with Christ, but with John the Baptist as his forerunner (vv. 6–8 and v. 15). If you remove these verses, the poem actually flows better. Probably, the author (or the editor) who added the poem in the first place made these additions himself.

The Teaching of the Prologue
Without the addition of the comments on John the Baptist, the poem is all about the Logos of God that existed with God in the beginning and that became a human in Jesus Christ. Christ is not named until near the end, in v. 17. But there is no doubt that the poem is about him, as is clear once you read it through from start to finish. Still, it is important to be precise in how one understands this poem and its presentation of Christ. The poem is decidedly not saying that Jesus preexisted his birth—and there is nothing about him being born of a virgin here. What preexisted was the Logos of God through whom God made the universe. It was only when the Logos became a human being that Jesus Christ came into existence. So Jesus Christ is the Logos that has become a human; but Jesus did not exist before that incarnation happened. It was the Logos that existed before.

Quite elevated things are said of this Logos, the Word. The

very beginning of the poem quickly calls to mind the beginning of the Bible, Genesis 1:1. Here in John we are told, "In the beginning was the Word," and that it was through this Word that "all things were made," including "life" and "light." How could a Jewish reader not immediately think of the creation story in Genesis? Genesis also starts with the words: "In the beginning"—the same Greek words later used in John. This opening of Genesis is all about creation. And how does God create the world and all that is in it? By speaking a word: "And God *said*, 'Let there be light. And there was light." It is God who creates light, and eventually, life, and he does so with his word. Now in the Prologue to John we have a reflection on that Word as a kind of hypostasis of God.

As in other Jewish texts, the Word is a being separate from God, and yet since it is God's word, his own outward expression of himself, it fully represents who he is, and does nothing else, and in this sense it is itself God. So John tells us that the Word was both "with God" and "was God." This Word was that which brought all life into existence and brought light out of darkness—just as in Genesis.

A careful reader at this point will be reminded of what some Jewish texts say about Wisdom, as the divine agent through whom God created the world, as in Proverbs 8. This comparison is indeed apt. As Thomas Tobin, a scholar of ancient Judaism, has summarized the matter, the following things are said both about Wisdom in various non–Christian Jewish texts and about the Logos in the Prologue to John:[17]

- Both were at the beginning (John 1:1; Prov. 8:22–23).
- Both were with God (John 1:1; Prov. 8:27–30; Wis. 9:9).
- Both were the agent through whom all things were made (John 1:3; Wis. 7:22).

- Both provide "life" (John 1:3–4; Prov. 8:35; Wis. 8:13).
- Both provide "light" (John 1:4; Wis. 6:12; 8:26).
- Both are superior to darkness (John 1:5; Wis. 7:29–30).
- Both are not to be recognized by those in the world (John 1:10; Bar. 3:31).
- Both have dwelled among people in the world (John 1:11; Sir. 24:10; Bar. 3:37–4:1).
- Both have been rejected by the people of God (John 1:11; Bar. 3:12).
- Both have tabernacled (i.e., dwelt in a tent) among people (John 1:14; Sir. 24:8; Bar. 3:38).

The Logos in the Christ poem of the Prologue of John, then, is being understood very much like Wisdom in other Jewish texts. As Tobin points out, the things said of the Logos here in John are also very similar to the portrait of the Logos found in the writings of Philo. In both cases, the Logos is reminiscent of Wisdom. In both, the Logos existed with God before the creation, "in the beginning"; and in both, it is called "God." For both, it is the instrument of creation and the means by which people become children of God.

No one should think that Philo, or the Jewish writings about Wisdom, are the actual literary source for the Prologue's poetic celebration of the Logos. My point instead is that what is said about the Logos here at the beginning of John is very similar to what Jewish authors were saying about both Logos and Wisdom. There is a crucial difference, however. In John's Gospel—and only there, among the texts I have been considering—the Logos becomes a specific human being. Jesus Christ is the incarnation of the Logos.

As I intimated before, the Prologue is not saying that Jesus preexisted, that he created the universe, that he became flesh.

Instead, it is saying that the Logos did all these things. Before all else existed, it was with God, and since it was God's own Logos, in that sense it actually was God. It was through the Logos that the universe and all that was in it was created and given life. And this Logos then became a human being: "And the Word became flesh and dwelt among us." That *in-fleshment,* or incarnation, of the Logos is who Jesus Christ was. When the Logos became a human and dwelt among his own people, his own people rejected him (John 1:11). But those who received him were the ones who were made "the children of God" (1:12). These were people who were not merely born into this physical world; they were born from God (1:13). That is because this Logos-made-flesh is the unique Son of God; he is superior even to the great lawgiver Moses since he is the only one who has ever dwelled with God— in his very bosom. And he is therefore the only one who has made the Father known (1:17–18).

In considering the far-reaching implications of this magnificent incarnation Christology, there is a clear downside that you may have detected just from my preceding remarks. If the Logos-made-flesh is the only one who truly knew God and made him known—far more so than Moses the lawgiver of the Jews—and if this one who revealed God has been rejected by his own people, what does that say about the Jews? According to this view, they have obviously rejected not only Jesus, but the Word of God who was God himself. And by rejecting "God" the Logos, have they not also, by implication, rejected God? The far-reaching, and rather horrific, implications of this view will be the subject of a later discussion in the epilogue. Some Christians came to argue that by refusing to recognize Jesus's true identity, the Jews rejected their own God.

One other point needs to be reemphasized at this stage however. If one uses the term *high Christology* to talk about this kind of incarnational view, the Prologue of John would be presenting a very high Christology indeed—higher than that even in the Philippians poem. For the author of that poem, as for Paul himself, Christ was some kind of angelic being before becoming a human—probably the "chief angel" or the "Angel of the Lord." And as a result of his obedience to God unto death, he was given an even more exalted state of being as one who was equal to God in honor and status as the Lord of all. This in itself is a remarkably exalted view of Jesus, the rural preacher from Galilee who proclaimed the coming kingdom of God and who, having ended up on the wrong side of the law, was crucified. But the Prologue of John has an even more elevated view of Christ. Here, Christ is not an angel of God, who was later "hyperexalted" or given a higher place than he had before he appeared on earth. Quite the contrary, even before he appeared, he was the Logos of God himself, a being who was God, the one through whom the entire universe was created.

Even though this view of Christ as the Logos made flesh is not found anywhere else in the Gospel of John, its views are obviously closely aligned with the Christology of the Gospel otherwise. That is why Christ can make himself "equal with God" (John 5:18); can say that he and the Father "are one" (10:30); can talk about the "glory" he had with the Father before coming into the world (17:4); can say that anyone who has seen him has "seen the Father" (14:9); and can indicate that "before Abraham was, I am" (8:58). This last verse is especially intriguing. As we have seen, in the Hebrew Bible when Moses encounters God at the burning bush in Exodus 3, he asks God what his name is. God tells him that his name is "I am." In John, Jesus appears to take the name upon himself. Here he does not receive "the name that is above every name" at his exaltation after his resurrection, as in the Philippians poem (Phil. 2:9). He already has "the name" while on earth. Throughout the Gospel of John, the unbelieving Jews understand full well what Jesus is saying about himself when he makes such claims. They regularly take up stones to execute him for committing blasphemy, for claiming in fact to be God.

Other Traces of Incarnation Christologies

BY NO STRETCH OF the imagination have I intended to provide a full, complete, and exhaustive evaluation of every Christological passage of the New Testament in my discussions so far. To do that would take a very long book indeed, and my objective is something else—to explain the two dominant Christological options of the early Christian movement: the older Christology "from below," which I am calling an exaltation Christology, arguably the very first Christological view of the very first followers of Jesus who came to believe he had been raised from the dead and exalted to heaven; and the somewhat later Christology "from above," which I am calling an incarnation Christology. We don't know how soon Christians started thinking of Jesus not merely as a man who had become an angel or an angel-like being, but as an angel—or some other divine being—who preexisted his appearance on earth. But it must have been remarkably early in the Christian tradition. This view did not originate with the Gospel of John, as I used to believe (as have a lot of other scholars). It was in place well before Paul's letters, as evidenced in the fact that the pre-Pauline Christ poem of Philippians attests it, as does Paul himself in scattered and sometimes frustratingly vague references throughout his writings. I don't think we can say for *certain* that this incarnation Christology dates earlier than the early 50s CE, but there's no reason it could not do so. Possibly it is much earlier. Once Christians thought of Jesus as an angel—and that could have happened very early, perhaps in the first years of the movement—the way was opened for the idea that he had always been an angel, and therefore a preexistent divine being. And so an incarnation Christology was born.

As we will see, eventually incarnation Christologies developed significantly and overtook exaltation Christologies, which came to be deemed inadequate and, eventually, "heretical." Already in some of the later writings of the New Testament we have elevated affirmations of the divinity of Jesus in Christological passages that apparently were written to counter earlier, objectionable views. This is the case, for example, with a passage attributed to Paul in the book of Colossians.

The Letter to the Colossians

I say this passage is *attributed to* Paul because scholars have long had reasons to think that this book was written by one of his later followers some time after Paul was dead.[18] I won't go into those reasons here. But I do want to note quickly that the book embraces Christological views that are astounding in their affirmation of who Christ really is. In particular the poetic section (another preliterary tradition perhaps?) in 1:15–20 has long fascinated scholars. Here, Christ is said to be the "image of the invisible God" (1:15)—a clear allusion to Jewish teachings of Wisdom as a hypostasis of God. Christ is called the "first born of all creation" (1:15), and we are told that "all things were created in him" (1:16). These "all things" are not just the material world, but all natural and supernatural beings "in heaven and on earth, visible and invisible, whether thrones or dominions or principalities or authorities" (1:16). Just as in the Prologue of John, Christ the Logos was made flesh; here, he is Wisdom made flesh. In fact "in him all the fullness of God was pleased to dwell" (1:19). We have now moved into an entirely different realm from the earlier exaltation Christologies.

The Letter to the Hebrews

Something similar could be said of the elevated Christological statements of the letter to the Hebrews, a book that was eventually admitted into the New Testament once church fathers had become convinced that Paul wrote it, even though it does not explicitly claim to be written by Paul and was almost certainly not written by him. The book begins with striking Christological claims. Christ is the "Son of God" who is the "heir of all things" and "through whom [God] created the world" (1:2). More than that, like the hypostases of Wisdom and Logos, Christ "reflects the glory of God and bears the very stamp of his nature, upholding the universe by his word of power" (1:3).

This may appear to be the kind of incarnational Christology found in the Gospel of John—and indeed it is very close in some respects. But a hint of exaltation Christology remains here as well, much as we found in the Philippians Christ poem. For here, after Jesus's death, we are told that he "sat down at the right hand of the Majesty on high, having become as much superior to angels as the name he has obtained is more excellent than theirs" (1:3–4). Once more, as in Philippians, we have an incarnational Christology mixed with a later exaltation. One of the major themes of the early part of Hebrews is that Christ in fact is superior to all angelic beings (e.g., 1:5–8; 2:5–9). In stressing this point, the unknown author quotes the passage from Psalm 45 that we had occasion to notice in Chapter 2, in which the king of Israel is called "God." Now the verse is taken to refer to Christ: "Your throne, O God, is forever and ever" (1:8).

The book of Hebrews wants to stress that Christ is superior to the angels in part because of its overriding emphasis: Christ is superior to simply everything in Judaism—angels, Moses, the Jewish priests, the Jewish high priest, the sacrifices in the temple, and on and on. Once again, we are confronted with the discomfiting situation. To make such exalted professions about Christ more or less forced the Christians to drive a wedge between their views and those of Jews, a matter to which we return in the epilogue.

Beyond Incarnation

AT THIS POINT IT is enough to note that exaltation Christologies eventually gave way to incarnation Christologies, with some authors—such as the anonymous writers of the Philippians Christ poem and the letter to the Hebrews—presenting a kind of amalgam of the two views. Eventually, however, incarnation Christologies emerged as dominant in the Christian tradition.

But this is not the end of the story of how Jesus became God. As we will see, innumerable developments occurred as theologians tried to work out the precise implications of these rather imprecise early claims made about Christ. One of the first issues to be addressed is one that may seem blindingly obvious to most readers as a potential problem. If Christ really was God, and God the Father was God, how could Christians claim that there was just one God? Aren't there two Gods? And if the Holy Spirit is also God, aren't there three Gods? If so, aren't Christians polytheists instead of monotheists?

Many of the struggles in the period after the New Testament period were over this precise issue. Numerous solutions to the problem were posed, several of which were eventually denounced as false teachings and heresies. But other solutions led theologians further onward and upward as they tried to refine their views, so as to affirm in the strongest terms their hard-fought convictions: Jesus was God; he was not God the Father; yet there was only one God.

CHAPTER 8

After the New Testament

Christological Dead Ends of
the Second and Third Centuries

OVER THE PAST FIVE years I have become re-enamored with French cinema, and among my favorite filmmakers is Eric Rohmer. I am especially taken by his two brilliant films *My Night at Maud's* (*Ma nuit chez Maud,* 1969) and *A Tale of Winter* (*Conte d'hiver,* 1992). The plots of both films are driven, in part, by a philosophical concept known as "Pascal's Wager," derived from the seventeenth-century philosopher Blaise Pascal.

Pascal's Wager is invoked in these two films through their explorations of personal relationships. Suppose a person has a decision to make in life—to do something or not. Even though there would be no downside in doing it, she would have only the slimmest of chances for success. Still, that success, should it happen, would lead to an amazingly positive outcome. Pascal's Wager says that given the choice, even if the odds for success are slim, it is better for her to take the risk: there is nothing for her to lose and a lot for her to gain.

When Pascal developed this idea, it was related not to existential decisions about personal relationships, as in Rohmer's films, but to theology. For Pascal, a man of the Enlightenment, it was important to decide whether or not to believe that God exists. There may be only a slim chance that he does. Still, if someone decides to believe, there could be a fantastic reward if he is right and no real downside if he is wrong. On the other hand, if he decides not to believe, no real benefits come from the decision, but there could be very real and harmful downsides (such as eternal punishment). And so, even though the chances of being right may be remote, it is better to believe than not to believe.

People have often told me that I should return to my Christian faith because of Pascal's Wager. Their logic is that if I believe in Christ, I could experience enormous benefits if it turns out that Christ really is the Son of God who brings salvation, and no downside if he is not; but if I choose not to believe, I could face enormous (eternal) bad consequences, with no upside. So it is better to believe than not to believe.

On the surface this may sound convincing, but I think it needs to be put into a broader perspective. The problem is that deciding for or against a particular religious point of view is not like flipping a coin, where there are only two possible options and outcomes. There are hundreds of religions in the world. You cannot choose for *all* of them, because some of them are exclusivistic and require a person's total commitment. So it is not an either/or proposition, as those who support Pascal's Wager sometimes imagine.

To put it in simple terms, if you were to choose *for* Christianity, that would mean choosing *against* Islam (to pick an example). But what if the Muslim view about God and salvation is right and the Christian view is wrong? Then it doesn't help to have taken Pascal's Wager and to have chosen Christianity.

Christianity has long been an exclusivistic religion—meaning that historically, a person who chose to be a follower of Christ could not also be a Muslim or a Hindu or a pagan. And this exclusivism does not merely keep a person from being a Christian and something else; it also keeps a person from being a different kind of Christian with a different kind of Christian belief. As it turns out, there are many different kinds of Christians, some of whom claim that if you do not adopt their particular version of the faith, you cannot be saved. I know of some Baptist churches that insist that if you are not baptized in *their* Baptist church, you are lost. Being baptized in some other Baptist church is not good enough—let alone in a Presbyterian, Lutheran, Methodist, or other kind of church. With hard-core conservative forms of Christianity like this, it is obviously not a matter of taking the "wager" and choosing between just two options. There are tons of options, any one of which might be "right."

This stress within Christianity that there is a right view and lots of wrong views; that the wrong views are found not only outside Christianity, but also inside it; and that wrong views could lead a person straight to the depths of hell, is not simply a modern invention. It goes back to the early years of the church. It was certainly in place in the second and third Christian centuries. By that time it had become exceedingly easy to castigate anyone as a "heretic" for holding to an alternative way of looking at God, and Christ, and salvation. Deciding who was right and who was wrong, and what views were true and what views were false, became an overpowering concern among the Christian leaders. This is because many Christians after the New Testament period had come to think that Christ was the only way of gaining salvation. Moreover, this salvation came only by having the correct understanding about God, Christ, salvation, and so on. For that reason, discerning right and wrong beliefs—ascertaining what was "orthodox" (right) and "heretical" (false)—became an obsession of many of the leaders of the early church.

Orthodoxy and Heresy in the Early Church

THERE WERE NUMEROUS VIEWS of Christ throughout the second and third Christian centuries. Some of Jesus's followers thought he was a human but was not (by nature) divine; others thought he was divine but not a human; others thought he was two different beings, one human and one divine; yet others—the side that "won" these debates—maintained that he was human and divine at one and the same time and yet was one being, not two. These debates, however, need to be placed in their broader context. For Christians were arguing not simply about the identity and nature of Christ, but about all sorts of other theological issues that were circulating at the time.

There were debates about God, for example. Some Christians maintained that there was only one God. Others argued that there were two Gods—that the God of the Old Testament was not the same as the God of Jesus. Yet others argued that there were twelve gods, or thirty-six gods, or even 365 gods. How could someone with those views even be Christian? Why didn't they simply read their New Testament and see that they were wrong? The answer, of course, is that the New Testament did not yet exist. To be sure, all of the books that were later collected and placed in the New Testament and deemed, then, to be holy scripture were in existence. But so were lots of other books—other Gospels, epistles, and apocalypses, for example—all of them claiming to be written by the apostles of Jesus and claiming to represent the "true" view of the faith. What we think of as the twenty-seven books of "the" New Testament emerged out of these conflicts, and it was the side that won the debates over what to believe that decided which books were to be included in the canon of scripture.[1]

There were other wide-ranging debates as well. Was the Hebrew Bible—the Jewish scriptures—part of the revelation of the true God? Or was it simply a sacred book of the Jews, of no relevance for Christians? Or even more extreme, was it authored by a lower, malevolent deity?

What about the world we live in? Was it the creation of the one true God? Or was it the inferior creation of the God of the Jews (who was not the God of the Christians)? Or was it a cosmic disaster and inherently evil?

The reason most Christians today would have no trouble answering any of these questions is that one perspective from early Christianity emerged as triumphant in the debates over what to believe and how to live. This is the side that insisted that there was only one true God; he had created the world, called the Jews to be his people, and given them his scriptures. The world had been created good, but it had become corrupt because of sin. Eventually, though, God would redeem the world and all of his true followers in it. This redemption would come through his Son, Jesus Christ, who was both God and human at one and the same time, the one who died for the salvation of all who believe in him.

That this view would emerge as triumphant was not at all a foregone conclusion in the early Christian centuries. But triumph it did, and it became the dominant Christian belief until now. Here, I focus on the debates concerning the views of Christ, especially as he was regarded as God.

Scholars often describe these theological debates as struggles between "orthodoxy" and "heresy." These are rather tricky terms, in no small measure because what they literally mean is not how they are used by historians who are today engaged in the study. Literally, the word *orthodoxy* means *right belief*. The word *heresy* literally means a *choice*—that is, a choice not to believe the "right belief." A synonym for heresy is *heterodoxy*, which literally means *different belief*—that is, different from the belief that is "right." The reason historians do not use these terms according to their literal meanings is that historians are not theologians (or if they are theologians, they are not practicing theology when they are writing history). A theologian may be able to tell you what the "right" thing to believe is, and what "wrong" things should not be believed. But the historian has no access—as a historian—to theological truth or to what is "right" in the eyes of God. The historian has access only to historical events. And so the historian can describe how some early Christians thought there was only one God and others thought there were two, or twelve, or thirty-six, or 365; but the historian cannot say that one of these groups was actually "right."

Still, historians do continue to use the terms *orthodoxy, heresy,* and *heterodoxy* to describe the early struggles over truth. This is not because historians know which side, ultimately, was right, but because they know which side, ultimately, prevailed. The side that eventually won the most converts and decided what Christians should believe is called "orthodox," because it established itself as the dominant view and thus *declared* it was right. A "heresy" or a "heterodoxy," from a modern historical perspective, is simply a view that lost the debate.

I stress this point because if, in this chapter, I describe a view as orthodox or as heretical, I'm not making a claim about what I think is true and right or false and wrong. I'm referring instead to a position that either came to dominate the tradition or lost the battle.

This chapter is mainly about the views that lost and came to be declared heresies; the next chapter explores those that won and came to be declared orthodox. I begin with three heretical views that were decisively ruled out of bounds by the emerging orthodox opinion. These views can be set out as three contrasting ways of understanding Christ. Some Christians denied that Christ was God by nature; for them, he was "only" a human who was adopted to be divine. Others denied that Christ could be human by nature; for them, he only "appeared" to be a man. Yet others denied that Jesus Christ was a single being; for them, he was two separate beings, one human and one divine. All three of these views ended up being theological "dead ends." A lot of people went down these paths, but they eventually led nowhere.[2]

The Path That Denies Divinity

ONE OF THE MOST interesting features of the early Christian debates over orthodoxy and heresy is the fact that views that were originally considered "right" eventually came to be thought of as "wrong"; that is, views originally deemed orthodox came to be declared heretical. Nowhere is this more clear than in the case of the first heretical view of Christ—the view that denies his divinity. As we saw in Chapter 6, the very first Christians held to exaltation Christologies which maintained that the man Jesus (who was nothing more than a man) had been exalted to the status and authority of God. The earliest Christians thought that this happened at his resurrection; eventually, some Christians came to believe it happened at his baptism. Both views came to be regarded as heretical by the second century CE, when it was widely held that whatever else one might say about Christ, it was clear that he was God by nature and always had been. It is not that the second-century "heresy-hunters" among the Christian authors attacked the original Christians for these views. Instead, they attacked the people of their own day for holding them; and in their attacks they more or less "rewrote history," by claiming that such views had never been held by the apostles at the beginning or by the majority of Christians ever. They were instead innovations that needed to be trounced and rejected by all true believers.

The Ebionites

Several groups in the second Christian century appear to have held on to the very ancient understanding of Christ as a human being who had been adopted by God at his baptism. It is unfortunate that we do not have writings from any of these groups that lay out their views in detail. Instead, for the most part, all we have are the writings of the Christian authors—usually "heresy-hunters," known to scholars as *heresiologists*—who opposed them. It is always difficult to reconstruct a group's views if all you have are writings by their enemies who are bound and determined to attack them. But sometimes that is all we have, and such is the case here. Scholars have long known that it is necessary to take the heresiologists' claims with a pound of salt. But even so, it does seem plausible in this case that some Christians continued to hold the views ascribed to them by their enemies. One such group has been known as the Ebionites.

The Ebionites are attacked by a number of our heresiologists, including one we will have occasion to discuss at greater length, a church leader in Rome from the early third century named Hippolytus. Throughout our sources the Ebionites are portrayed as Jewish Christians—that is, Christians who continued to think it was necessary for the followers of Jesus to keep the Jewish law and Jewish customs, that is, to retain (or acquire) a Jewish identity. There was a certain logic to this view: if Jesus was the Jewish messiah sent from the Jewish God to the Jewish people in fulfillment of the Jewish law, then it makes sense that he embraced a Jewish religion and that to be his follower a person needs to be Jewish. But as Christianity increasingly became gentile (non-Jewish), it also makes sense that it eventually departed from its Jewish roots and came to oppose key aspects of Judaism, as we will see at greater length in the epilogue.

Some scholars have maintained that the Ebionites could trace their theological lineage back to the earliest followers of Jesus, the

Jewish believers who congregated in Jerusalem in the years after Jesus's death around the leadership of his brother James. In terms of their Christological views, the Ebionites do indeed appear to have subscribed to the perspective of the first Christians. According to Hippolytus, in his lengthy book *Refutation of All Heresies,* the Ebionites maintained that they could be made right with God, or "justified," by keeping the Jewish law, just as Jesus himself was "justified by fulfilling the law." Being made right with God, then, was a matter of following Christ's example, and anyone who did so also became a "Christ." In this view, Christ was not different "by nature" from everyone else. He was simply a very righteous man. Or as Hippolytus puts it, the Ebionites "assert that our Lord Himself was a man in a like sense with all (the rest of the human family)" (*Refutation* 22).[3]

In the opinion of Hippolytus and his orthodox peers, nothing could be farther from the truth. For them, Christ was God—not because he was exalted to a divine status, but because he was a preexistent divine being who had always been with God and was equal with God, even before he was born.

The Theodotians (Roman Adoptionists)

Another group that held to such "adoptionist" views—the view that Christ was not by nature divine but was adopted to be God's son—emerged not out of Jewish Christianity, but from purely gentile stock. This was a group known as the Theodotians, named after their founder, a shoemaker, who happened also to be an amateur theologian, named Theodotus. Since they were centered in Rome, scholars sometimes refer to this group as the Roman Adoptionists.

The followers of Theodotus did think that Christ was unlike other humans in that he was born of a virgin mother (and so they may have accepted either the Gospel of Matthew or the Gospel of Luke as scripture). But other than that, as Hippolytus tells us, for them "Jesus was a (mere) man" (*Refutation* 23). Since Jesus was unusually righteous, at his baptism something special happened: the Spirit of God came upon him, giving him the power to do his great miraculous deeds. As Hippolytus presents it, the Theodotians were split among themselves concerning Jesus's relationship to God: some of them maintained that Jesus was a "mere man" who was empowered by the Spirit he received at the baptism; others apparently believed that at that point Jesus became divine; yet others maintained that "he was made God after the resurrection from the dead" (*Refutation* 23).

The longest refutation of the Theodotians' perspective comes in the writings of Eusebius, whom we have already met as the "father of church history." As happens so frequently throughout his ten-volume work on the history of the church, Eusebius quotes at length an earlier writing that attacks a heretical view, without, however, indicating who the author was. A later church father called the writing in question "The Little Labyrinth" and indicated that it was produced by the great theologian Origen, whose own Christological views I will discuss below. As it turns out, some modern scholars have argued that it was instead written by Hippolytus. In either event, this source appears to have been written in the early third century, and it is directed against the adoptionists who maintained that "the Savior was merely human."

The author of "The Little Labyrinth" indicates that Theodotus the shoemaker had a follower who was a banker and who was also called, remarkably enough, Theodotus. Another member of the group was a man named Natalius, who was induced to become the bishop of the group when he was told that he would receive 150 denarii a month for his troubles (a sizable amount of money at the time). But then in an interesting anecdote we are told that Natalius was driven from the sect by an act of God, who sent him some very graphic nightmares in which he "was whipped all night long by holy angels and suffered severely, so that he got up early, put on sackcloth, sprinkled himself with ashes, and without a moment's delay prostrated himself in tears before the Roman bishop Zephyrinus" (Eusebius, *Church History* 5.28).[4]

The author of "The Little Labyrinth" indicates that the Theodotians maintained that their view—that Jesus was completely human, and not divine, but that he was adopted to be the Son of God—had been the doctrine taught by the apostles themselves and by most of the church in Rome until the time of Bishop Victor, at the end of the second century. Historically, as we have seen, the Theodotians may well have had a point: some such understanding does indeed appear to have been among the earliest Christian beliefs. Whether it was the view held by most Roman Christians until near their own time is not as clear. The author of "The Little Labyrinth" refutes the claim by pointing out that renowned Christian authors from the time of Justin Martyr, who was writing in Rome around 150 CE, held a different view: "in every one of these Christ is spoken of as God."

In Chapter 9 we will see that this author is right: Justin did see Christ as a preexistent divine being. But Justin was writing 120 years after the "earliest" Christians and cannot, of course, be used to show what the followers of Jesus were saying in the years just after Jesus's death, more than a century earlier.

It is worth observing that "The Little Labyrinth" accuses the Theodotians of altering the texts of the New Testament they were copying in order to insert their own adoptionist views into them. It is an interesting passage and worth quoting at length:

> *They laid hands unblushingly on the Holy Scriptures, claiming to have corrected them. In saying this I am not slandering them,*

as anybody who wishes can soon find out. If anyone will take the trouble to collect their several copies and compare them, he will discover frequent divergencies; for example, Asclepiades' copies do not agree with Theodotus'. A large number are obtainable, thanks to the emulous energy with which disciples copied the "emendations" or rather perversions of the text by their respective masters. Nor do these agree with Hermophilus' copies. As for Apolloniades, his cannot even be harmonized with each other; it is possible to collate the ones which his disciples made first with those that have undergone further manipulation, and to find endless discrepancies. . . . They cannot deny that the impertinence is their own, seeing that the copies are in their own handwriting, that they did not receive the Scriptures in such a condition from their first teachers, and that they cannot produce any originals to justify their copies. (Eusebius, Church History *5.28)*

This became a standard charge among the orthodox heresy-hunters of the early Christian centuries—that the heretics altered their texts of scripture in order to make them say what they wanted them to say. But two points need to be stressed when evaluating these claims. The first is that many texts of scripture actually did support such heretical views, as we saw in Chapter 6 when we talked about exaltation Christologies (e.g., Rom. 1:3–4; Acts 13:33). The second is that even though the orthodox claimed that this kind of manipulation of texts was a heretical activity, in the manuscripts of the New Testament that survive today almost all the evidence points in the other direction, showing that it was precisely orthodox scribes who modified their texts in order to make them conform more closely with orthodox theological interests. Certain heterodox scribes may have done the same, but among our surviving manuscripts there is almost no evidence to demonstrate that they did so.[5]

In any event, these adoptionist views were rejected by the orthodox theologians of the second and third centuries, whose views had firmly moved into the camp of incarnational Christologies, in which Christ was understood by nature to be a preexistent divine being who had become human.

The Path That Denies Humanity

WE HAVE SEEN THAT those holding adoptionist views of Christ claimed to represent the earliest views of Jesus's own apostles. Of course, every group representing every view of early Christianity claimed that its views were the original teachings of Jesus and his earthly followers—but in the case of the adoptionists, they may well have been right. The view we consider now is in some ways the polar opposite: it maintained that rather than being completely human, and so not—by nature—divine, Christ instead was completely divine, and so not—by nature—human. Eventually, this view came to be labeled *docetism,* from the Greek word *dokeo,* which means *to seem* or *to appear.* According to this view, Christ was not really a man but only "appeared" to be. He in fact was completely God. And God, for these believers, could not be a human any more than a human can be a rock.

This understanding too can be traced back to early times, though not nearly as early as the adoptionist understanding rooted in exaltation Christologies. Docetic views, when first we meet them, appear to have emerged out of incarnation Christologies later in the first century—but still during the times of the New Testament. One would be hard-pressed to see them as views adopted by the original followers of Jesus, however. As we have seen, there may be some reason to suspect that Paul held to some such views—but it is very difficult to say. Paul does speak about Christ coming in the "likeness of sinful flesh" (Rom. 8:3) and to have been "in appearance" as a human (Phil. 2:7), but he never spells out clearly his views about the humanity of Jesus. He does, however, say that Christ was actually "born of a woman" (Gal. 4:4), and that does not sound like the sort of thing most docetists would want to claim.

As a result, the first clear attestation of a docetic view comes only near the end of the New Testament period, in the book known as 1 John. The author of this anonymous work was traditionally said to be Jesus's disciple John, the son of Zebedee. The book was almost certainly not written by him, though, and it makes no claim to be written by him. What is clear is that the book is directed against members of this author's community—or rather former members who have split off from the larger group because of a difference of opinion concerning the nature of Christ's existence. Those who have left the community to found their own church do not believe that Christ "came in the flesh"; that is, they do not believe he was a real flesh-and-blood human being.

The Docetists Opposed in 1 John

The author of 1 John explicitly refers to a group of former members of the community who have left, whom he calls *antichrists*—that is, "those opposed to Christ": "Now many antichrists have come, from which we know that it is the last hour. They went out from us but they were not of us; for if they had been of us they would have remained with us. But they went out in order that they all might be shown not to be of us" (1 John 2:18–19).

It is clear from this passage that the opponents of Christ were once in this author's church, but they left. The author maintains that they never really were of like mind with those who remained in the community. But what was the issue that made them leave? On another occasion the author mentions the "antichrists," but this time he tells us what it is they believed that was at odds with his own views and the views of the wider community: "By this you know the Spirit of God. Every spirit that confesses that Jesus Christ has come in the flesh is from God; and every spirit that does not confess Jesus is not from God. This is the spirit of the antichrist, which you have heard is coming and now is in the world already" (4:2–3).

And so, only those who acknowledge that Christ came "in the flesh" can be considered true believers. The antichrists who have left the community apparently did not make this acknowl-edgment. Scholars debate the meaning of this passage, but it is easiest to assume that those who have split from the community deny the real fleshly existence of Christ. This would explain as well why the author begins his book the way he does, by stress-ing that Christ had a real, bodily, tangible existence: "What was from the beginning, what we have heard, what we have seen with our eyes, what we beheld and our hands handled, concern-ing the word [Logos] of life; and the life has been manifested and we have seen and witnessed and report to you the eternal life that was with the father and has been manifest to us" (1:1–2).

He goes on to say that he is referring to the Son of God, Jesus Christ (1:3). Why does he stress the tactile existence of Christ as one who could be seen, heard, and handled? Precisely because the antichrists have denied it. You may be struck by the fact that this opening to the book of 1 John sounds vaguely like the opening of the Gospel of John, which also starts with "in the beginning" and also refers to the word/Logos of God that provided life and became a human (John 1:1–14). Why the similarities? It is widely believed among scholars that 1 John was written by someone living in the same community in which the Gospel of John was written and circulated. As we saw, the Prologue of John stressed that Jesus was the incarnation of the preexistent Word of God who was both with God and was himself God. This incarnation Christology is one of the "highest" views of Christ to be found in the New Testament. How can we explain the view of the antichrist, which is "higher" still—so high that Christ is completely divine and not at all human? Some scholars have maintained that within the community that produced the Gospel of John, some believers took the Christological views of the Gospel to an extreme—or at least to what they considered to be a logical conclusion—and maintained that Jesus was so much God that he could not really have been a man. The book 1 John was written, then, to counter that view by insisting that "Jesus Christ came in the flesh" and that anyone who refused to acknowledge his fleshly existence was in fact an antichrist.

The Docetists Opposed by Ignatius

The view embraced by the antichrists dismissed in 1 John came to be widely held in some Christian groups of the second century. A similar view was opposed by one of the most interesting authors from just after the New Testament period, a Christian bishop of the large church in Antioch, Syria, named Ignatius. We wish we knew a good deal more than we do about Ignatius's life. What we do know is that he was arrested in Antioch for Christian activities around 110 CE and was sent to Rome to be executed by being thrown to wild beasts. On his journey to Rome, Ignatius wrote seven letters that still survive. They are, needless to say, fascinating reading, as they were written in some haste by a Christian who was staring a gory martyrdom in the face. The letters were written to various churches, most of which had sent representatives to meet Ignatius along his journey. Ignatius had learned of the inner workings of these churches and was writing to help them deal with their problems. One of the major problems he heard about was that some of these communities were having conflicts over the nature of Christ, as some of their members were embracing a docetic Christology.

Ignatius takes a strong stand against any such understanding that Christ was not a real flesh-and-blood human being who physically suffered and died. And one can imagine why he was so adamant in his opposition to such views. If Christ did not *really* experience pain and death—that is, if he was only a phantom of some kind without a real body or physical sensation—what would be the sense of Ignatius himself going through torture and death as a follower of Christ? For Ignatius, Christ was a man like all men. He was God too, to be sure. But he had a real body, he could feel real pain, and he could experience real death.

And so Ignatius tells his Christian readers in the city of Tralles that they are to "be deaf when someone speaks to you apart from Jesus Christ." For Christ "was truly born, both ate and drank, was truly persecuted at the time of Pontius Pilate, was truly crucified and died" (*To the Trallians* 9).[6] He goes on to attack people he calls "atheists." He labels them "unbelievers" and indicates they "say that he only appeared to suffer (it is they who are the appearance)." For if they are right that Christ was only an appearance, "why am I in bondage, and why also do I pray to fight the wild beasts? I am then dying in vain and am, even more, lying about the Lord" (*To the Trallians* 10).

Ignatius says something similar to the Christians in the town of Smyrna: "For [Christ] suffered all these things for our sake, that we might be saved; and he truly suffered . . . not as some unbelievers say, that he suffered only in appearance. They are the ones who are only an appearance" (*To the Smyrneans* 2). That is to say, Christ was not deceitful, only pretending to be a fleshly being when he wasn't; it is Ignatius's docetic opponents who are deceitful. Ignatius then insists that Christ not only died in the flesh, he was raised in the flesh, as proved by the fact that "after his resurrection he ate and drank with them as a fleshly being" (*To the Smyrneans* 3). Christ was not simply disguised in human form; instead, it is the docetists who are "wild beasts in human form." If Christ was "only in appearance, I also am in chains only in appearance. But why then have I handed myself over to death, to fire, to the sword, to wild beasts?" For Ignatius, since salvation comes to the human body, it must be experienced in the human body; and it must have been accomplished by Christ's own actual human body. Otherwise, it is just an empty and apparent salvation.

The Marcionites

The best known docetist of the second Christian century was a famous preacher and philosopher, who was eventually branded as an arch-heretic, named Marcion. It is much to be regretted that we do not have any writings from Marcion's hand, as he was tremendously influential on Christianity in his day, establishing churches throughout the Christian world that embraced his distinctive teachings. Unfortunately, we know of these teachings only from what his orthodox enemies said about them in their refutations. These refutations are, in any event, extensive. The heresiologist Tertullian, whom I will discuss at greater length below, wrote a five-volume work against Marcion that we still have today. This serves as our chief source of information about this great heretic.[7]

Unlike the antichrists mentioned in 1 John, Marcion did not take his theological cues from the Gospel of John but from the writings of the Apostle Paul, whom he considered to be the great apostle who alone understood the real meaning of Jesus. Paul in particular stressed that there was a difference between the Jewish law and the gospel of Christ. For Paul, following the dictates of the law could not make a person right with God; only faith in the death and resurrection of Jesus could do that. Marcion took this differentiation between law and gospel to an extreme by saying that in fact they were completely at odds with one another. The law was one thing, the gospel another. And that was for a very clear and, to Marcion, obvious reason: the law was given by the God of the Jews, but salvation was given by the God of Jesus. These were, in fact, two different gods.

Even today, some people—often Christian people—think of the God of the Old Testament as a God of wrath and the God of the New Testament as a God of mercy. Marcion honed this view to a razor-sharp edge. The God of the Old Testament created this world, called Israel to be his people, and then gave them his law. The problem was that no one could possibly keep the law. The God of the law was not evil, but he was mercilessly just. And the just punishment for breaking his law was condemnation to death. That was the punishment everyone deserved, and it is the punishment everyone received. The God of Jesus, on the other hand, was a God of love, mercy, and forgiveness. This God sent Jesus into the world in order to save those who had been condemned by the God of the Jews.

But if Christ belonged to the spiritual loving God rather than to the just Creator God, that must mean he did not belong in any sense to the creation itself. Christ could not, therefore, have actually been born and could not actually have any attachment to this material world, which was the world created by and judged by the God of the Jews. And so Jesus came into the world not as a real human being with a real birth. He descended from heaven in the appearance of a full-grown adult, as a kind of phantom who only appeared to have human flesh. But it was all an appearance, designed, evidently, to fool the Creator God. Jesus's "apparent" death was accepted as the payment of the sins of others, and through seeming to die, the phantom Jesus from the spiritual God managed to bring salvation to those who believed in him. But he didn't really suffer and he didn't really die. How could he? He didn't have a real body. It was all an appearance.

In response, the opponents of Marcion among the orthodox insisted that the God who created the world was the same God who had redeemed the world; the God who gave the law was the God who sent Christ in fulfillment of the law; and Christ was an actual, full, flesh-and-blood human who did not *seem* to suffer and die but who *really did* suffer and die, shedding real blood and feeling real pain, so that he could bring real salvation to real people who desperately needed it. The orthodox view that triumphed over Marcion and other docetic Christians like him insisted that even though Christ was divine, he was also actually, really human.

The Path That Denies Unity

SO FAR WE HAVE explored two Christological extremes—on one hand were adoptionists, who claimed that Christ was human but not, by nature, divine; on the other were docetists, who claimed that Christ was divine but not, by nature, human. The orthodox position, as we will see, claimed that both sides of this dispute were right in what they affirmed and wrong in what they denied: Christ was divine by nature—actually God—and he was human by nature—actually man. But how could he be both? One solution to this problem was deemed completely wrong-headed and heretical: that Jesus Christ was in fact two entities, a human Jesus who temporarily came to be inhabited by a divine being, who departed from him before his death. Some such view was held by a variety of Christian groups that modern scholars have called *Gnostic.*

Christian Gnosticism

There have been long, hard, and heated debates among scholars in recent years concerning the nature of the religious phenomenon known as Gnosticism.[8] If nothing else, these debates have shown that we can no longer speak simply of Gnostic religions as if there were a monolithic set of beliefs shared by a wide range of religious groups, all of whom can fairly be labeled Gnostic. Some scholars think that the term *Gnosticism* has been so broadly defined that it is no longer of any use at all. Others have more plausibly suggested that we need to define Gnosticism very narrowly and refer only to a certain group as Gnostic and to call other, roughly similar groups by other names. Since this is not a book about Gnosticism per se, I do not need to go into great detail about these scholarly disagreements, important as they are. Instead I will simply indicate what I mean by Gnosticism and briefly discuss the kind of Christological view found among surviving Gnostic texts.

The term *Gnosticism* comes from the Greek word for knowledge, *gnosis*. As we have seen, Christian Gnostics maintained that salvation came not through faith in the death and resurrection of Jesus, but through proper "knowledge" of the secrets Christ revealed to his followers. For many centuries we knew about Gnostics only from the writings directed against them by such Christian heresiologists as Irenaeus, Hippolytus, and Tertullian. We now know that even if we take the reports of these heresy-hunters gingerly and treat them with a rigorously critical eye, they still can mislead us as to the real character of Gnostic views. We know this because actual writings by Gnostics themselves have turned up. Now we can read what the Gnostics have to say about their own views.

The most significant find of such writings in modern times was a collection of books uncovered by Egyptian farmhands digging for fertilizer near the town of Nag Hammadi.[9] This collection is called the Nag Hammadi Library. It contains thirteen books that are ancient anthologies of texts, most of them Gnostic writings produced by Gnostics and for Gnostic readers. Altogether the books contain fifty-two treatises—forty-six if you eliminate duplicates. They are written in the ancient Egyptian language known as Coptic; originally the books were apparently all authored in Greek, so the surviving copies are later translations. The books in which these treatises were found were manufactured in the fourth Christian century; the treatises themselves were composed much earlier, probably in the second Christian century. Studies of these books abound in scholarship. For our purposes, I briefly summarize the basic view set forth in these texts to help us make sense of the Christology that Gnostic Christians commonly shared.

Gnostic Christians did not think that this world was the creation of the one true God, making their views roughly similar to those of Marcion. But unlike Marcion, Gnostics subscribed to extensive mythological explanations for how the world came into being. Its origin was traced far into eternity with the generation of numerous divine beings who made up the divine realm. At some point—when the divine realm was all that existed—a cosmic catastrophe occurred that led to the formation of divine beings who were imperfect and not fully formed. One or more of these lower, imperfect, and (often seen as) ignorant divinities created this material world that we inhabit.

Gnostic texts do not explain the logic lying behind this view of the origin of the world, but it is not hard to detect. Does anyone really want to assign responsibility for this world, filled with so much pain and suffering, to the one true God? This is a world with hurricanes, tsunamis, floods, droughts, epidemics, birth defects, famine, war, and on and on. Surely a good and powerful God is not responsible for this cesspool of misery and despair. The world is a cosmic disaster, and the goal of religion is to escape this disastrous world.

According to Gnostics, the world is a place of imprisonment for sparks of the divine that originated in the divine realm but have come to be entrapped here. These sparks want and need to escape their material entrapment. They can do so by learning the secrets of who they really are, where they came from, how they got here, and how they can return.

You may wonder what any of this has to do with Christianity. According to the Christian Gnostics, this view of the world was taught by Christ himself. Christ is the one who came into the world to teach heavenly secrets that can liberate the divine sparks entrapped in matter.

A "Separationist" Christology

Apparently, some Gnostics held to a docetic understanding, that Christ—who could not belong to this evil material world—came to the earth as a phantom, much as Marcion had said. Marcion himself should not be thought of as a Gnostic; he held that there were only two gods, not many; he did not think of this world as a cosmic disaster, but as the creation of the Old Testament God; and he did not think divine sparks resided in human bodies that could be set free by understanding the true "gnosis." Moreover, his docetic view does not appear to have been the *typical* view of Gnostics. Rather than thinking that Christ was completely divine but not human, most Gnostics appear to have thought that Jesus Christ was two entities: a human Jesus who was temporarily inhabited by a divine being. For them, there was a "separation" between Jesus and the Christ. We might call this a *separationist* Christology.

Because the man Jesus was so righteous, a divine being from the heavenly realm came into him at his baptism. This is why the Spirit descended upon Jesus and—as Mark's Gospel says—came "into" him at that point (the literal meaning of Mark 1:10). And this is why he could begin doing his miracles then—not earlier—and delivering his spectacular teachings. But the divine cannot, of course, suffer and die. So, before Jesus died on the cross, the divine element left him. This is attested, some Gnostics claimed, by Jesus's final words: "My God, my God, why have you left me behind?" (the literal meaning of Mark 15:34). Jesus was abandoned by his divine element on the cross.

One of the Nag Hammadi texts that espouses this kind of Gnostic separationist Christology most poignantly is the book we considered in Chapter 5 called the *Coptic Apocalypse of Peter,* which is allegedly narrated by none other than Jesus's closest disciple, Peter. In the final portion of the text, Peter is said to be speaking with Jesus, the Savior, when suddenly he sees a kind of double of Christ who is seized by his enemies and crucified. Peter is understandably confused and asks Christ: "What am I seeing O Lord? Is it you yourself whom they take?"[10] His confusion increases because then he sees yet another Christ figure above the cross and asks in his dismay: "who is this one above the cross, who is glad and laughing? And is it another person whose feet and hands they are hammering?" (*Apocalypse of Peter* 81).

Christ replies that the person above the cross is "the living Jesus" and that the person being nailed to the cross "is his physical part." And so, there is a radical disjuncture between the physical, human Jesus and the Jesus who is "living." The physical being is said to be "the home of demons, and the clay vessel in which they dwell, belonging to Elohim" (that is, God). The physical Jesus belongs to this material world and the inferior God who created it. But not the living Jesus: "But he who stands near him is the living Savior, the primal part in him whom they seized. And he has been released. He stands joyfully looking at those who persecuted him." In other words, the divine element—the living Christ—has been set free from its material shell. And why does the living Jesus find the scene so amusing? "Therefore he laughs at their lack of perception, and he knows that they are born blind. Indeed therefore, the suffering one must remain, since the body is the substitute. But that which was released was my incorporeal body" (*Apocalypse of Peter* 83).

Here then is a separationist Christology. The "real" Christ, the "living Jesus," is the divine element that only temporarily inhabited the body. It was this lower, inferior part, the "home of demons," that was crucified. It is not the dying Jesus who brings salvation; salvation comes through the living Jesus who cannot be affected by suffering and who can never die. Those who don't understand, who think that it is the death of Jesus that matters, are the object of Christ's ridicule. Obviously, this would include church leaders who insisted that the real suffering and death of Jesus was the one thing that brought salvation. For this Gnostic author, these church leaders were not only misguided; they were a joke.

But the Gnostics did not have the last laugh. For a variety of complex social, cultural, and historical reasons, the Gnostic form of Christianity did not succeed in winning the majority of converts to its perspective. Orthodox church writers such as Irenaeus, Hippolytus, and Tertullian ended up winning the day. These orthodox authors attacked the Gnostics for their divisive views based on a divisive set of theological beliefs: Gnostics, the orthodox charged, separated the true God from creation; they separated human bodies from their souls; and they separated Jesus from Christ. But in fact the one God had made the world, which is a place of suffering not because it was created evil, but because it has fallen as a result of sin. This was not God's fault. This one God had made humans body and soul, and they would be saved body and soul. The true God had sent his Son into the world, not in the mere appearance of human flesh and not as a temporary inhabitant of a human body. God was one and his Son was one, body and soul, flesh and spirit, human and divine.

Early Christian Hetero-Orthodoxies

BY THE END OF the second century it appears that a majority of Christians had not accepted the views of the adoptionists, the docetists, or the Gnostics. All these views were widely seen as theological dead ends—or worse, theological heresies that could lead to eternal damnation. Most Christians instead embraced the understanding that came to be—at least in the next century—the dominant view throughout Christendom: that Christ was a real human being who was also really divine, that he was both man and God, yet he was not two separate entities, but one. How, though, could that be? If he was human, in what sense was he divine? And if he was divine, in what sense was he human? This was the theological conundrum Christian thinkers had to resolve. It took them a very long time indeed to do so. Before settling on one solution, Christian thinkers proposed a number of solutions that may have seemed appropriate and satisfying at the time, but that in the long run came to be rejected as inappropriate, dissatisfying, and even heretical. This is one of the hard-and-fast ironies of the Christian tradition: views that at one time were the majority opinion, or at least that were widely seen as completely acceptable, eventually came to be left behind; and as theology moved forward to become increasingly nuanced and sophisticated, these earlier majority opinions came to be condemned as heresies. We have seen this movement already with the exaltation Christology that was the original form of Christian belief. By the second century it was widely deemed heretical.[11] Later understandings of the second century were acceptable and dominant in their day, but they too came to be suspect and even spurned.

Since these later understandings embraced the principal orthodox concerns—to see Jesus as both human and divine, and as one being not two—yet came to be condemned as heretical, I have coined a new term for them: I call them *hetero-orthodox* (literally "other-orthodox"). Here I consider two such understandings that played an important role in the formation of later Christological thinking.

Modalism

The first was the view that evidently was held by a majority of Christians at the beginning of the third century—including the most prominent Christian leaders in the church, the bishops of the church of Rome (i.e., the early "popes"). Modern scholars sometimes call this view *modalism*.

Christians in the period by and large insisted on maintaining two separate views that on the surface may seem, and did seem to others, to be contradictory. The first was monotheism: there is only one God. There are not two gods, as for Marcion, or an entire realm of gods, as for the Gnostics. There is one God and only one God. But the second view was that Christ was God. It wasn't merely that Christ was a human who had been adopted to a status of divine power, as in the (now primitive) exaltation Christologies. It was that he was a preexistent divine being who was by his very nature, in some sense, God. But if God the Father is God, and Christ is God, how is it that there are not two Gods?

The Modalist View

A modalist Christology explained it. According to modalists, Christ was God and God was God because they were the same person. For those who took this position, God exists in different *modes* of being (hence *modalism*), as the Father, and as the Son, and as the Spirit. All three are God, but there is only one God, because the three are not distinct from one another but are all the same thing, in different modes of existence. Let me explain by analogy: I am a different person in my different relationships, even though I am the same person. I am a son in relationship to my father, and a brother in relationship to my sister, and a father in relationship to my daughter. I am son, brother, and father. There are not three of me, however, but only one of me. God is like that. He is manifest as Father, Son, and Spirit; but there is only one of him.

According to Hippolytus, this view was held by one of the bishops of Rome named Callistus (bishop from 217 to 222 CE): "That the Father is not one person and the Son another, but that they are one and the same." Moreover, "That Person being one, cannot be two" (Hippolytus, *Refutation* 7). The conclusion for modalists was clear and straightforward: "If therefore I acknowledge Christ to be God, He is the Father Himself, if he is indeed God; and Christ suffered, being Himself God; and consequently the Father suffered for He was the Father Himself" (Hippolytus, *Against Noetus* 2). Or as an adversary, Tertullian, put it, "the devil" has put forward the view that "the Father Himself came down into the virgin, was Himself born of her, Himself suffered, indeed was Himself Jesus Christ" (*Against Praxeas* 1).[12] The opponents of the modalist view sometimes mockingly referred to modalists as "patripassianists"—that is, those who maintain that it was the Father (Latin, *pater*) who suffered (Latin, *passus*).[13]

As might well be imagined, the supporters of this view could appeal to scripture as the source for their teaching. For example, in Isaiah 44:6 God declares, "I am the first and the last; and beside me there is no other." This surely must mean what it says—there is literally no other God besides the God of the Old Testament. But at the same time, the Apostle Paul, in Romans 9:5, speaks of "Christ . . . who is over all, God blessed forever." If there is only one God, and Christ is God, then Christ is the God of the Old Testament. God the Son and God the Father are one God—not two separate beings, but the same being.

Those who embraced this view attacked anyone who thought that Christ could be a God separate from God the Father. As Hippolytus admits, the modalists who objected to his own view—that the Son and the Father were two separate beings—"called us worshippers of two gods" (*Refutation* 6). Or as Tertullian says, "They are constantly throwing out against us that we are preachers of two gods and three gods, while they take to themselves pre-eminently the credit of being worshippers of the One God" (*Against Praxeas* 3).

It is no wonder that the modalist understanding was so popular. Hippolytus notes, with some chagrin, that it was not only the view held by the bishops of Rome, but it had "introduced the greatest confusion among all the faithful throughout the world" (*Refutation* 1). Tertullian admits that the "majority of believers" have trouble accepting his own view but prefer the view of the modalists (*Against Praxeas* 3).

But Hippolytus and Tertullian were no pushovers. Quite the contrary, they were forceful polemicists and aimed their attacks not only at such "obvious" heretics as Marcion and the Gnostics, but also at those who seemed to be orthodox in affirming both the humanity and divinity of Christ but who nonetheless pressed the logic of their positions to a point that created its own kind of heresy. As a result of this controversy, Hippolytus, one of the leaders of the church of Rome, withdrew with a group of like-minded Christians from the larger church and was elected as a kind of sectarian bishop. He is known to history as the first antipope. In that role, he saw himself as the advocate of orthodoxy and maintained that the more broadly recognized bishops of Rome were heretics.

For his part, Tertullian was the best-known author from the important church in Carthage, North Africa. He was famous as a Christian apologist (that is, a defender of the faith against pagan intellectual attacks), heresiologist, essayist, and all-around polemicist. He was one of the most important theologians of the early third century, and no controversy drove him to develop his own theological views with greater sophistication than his opposition to the modalists. It was in the context of the ensuing back and forth that Tertullian became the first Christian author to adopt the term *Trinity* as a way of understanding the relationship of the Father, Son, and Holy Spirit—who were distinct in number from one another even if they stood together as One.

The Opposition by Hippolytus and Tertullian

Hippolytus had a good deal to say about the shortcomings of a modalist view, but for the most part it came down to a very basic point: scripture portrays Christ as a separate being from God the Father, so they cannot be one and the same. And so, for example, John 1:18 says, "No one has seen God at any time; the only Son who is in the bosom of the Father, has made him known." Obviously, Christ was not in his own bosom. In Matthew 11:27 Christ says "all things are given me by the Father," and he clearly was not giving these things to himself. On occasion Hippolytus pushes the point of Greek grammar: in John 10:30 Jesus says, "I and the Father are one." As Hippolytus points out—in an ancient equivalent to the view that it "all depends on what the meaning of the word is is"—the verb used is the plural *are,* not the singular *am.* Jesus does not say "I am the Father" or "the Father and I am one." He says "the Father and I *are* [plural] one."

Even more trenchant are the biting comments of Tertullian, who more than any polemicist of his time had no qualms about attacking his opponents with all the vicious wit at his disposal. He mocks those who say, in effect, that God the Father "Himself made Himself a Son to Himself." In his words:

> *It is one thing to have and another thing to be. For instance, in order to be a husband, I must have a wife; I can never myself be my own wife. In like manner, in order to be a father, I have a son, for I never can be a son to myself, and in order to be a son, I have a father, it being impossible for me ever to be my own father. (Against Praxeas 10)*

> *For if I must be myself my son, who am also a father, I now cease to have a son, since I am my own son. But by reason of not having a son, since I am my own son, how can I be a father? For I ought to have a son, in order to be a father. Therefore I am not a son, because I have not a father, who makes a son. (Against Praxeas 10)*

Here we have a heresiological version of Abbott and Costello's "Who's on First?" Tertullian, like Hippolytus, could also appeal to scripture:

> On my side I advance the passage where the Father said to the Son, "Thou art my Son, this day have I begotten Thee." If you want me to believe Him to be both the Father and the Son, show me some other passage where it is declared, "The Lord said unto Himself, 'I am my own Son, today have I begotten myself.'" (Against Praxeas 11)

The Resultant Doctrine of the Trinity

Even though Hippolytus and Tertullian vigorously attacked the modalist position, they did want to hold on to the theological affirmations that created it in the first place. They, like their modalist opponents, agreed that Christ was God, and that God the Father was God, but that there was only one God. In order to retain this view while rejecting the modalist option, Hippolytus and Tertullian developed the idea of the *divine economy.* The word *economy* in this usage does not refer to a monetary system but to a way of organizing relationships. In the divine economy there are three persons—the Father, the Son, and the Holy Spirit. These are three distinct beings, but they are completely unified in will and purpose. As we will see in the next chapter, at the end of the day these affirmations are difficult—one might say impossible—to hold in mind simultaneously, but they are affirmed nonetheless in a way that at the very least can be called paradoxical. The three are one. As Hippolytus expresses his view of the economy:

> The Father indeed is One, but there are Two Persons, because there is also the Son; and then there is the third, the Holy Spirit. The Father decrees, the Word executes, and the Son is manifested, through whom the Father is believed on. . . . It is the Father who

commands, and the Son who obeys, and the Holy Spirit who gives
understanding. The Father who is above all, and the Son who
is through all, and the Holy Spirit who is in all. And we cannot
otherwise think of one God, but by believing in truth in Father and
Son and Holy Spirit. (Against Noetus 14)

Hippolytus termed this three-in-one God the *triad*. Tertullian, as I have noted, called it the Trinity. In his view, the "one
only God has also a Son, His Word, who proceeded from Himself, by whom all things were made." This Son was "both man
and God, the son of man and the Son of God" (*Against Praxeas* 2).
By now, as is clear, "son of man" is no longer an apocalyptic term,
but a designation of humanity, as "Son of God" is a designation
of divinity.

For Tertullian, the relationship of the Father and the Son is
worked out in the divine economy, in which the Spirit too plays
a distinctive role. This economy "distributes the Unity into a
Trinity, placing in their order the three Persons—the Father, the
Son, and the Holy Spirit; three however, not in condition, but in
degree; not in substance, but in form; not in power, but in aspect;
yet of one substance and of one condition, and of one power, inasmuch as He is one God" (*Against Praxeas* 2).

Tertullian goes on to stress that the three within the godhead
are "susceptible of number without division." Later he indicates
that this is "the rule of faith" that Christians adhere to: "The
Father is one, and the Son one, and the Spirit one, and that they
are distinct from each other." The diversity, though, does not
mean separation: "it is not by division that He is different, but
by distinction; because the Father is not the same as the Son,
since they differ one from the other in the mode of their being"
(*Against Praxeas* 9).

Even though Hippolytus and Tertullian are well on the way to
the orthodox doctrine of the Trinity, they are not there yet. This

is clear to anyone conversant with the fourth-century debates that I discuss in the next chapter and who reads from Tertullian the following: "Thus the Father is distinct from the Son, being greater than the Son, inasmuch as He who begets is one, and He who is begotten is another" (*Against Praxeas* 9). Later orthodox theologians would have found this view completely inadequate. In stressing that the Father was "greater" than the Son, Tertullian articulated a view that would later be deemed a heresy. Theology, in these early years of the formation of Christian doctrine, could not stand still. It progressed and got more complicated, sophisticated, and refined as time went on.

The Christology of Origen of Alexandria

With no early thinker is this more clear than with Origen of Alexandria—the greatest Christian theologian before the debates of the fourth century. Although he was an orthodox thinker in his time, he was condemned in later centuries for perpetrating heresy.

Origen, born and raised in Alexandria, Egypt, was unusually precocious. Already at a young age he was appointed head of the school that educated converts, the famous catechetical school. He was brilliant, learned, and massively well read. He was also incredibly prolific. According to the church father Jerome, Origen's biblical commentaries, treatises, homilies, and letters totaled some two thousand.[14]

Origen delved into theological areas that had not yet been examined by any of his predecessors in the faith, and as a result he came up with many distinctive and highly influential ideas. Later theologians questioned his orthodoxy, and he was faulted for developing ideas that subsequently led to the major theological schism that I discuss in the next chapter, the Arian controversy. But he was working in virgin territory. He accepted the orthodox views of his day—including the Christological perspective claiming that Christ was divine and human at the same time, and yet was one person, not two. But Origen worked out that doctrine in a way that took him into theological arenas never before explored.

Among his abundant writings, none is more interesting than his book *On First Principles,* written around 229 CE when Origen was just over forty years old. This was the first attempt we have of a *systematic theology,* that is, a methodical attempt to deal with the major theological views of the church, both to establish what "all" Christians were supposed to believe and to speculate on how to understand the considerable number of gray areas not yet worked out by the orthodox thinkers of his day.

Origen begins his book by stressing that Christ is to be understood as God's Wisdom, which existed always with God the Father (since God always had wisdom), without beginning. Christ is also God's Word, since he is the one who communicates to the world all that is involved with God's Wisdom. For Origen, Christ was not only a preexistent divine being; he was always with God the Father, and since he is God's own Wisdom and Word, he was himself God by nature, and always has been. He was the one through whom God created all things.

This, then, naturally raises the question of how it is that "this mighty power of the divine majesty" can have become a human, "to have existed within the compass of that man who appeared in Judea" (*On First Principles* 2.6.2).[15] Origen himself stands in awe of the question of incarnation: "The human understanding with its narrow limits is baffled; and struck with amazement at so mighty a wonder knows not which way to turn, what to hold to, or whither to betake itself. If it thinks of God, it sees a man; if it thinks of a man, it beholds one returning from the dead with spoils after vanquishing the kingdom of death" (*On First Principles* 2.6.2).

How exactly did this divine figure become human? How, in becoming human, did it not diminish its divinity? And how can the human be divine without ceasing to be human? Origen's solution is one of the ideas that ended up making him susceptible to the charge of heresy. He came to believe in the *preexistence of souls.* In this view, not only did Christ preexist his appearance on earth as a human, so did everyone else.[16]

Origen maintained that in the remote past, way back into eternity, God created an enormous number of souls. He made these souls in order to contemplate and participate with the Son of God, who was God's Word and Wisdom. But virtually all of these souls failed to do what they were designed to do and fell away from their adoring contemplation of the Word and Wisdom of God. Some fell away further than others. Those who fell the furthest became demons. Those who fell not so far became angels. And those who fell somewhere in between the two became human beings. Becoming a demon, a human, or an angel was a kind of punishment for the soul. That is why there are ranks and divisions among these three kinds of being, with some greater than others. Among humans, that is why some people are born with birth defects or disadvantages in life. It is not because God is capricious in how he deals with people; it is because some people are being punished more severely for the greater sin they committed before coming into human existence.

There was one soul, however, out of all the multitude, that did not fall away. Understanding this soul is the key to Origen's Christology. This one soul clung with absolute devotion to the Word and Wisdom of God in a state of constant contemplation, "in a union inseparable and indissoluble." Its unceasing contemplation had a profound effect on this soul. The best analogy that Origen can draw is of a piece of iron placed into the blazing coals of a very hot fire. After a long while, the iron—even though it is not itself "fire"—nonetheless takes on all the characteristics of fire. Touching it would produce no different effect from touching the fire itself. That's what happened to this soul. It "was forever placed in the Word, forever in the Wisdom, forever in God." It, in effect, became "God in all its acts and feelings and thoughts; and therefore it cannot be called changeable or alterable, since by being ceaselessly kindled it came to possess unchangeability through its unity with the Word of God" (*On First Principles* 2.6.6).

This one soul was the means by which God could establish contacts with the fallen souls who had become human as a means of punishment. For this one soul, thoroughly infused with Christ, the Word and Wisdom of God, became a human. Since it was "at one" with God (like the iron in the fire), in its incarnate state, as the man Jesus, it too could rightly be called the Son of God, the Wisdom of God, the power of God, the Christ of God; and since it was human, it could be named Jesus and be called the Son of Man.

How is it that Jesus Christ can on the one hand have a rational soul, like all other humans, and yet still be a manifestation of the Son of God on earth? It is because "this soul which belongs to Christ so chose to love righteousness as to cling to it unchangeably and inseparably in accordance with the immensity of its love; the result being that by firmness of purpose, immensity of affection and an inextinguishable warmth of love all susceptibility to change or alteration was destroyed, and what formerly depended upon the will was by influence of long custom changed into nature" (*On First Principles* 2.6.5).

Here then is a highly sophisticated, if greatly speculative, understanding of the incarnation and nature of Christ, arguably the most advanced early attempt to understand how Christ could be both human and divine. But it too would be surpassed in the years to come, as theologians worked to refine their views and to rule out of court any views that they considered either heretical or bordering on heretical.[17]

The Dead Ends and Broad Avenues of Early Christologies

WHEN THE HERESIOLOGISTS OF the second, third, and fourth centuries discussed the "heretics" whom they considered to be a threatening presence in their midst, they described them as demon-inspired, evil propagators of falsehood. The reality, though, is that virtually no heretic then or since has considered himself or herself to be a "heretic," in the sense that the ancient heresiologists used the term, as referring to someone who propagated error. No one thinks they are propagating error, just as no one thinks that their views are "wrong." Anyone who thinks their views are wrong changes those views so that they become right. Almost by definition, everyone thinks that their views are "orthodox"—at least in the theological sense of "right teachings."

This is one of the reasons why historians do not use the terms *heresy, heterodoxy,* and *orthodoxy* in the value-laden theological sense to describe which views are right and which are wrong. People always think they are right. So historians use the terms in a neutral sense, to describe the views that ended up being declared true by the majority of believers—or at least the majority of church leaders—and those that ended up being declared false.

But since everyone who propounded one view or another in the early church believed that their views were right, there is very little reason to suppose that anyone meant to cause harm by advancing the views they did. Virtually everyone in the early church whom we know of believed they were doing the right things and intended to understand the secrets of the Christian religion correctly. But history is not always kind to good intentions.

Christians wanted to affirm certain beliefs. But in some instances, if those affirmations were pressed to an extreme, they did not allow Christians to affirm other beliefs that they or other Christians also wanted to affirm. We have seen, for example, that some Christians wanted to affirm that Christ was human, but they did so to such an extent that they refused to acknowledge he was divine. Others wanted to affirm that he was divine and did so to such an extent that they refused to acknowledge he was human. Others tried to get around the problem by claiming that he was two different things: part of him was human and part of him was divine; but this solution brought division and disunity instead of harmony and oneness. Others wanted to affirm that since there can be only one God, Jesus could be divine only if he himself was that one God come to earth. But that solution ended up causing Christians to say that Jesus begot himself as the father to his own son, along with other equally confusing formulations. Some superscholars of the day such as Origen tried to resolve the problems in more sophisticated ways, but these views also led to ideas that were later deemed objectionable, such as the view that all of us have souls that preexisted and were brought into the world as a form of punishment.

I should stress that these issues were not merely intellectual games that a group of cerebral Christian theologians were playing. They evidently mattered to ordinary Christians as well, and not just because they wanted to get their beliefs "right"; it was also because they wanted to know how to worship properly.[18] Should Jesus be worshiped? If so, should he be worshiped as God, or as a subsidiary divinity? Or is God the Father alone to be worshiped? And is the God who is to be worshiped the same God who created the world, or some other deity? If Jesus is to be worshiped and God the Father is to be worshiped, how does one avoid the conclusion that the Christians worship two Gods?

Throughout all these debates, we see Christian thinkers

trying to figure it all out, wanting to make certain affirmations that they took to be gospel truth. What resulted was not so much confusion, as considerable nuance and sophistication. Eventually a Christology emerged that affirmed at one and the same time aspects of what opposing heresies affirmed, while refusing to deny what they denied. This led to a significantly refined but highly paradoxical understanding of how it is that Jesus could be God.

CHAPTER 9

Ortho-Paradoxes on the Road to Nicea

AFTER I STOPPED BEING an evangelical Christian, I worshiped for years in liberal Christian churches. Most people in these congregations were not literalists: they did not think either that the Bible was literally true or that it was some kind of infallible revelation of the word of God. And even though they said the traditional Christian creeds as part of their worship services, many of these people did not believe what they said—as I learned from talking with them. Moreover, many people never gave a passing thought even to what the words meant or why they were in the creed in the first place. For example, the famous Nicene Creed begins with the words:

> We believe in one God,
> the Father, the Almighty,
> maker of heaven and earth,
> of all that is, seen and unseen.

In my experience, many Christians who say these words have no idea why they are there. Why, for example, would the creed stress that there is "one God"? People today either believe in God or they don't. But who believes in two Gods? Why say there is only one? The reason has to do with the history behind the creed. It was originally formulated precisely against Christians who claimed there were two Gods, like the heretic Marcion; or twelve or thirty-six gods, like some of the Gnostics. And why say that God had made heaven and earth? Because lots of heretics claimed this world was not created by the true God at all, and the creed was designed to weed such people out of the church.

The creed especially has a lot to say about Christ.

We believe in one Lord, Jesus Christ.

Again, why say there is one of him? How many could there be? Here, too, it is because Gnostic Christians were saying that Christ was several beings, or at least two: a divine being and a human being who were only temporarily united. The creed continues with a long string of affirmations about Christ:

> *the only Son of God,*
> *eternally begotten of the Father,*
> *God from God, Light from Light,*
> *true God from true God,*
> *begotten, not made,*
> *of one Being with the Father.*
> *Through him all things were made.*
> *For us and for our salvation*
> *he came down from heaven:*
> *by the power of the Holy Spirit*
> *he became incarnate from the Virgin Mary,*
> *and was made man.*
> *For our sake he was crucified under Pontius Pilate;*
> *he suffered death and was buried.*

On the third day he rose again
in accordance with the scriptures;
he ascended into heaven
and is seated at the right hand of the Father.
He will come again in glory to judge the living and the dead,
and his kingdom will have no end.

Every one of these statements was put into the creed to ward off heretics who had different beliefs, for example, that Christ was a lesser divine being from God the Father, or that he was not really a human, or that his suffering was not important for salvation, or that his kingdom would eventually come to an end—all of them notions held by one Christian group or another in the early centuries of the church.

But these views tend to be far less important to liberal-minded Christians today, at least the ones in my experience. On several occasions over the past few years, when giving lectures in liberal and open churches throughout the country, I have said that of the entire creed, I can say only one part in good faith: "he was crucified under Pontius Pilate; he suffered death and was buried." For me, personally, not being able to say the (rest of the) creed—since I don't believe it—prevents me from joining such congregations. But members of these congregations—and even clergy—often tell me that this should not be an obstacle. A lot of them don't believe it either! At least not in any literal way.

This would never have been true in the fourth-century context in which such expressions of faith were initially produced. For the church leaders who formulated them, not only the very basic literal meaning of these statements mattered (God exists; Christ is his Son; he was God; but he became a human; he died for others and rose from the dead; etc.); the deeper nuances mattered as well—every word was to be taken as literally true and important, and contrary statements were to be rejected as both heretical and dangerous. Heretics with slightly different views were in danger of eternal damnation. This was serious business in the theological environment of the fourth Christian century. With respect to Christology, as we will see in this chapter, it was concluded that Christ was a separate being from God the Father, who had always existed alongside God, who was equal with God and always had been equal with God, who became a human, not in part, but completely, while not abandoning his status and power as God. This view seems internally inconsistent and contradictory—how can Christ be God and God the Father be God if there is only one God? And how can Christ be fully divine and fully human at the same time? Wouldn't he need to be partly human and partly divine?

Rather than seeing these statements as inherently contradictory, perhaps it is more useful to see them as the paradoxes that resulted from the debates over Christ's being. And since they are the paradoxes that came to figure so prominently in specifically orthodox Christianity, I have coined a new term for them. I call them *ortho-paradoxes*. As a way of summing up our discussion to this point, I lay out these paradoxes in greater detail before looking at some of the important theologians in the early church who helped to shape them, leading up to the first major church council that met in order to resolve some of these issues, the famous Council of Nicea in 325 CE.

The Ortho-Paradoxes

THE PARADOXES OF ORTHODOX Christianity emerged from two brutal facts. First, some passages of scripture appear to affirm completely different views. Orthodox thinkers realized that it was necessary to affirm all of these passages, even though they appeared to be at odds with one another. But affirming these different passages, at one and the same time, necessarily led to paradoxical affirmations. Second, different groups of heretics stated views in direct opposition to one another, and the orthodox thinkers knew that they had to reject each of these views. This meant that the orthodox had to attack a view from one side as wrong while also attacking the opposite view as wrong. But both of two opposing views cannot be completely wrong, or nothing is right, and so the orthodox—in attacking opposing views—had to affirm *part* of each view as being right and the rest as being wrong. The result was a paradox that each of the opposing sides was wrong in what it denied but right in what it affirmed. It's a little hard to get one's mind around without concrete examples, so I now explain how both of these factors led to the resultant ortho-paradoxes—one having to do with the nature of Christ (that is, whether he was God or man or both) and the other having to do with the nature of the godhead (that is, how Christ could be God if only God the Father was God).

The Christological Ortho-Paradox

When it comes to the nature of Christ—the question of Christology—one can point to clear passages in scripture that say he is God. As we have seen, for example, in the Gospel of John, Jesus declares: "Before Abraham was, I am" (John 8:58, invoking the name of God from Exod. 3); "I and the Father are one (10:30); "Whoever has seen me has seen the Father" (14:9). And at the end of the Gospel, doubting Thomas declares that Jesus is "my Lord and my God" (20:28).

But other passages of the Bible say that Jesus is human. And so, John 1:14 says that "the Word became flesh and dwelt among us." First John 1:1–4 claims that Christ can be seen, and heard, and handled. First John 4:2–3 indicates that anyone who denies that "Christ came in the flesh" is an antichrist. And, of course, throughout the Gospels of the New Testament Jesus is portrayed as human: he is born, he grows up, he eats, he drinks, he suffers, he bleeds, and he dies.

The resulting ortho-paradox was driven by the positions that the orthodox were compelled to stake out when opposing the contradictory views of their opponents and the biblical texts. The adoptionists were right to affirm that Jesus was human but wrong to deny that he was God; the docetists were right to affirm that Jesus was divine but wrong to deny that he was human; the Gnostics were right to affirm that Christ was both divine and human but wrong to deny that he was a single being.

And so, if you put together all the orthodox affirmations, the result is the ortho-paradox: Christ is God; Christ is a man; but he is one being, not two. This became the standard Christological affirmation of the orthodox tradition.

As we will see, this did not settle the issue of who Christ was for the orthodox. It instead led to more questions, and "false beliefs" continued to propagate—not against any of the standard orthodox claims, but against various ways of *understanding* these claims. As time went on, heresies became increasingly detailed, and the orthodox affirmations became increasingly paradoxical.

The Theological Ortho-Paradox

The theological debates more broadly dealt with the implications of orthodox Christology for understanding the nature of God—if Christ is God, and the Spirit is God, yet God the Father alone is God, then is God one being, or two, or three?

Here again, some scriptural passages seem to stand at odds with one another. Isaiah 45:21 is quite explicit: "There is no other god besides me, a righteous God and a Savior; there is no one besides me." On the other hand, in some passages, God is spoken of in the plural. In Genesis, when God creates the first human, he says, "Let us make humankind in our image, according to our likeness" (1:26). But to whom is God talking when he says "us" and "our"? In Psalm 45:6, God is speaking to someone else and says, "Your throne, O God, endures forever and ever." Who is this other God? In Psalm 110:1 we are told, "The LORD says to my Lord, 'Sit at my right hand until I make your enemies your footstool.'" Is there more than one Lord? How can there be if, as Isaiah says, there is only one?

More specifically, if Christ is God, and God the Father is God, in what sense is there only one God? And if one adds the Holy Spirit into the mix, how does one escape the conclusion either that Christ and the Spirit are not God, or that there are three Gods? In the end, the orthodox settled for the paradox of the Trinity: there are three persons, all of whom are God, but there is only one God. One God, manifest in three persons, who are distinct in number but united in essence. This too became the standard doctrine of the orthodox tradition, and as happened with the Christological ortho-paradox, it also led to further disputes, heretical interpretations, and nuanced refinements.

For the rest of this chapter we examine some of the Christian thinkers who stood in the orthodox tradition to see how they worked out these various Christological and theological views in their writings. I do not try to cover every important orthodox theologian of the early Christian centuries, and I do not mean to suggest that the figures I discuss here were aware of each other's work. But these thinkers all stand within the very broad stream of "orthodox" tradition. In the preceding chapter we saw how Hippolytus and Tertullian hammered out certain orthodox views. Now we look at a range of other thinkers standing in the same orthodox line. We start at a relatively early point, even before Hippolytus, in the mid-second century, and move from there through theologians all the way up to the famous Council of Nicea, convened by the emperor Constantine in 325 CE in order to resolve the outstanding theological controversies of his day.

Justin Martyr

JUSTIN CAN RIGHTLY BE considered the first true intellectual and professional scholar in the church. Before becoming a Christian, he was already trained in philosophy, and he himself narrates how he came to be a Christian in an autobiographical account in one of his surviving works. Originally from Palestine, Justin moved to Rome in the middle of the second century in order to set up a kind of Christian philosophical school, possibly around 140 CE. His surviving works include two "apologies." In this context an *apology* does not mean "saying you're sorry." It comes from a Greek word that means *defense* and is used as a technical term to refer to an intellectual defense of the faith with regard to the charges leveled against it by its enemies. We also have from his hand a book called the *Dialogue with Trypho,* in which Justin records a conversation that he allegedly had—it is possibly fictitious—with a Jewish scholar over the legitimacy of the claims of the Christians that Jesus was the messiah anticipated by the Jewish scriptures.

Eventually Justin was arrested and condemned for his Christian beliefs and activities. We do not have a reliable account of his trial and execution, but it is clear that he was condemned and died around the year 165—earning him the sobriquet Martyr.

The orthodox of later times considered Justin to be a proponent of their views. As one would expect, his exposition of theology is highly intelligent—he was, after all, a philosopher—but by later standards it came to seem rather unsophisticated and unnuanced. Theology takes a long time to develop, and once it does, earlier views, even intelligently expressed ones, can appear unrefined and even primitive.

Here we focus on our central concern and consider what Justin had to say specifically about Christ and his character. Justin held to the view that Christ was a preexistent divine being who was, in his words, the "first begotten of God" (*1 Apology* 46).[1] Christ was begotten—that is, brought into existence—before the creation of the world (*2 Apology* 5), and in time he became a human being for the sake of believers and in order to destroy the evil demons who were opposed to God (*2 Apology* 6).

There are two principal ways that Justin understands Christ as a divine being, both of which harken back to earlier views we have already explored. Justin develops these views in more sophisticated ways than seen in the New Testament itself. He saw Christ both as the preincarnate Angel of the Lord and as the Logos (Word) of God made flesh.

Christ as an Angel of God

In several places throughout his writings Justin speaks of Christ as the Angel of the Lord who appeared in the Old Testament. In Chapter 2 we saw that there is some ambiguity in the famous passage of Moses and the burning bush: the "Angel of the Lord" speaks with Moses, but then the narrative shifts to indicate that in fact it is "the Lord" who is speaking with him. Justin is keen to explain this textual conundrum in Christological terms. The reason this divine figure is both the Angel of the Lord and the Lord, at the same time, is that it is not God the Father who is there in the bush, but it is Christ, who is fully divine. First Justin establishes that the angel is no mere angel, but God: "Do you not see that He whom Moses speaks of as an Angel who conversed with him from the fiery bush is the same who, being God, signifies to Moses that He is the God of Abraham, of Isaac, and of Jacob?" (*Dialogue* 59). But then he argues that this "God" could not have been God the Father: "No one with even the slightest intelligence would dare to assert that the Creator and Father of all things left His supercelestial realms to make himself visible in a little spot on earth" (*Dialogue* 60). And so who was this God? It was Christ, the angel who later was to become human.

Christ was also one of the three angels who appeared to Abraham at the oaks of Mamre in Genesis 18, another passage we have considered. Because this "angel" is also a "man" but is called "the Lord," it is clear to Justin: "There exists and is mentioned in Scripture another God and Lord under the Creator of all things who is also called an Angel." This one "appeared to Abraham, Jacob, and Moses, and is called God, [and] is distinct from God, the Creator; distinct, that is, in number, but not in mind" (*Dialogue* 56). These patriarchs did not see God the Father but "God the Son . . . His angel" (*Dialogue* 127).

God the Son, then, is the one to whom God the Father is speaking in the Old Testament when he says, "Let us make humankind in our own image" (Gen. 1:26); he is the one to whom God speaks in the psalms when he says, "Your throne, O God, endures forever and ever" (Ps. 45:6); and he is the one to whom the text refers when it says "The LORD says to my Lord, 'Sit at my right hand . . .'" (Ps. 110:1).

Christ as the Logos of God

For Justin, Christ was not only the Angel of the Lord, however; he was also the Word (Logos) of God who became human. It appears clear that Justin was influenced by the Christology found in the Gospel of John, a book that he rarely, if ever, actually quotes, surprisingly enough. But Justin's Logos Christology is more advanced and philosophically developed than that found in the Fourth Gospel.

Justin maintains that the Logos of God is the "reason" that can be found within anyone who uses reason to understand the world (*1 Apology* 5). This means that all humans have a share in the Logos, since all humans use reason. But some have a greater share of it than others. Philosophers, in particular, are skilled in using their reason. But even philosophers do not have a full knowledge of God's Logos. If they did, they would not spend so much time contradicting one another (*2 Apology* 10). Still, some philosophers were closely attuned to God's truth, as revealed to them through the Logos within them; this would include above all that great Greek philosopher Socrates. For this reason, Justin maintained that a philosopher like Socrates should be considered to be a pre-Christian Christian (*1 Apology* 46).

Most important, though, this Logos was known to and proclaimed by the Hebrew prophets of the Old Testament (*2 Apology* 10). And it eventually became a human being, Jesus Christ (*1 Apology* 1.5). Christ, then, is the incarnate Logos that created the world and manifested itself in the world in human reason that seeks to understand the world. It is in Christ himself that "reason" is fully incarnate. Those who accept and believe in Christ, therefore, have a fuller share of Logos/reason than anyone else—even the greatest philosophers of antiquity. Moreover, since he is the incarnation of God's own Logos, Christ deserves to be worshiped along with God (*1 Apology* 6).

Justin was especially concerned to deal with the question of whether Christ is in any sense a being distinct from God the Father, and if so, how one is to imagine the relationship of Christ, the incarnate Word, to God the Father himself. In one place Justin considers Christ as the Word in relation to words we ourselves use. When we speak a word, in some sense that word has an existence independent of us (as we discover when someone misunderstands a word we have spoken); on the other hand, the word we utter owes its existence entirely to us, since we are the ones who utter the word. The Logos of God is like that: it comes forth from God, and so belongs entirely to God, but it takes on its own kind of existence once it comes forth.

In another place Justin likens Christ's relationship to God to a fire that is used to start another fire. The second fire exists independently of the first, but it could not have come into existence without the other. Moreover, when it is started, the new fire does not diminish anything of the first fire, making it less than it was to begin with. The first fire is just the same as it was before. But the second fire is just as fully fire as the first. And that's how it is with God and Christ. Christ came forth from God and became his own being, and yet God was not diminished in the slightest when that happened (*Dialogue* 61). Thus Justin stresses that Christ is a separate being from God and is "numerically distinct from the Father" (*Dialogue* 129); but Christ is at the same time fully God.

One might suspect that Justin has moved into tricky waters with these explanations, since they could be taken to mean that Christ did not always exist (a view that later came to be declared a heresy) and that he was a kind of second God created by God the Father and who was, therefore, subordinate to God the Father (views also declared heresies). Justin is living before later theologians worked out the nuances of these views.

There is some question, in fact, about whether Justin can rightly be thought of as embracing a doctrine of the Trinity. He does not yet talk about the three divine beings, Father, Son, and Spirit, as being all equal and the "three" being "one." He does say that God is worshiped first, the Son second, and the prophetic Spirit third (*1 Apology* 1.13). But this again seems to suggest a hierarchy of divinity, with God at the top and the others in lower places beneath him; and elsewhere Justin claims that God alone is "unchanging and eternal" and the Son is subordinate to the Father (*1 Apology* 13). So too he indicates that Christians worship God, the Son, angels, and the Spirit—clearly not a Trinitarian view (*1 Apology* 13). If nothing else, one can say that Justin represents a development *toward* the orthodox Christological and Trinitarian paradoxes.

Novatian

MOVING THE CLOCK FORWARD a hundred years to the middle of the third century, we come to the writings of a leader of the Roman church named Novatian (210–278 CE). Like Hippolytus, whom we met in the previous chapter, Novatian was the head of a schismatic movement in the church and was elected as a kind of antipope. His theology, however, was completely orthodox in its day. Novatian's most famous work is a treatise on the Trinity, in which he foreshadows ideas that theologians after his time developed; he still has not worked out the implications of a Trinitarian view with the nuance that later thinkers would. He, like Justin before him, still understands Christ to be a divine being subordinate to God the Father. But his chief concern is to show that Christ is fully God and yet is not the same as the Father. In other words, he develops his views in relation to the heresies that were still affecting his own day, adoptionism and modalism.

In some ways these heresies were at the opposite ends of the theological spectrum, one of them claiming that Christ was not God by nature at all, but only human, and the other claiming that Christ was not only God, but was actually God the Father. At the same time, one could argue that the very same monotheistic concern was driving both of these very different Christologies. The adoptionists, who said that Christ was not by nature God, did so in part to preserve the idea that there was only one God; the same concern lay behind the view of the modalists—that Christ was indeed God by nature, because he was God the Father made flesh, so here too there was only one God. Novatian saw these two contrary views as fundamentally related, as flip sides of the same heretical coin. As he puts it, Christ himself was crucified between these two thieves (of heresy).

Novatian is quite explicit that he is opposing these views that were intent on preserving the oneness of God. At one point he states that when the heretics "perceived that it was written that 'God is one,' they thought that they could not otherwise hold such an opinion than by supposing that it must be believed either that Christ was man only or really God the Father" (*Trinity* 30).[2] And so both views were driven by those who objected to the idea that Christ could be a separate God from God the Father, since otherwise there would be "two gods."

In response, Novatian wants to emphasize that Christ indeed is God, that he is distinct from God the Father, but that he is in perfect unity with him: "[Christ], then, when the Father willed it, proceeded from the Father, and He who was in the Father came forth from the Father; and He who was in the Father because He was of the Father, was subsequently with the Father, because He came forth from the Father" (*Trinity* 31).

The complete unity of Christ with God is qualified, however, because for Novatian, as for the orthodox before him (but not so much afterward), Christ is not actually equal with God, but is subordinate to him, a divine being who came into existence at a certain time, begotten by God at some point before the creation. This is because there cannot be, in Novatian's view, two different beings who are both "unborn" or "unbegotten" and "without beginning" and "invisible." Novatian's reasoning has a certain force to it: "For if [Christ] had not been born— compared with Him who was unborn, an equality being manifested in both—He would make two unborn beings, and thus would make two Gods" (*Trinity* 31).

Very much the same thing can be said if he was "not begotten" like the Father, or was "formed without beginning as the Father" or "invisible" like the Father. In all these cases, Christ would necessarily be "equal" with the Father, which would mean that there would not be one God but "two Gods." And that, for Novatian, cannot be. As a result, Christ is best seen as a subordinate divinity who was begotten by God the Father before the creation:

[Christ] therefore is God, but begotten for this special result, that He should be God. He is also the Lord, but born for this very purpose of the Father, that He might be Lord. He is also an Angel, but he was destined of the Father as an Angel . . . For all things being subjected to [Christ] as the Son by the Father, while He Himself, with those things which are subjected to Him, is subjected to His Father. He is indeed proved to be the Son of His Father, but He is found to be both Lord and God of all else. (Trinity 31)

Novatian was more or less driven to this view by his opposition to heresies that declared that since there can be only one God, then Christ either was not God or was God the Father himself. The natural solution, then, was to say that Christ indeed was God, but there are not two Gods because he was begotten by God (not eternal with him) and subordinate to him (rather than equal with him). In Novatian's day, this view could count as orthodoxy. But it was not long before this orthodox position came to be declared a heresy. In its stead, the orthodox theologians of the fourth century asserted a more complete paradox: that Christ was fully, not partially, God; that he had always existed; and that he was equal with God the Father. But together they, along with the Spirit, made up just one God.

Dionysius of Rome

A STEP TOWARD WHAT was to become the established orthodox view can be seen in a short letter by the bishop of Rome, Dionysius, who was writing just about a decade after Novatian (ca. 260 CE). His letter was directed to a bishop of Alexandria, Egypt, who happened to have the same name. This other Dionysius had taken a strong stand against modalism—which he called by the name of the most famous of the later modalists, a man named Sabellius (so sometimes modalism was termed *Sabellianism*). But in opposing the Sabellian position that there was only one God in three modes of existence, Dionysius of Alexandria had gone too far in the other direction, at least in the opinion of Dionysius of Rome. He was in danger of claiming that the Father, Son, and Spirit were so distinct from one another that they could be seen as three different Gods. But any kind of polytheism—or in this case, tritheism—was a heresy to be avoided. So Dionysius of Rome wrote a letter to his namesake in Alexandria to help provide greater nuance to his theological views, affirming that Christ is God and is a separate being from God the Father, but is so united with him that they form an absolute unity.

Dionysius of Rome states the situation that he has heard about in the theological disputes occurring in Alexandria: "I learn that there are some of you . . . who are, one might say, diametrically opposed to the views of Sabellius; he blasphemously says that the Son is the Father and the Father the Son, while they [those who oppose Sabellius] in a manner preach three Gods, dividing the sacred Monad into three substances foreign to each other and utterly separate."[3] In response, Dionysius of Rome gives his own corrective, which stresses that the three are one: "The Divine Word must of necessity be united to the God of the Universe, and the Holy Spirit must have his habitation and abode in God; thus it is absolutely necessary that the Divine Triad be summed up and gathered into a unity, brought as it were to an apex, and by that Unity I mean the all sovereign God of the Universe."

Three beings make up a "Divine Triad." But they are so harmonious that they can be seen as a "unity," and this unity is itself the "God of the universe." This unity, for Dionysius of Rome, signifies that the Son of God is not a creature made or begotten by God, but that he is eternal with God and that he shares all the attributes of God the Father, as his Word, and Wisdom, and Power. For Dionysius of Rome the logic for this is compelling: "for if the Son came into being there was [a time] when these attributes were not; therefore there was a time when God was without them; which is most absurd."

By refusing to "divide into three deities the wonderful and divine Monad," and yet insisting that they are in fact three different beings united together into one, Dionysius reaches the desired theological result: "For thus both the Holy Triad and the holy preaching of the Monarchy will be preserved."

Obviously, we are moving into some deep theological waters. There need to be three divine beings. But the three need to be one, not three. The question of how this can be became the major theological obsession of the fourth century. It all started with a controversy in Alexandria, in which a priest had serious disagreements on the matter with his bishop. The priest embraced a view that seems very similar to that endorsed earlier by the orthodox Novatian and others in the orthodox tradition, but it came to be condemned as one of Christianity's most notorious heresies. This heresy was called *Arianism,* named after the priest with whom it allegedly originated, Arius.

Arius of Alexandria

ARIUS WAS BORN AROUND 260 CE, right about the time Dionysius of Rome and Dionysius of Alexandria were engaged in their back-and-forth over questions of Christology. Arius came from Libya but eventually moved to the city of Alexandria and became intimately involved with the vibrant Christian community there. In 312 he was ordained as a priest and was placed in charge of his own church. In that capacity Arius was answerable to the bishop of Alexandria, who, for most of his time there, was a man named Alexander.

The controversy over Arius's teachings broke out in 318 CE.[4] We know about the dispute from a letter written in 324 by none other than the Roman emperor Constantine, who had converted to Christianity in the same year Arius was ordained (312 CE) and who, in the years that followed, became increasingly committed to seeing that the Christian church should become unified, in no small measure because he saw the church as a potentially unifying force in his fragmented empire. By 324 the church was not at all unified, and much of the rancor and debate focused on the controversial teachings of Arius.

According to Constantine's letter, Bishop Alexander had asked his priests for their opinions about the theology expressed in a particular passage in the Old Testament. Constantine does not indicate which passage this was, but scholars have plausibly argued that it was Proverbs 8, a text we have encountered on a number of occasions, in which Wisdom (whom Christians identified as Christ) is portrayed as speaking, indicating that she was a fellow worker with God in the beginning, at the time of creation.

Arius's interpretation was one that may well have been acceptable in the theological climate of orthodox Christianity during the century or so before his day, but by the early fourth century it proved to be highly controversial. He, like other interpreters, understood the Wisdom of God to be the same as the Word of God and the Son of God—that is, the preexistent divine Christ who was with God at the beginning of the creation. But in Arius's opinion, Christ had not always existed. He had come into existence at some point in the remote past before the creation. Originally, God had existed alone, and the Son of God came into existence only later. He was, after all, "begotten" by God, and that implied—to Arius and others who were like-minded—that before he was begotten, he did not yet exist. One further implication of this view is that God the Father had not always been the Father; instead, he *became* the Father only when he begot his Son.

In Arius's view, everything except for God himself had a beginning. Only God is "without beginning." And this means that Christ—the Word (Logos) of God—is not fully God in the way that God is. He was created in God's own image by God himself; and so Christ bears the title God, but he is not the "true" God. Only God himself is. Christ's divine nature was derived from the Father; he came into being at some point before the universe was made, and so he is a creation or creature of God. In short, Christ was a kind of second-tier God, subordinate to God and inferior to God in every respect.

As we have seen, Christological views such as this were not merely academic exercises but were connected at a deep level with Christian worship. For Arius and his followers it was indeed right to worship Christ. But was Christ to be worshiped as one who was on a par with God the Father? Their answer was clear and straightforward: absolutely not. It is the Father who is above all things, even the Son, by an infinite degree.

Bishop Alexander was not at all pleased with this response and considered such views heretical and dangerous. In the year 318 or 319 he deposed Arius from his position and excommunicated him along with about twenty other church leaders who were Arius's supporters. As a group these exiles went to Palestine, and there they found several church leaders and theologians who were willing to support them in their cause, including a figure with whom we are already familiar: Eusebius of Caesarea.

Before explaining the alternative view embraced by Bishop Alexander, and describing the events that led up to the Council of Nicea that Emperor Constantine called to try to resolve these issues, I set forth Arius's teachings in some of his own words. You may have noticed that we very rarely have the writings of the heretics themselves. In most instances we have to rely on what the orthodox opponents of heretics said, since the heretics' own writings were generally destroyed. With Arius, we are in the happy position of having some of his own words, some of them in letters he wrote and others in a kind of poetic work he produced called the *Thalia*. Unfortunately, the actual text of the *Thalia* is not preserved for us in a surviving manuscript, but it is quoted by a very famous church father of Alexandria, Athanasius. And it appears that when Athanasius quotes these passages, he does so accurately. I present a few that show Arius's particular views of Christ as not equal with God the Father but fully subservient to him:

> *[The Father] alone has neither equal nor like, none comparable in*
> *glory.*

> *[The Son] has nothing proper to God in his essential property*
> *For neither is he equal nor yet consubstantial with him.*

> *There is a Trinity with glories not alike;*
> *Their existences are unmixable with each other;*
> *One is more glorious than another by an infinity of glories.*

> *Thus the Son who was not, but existed at the paternal will,*
> *Is only begotten God, and he is distinct from everything else.*[5]

Unlike the unbegotten Father, Christ, the Son of God, is the "begotten God." He is greater than all else. But he is removed from the greatness of the Father by an "infinity of glories" and so is not "comparable in glory" to the Father.

In a letter defending his views to Bishop Alexander, Arius is even more explicit about his understanding of the relationship of God and Christ: "We know there is one God, the only un-begotten, only eternal, only without beginning, only true, who only has immortality. . . . Before everlasting ages he begot his unique Son, through whom he made the ages and all things. He begot him . . . a perfect creature of God, but not as one of the creatures—an offspring, but not as one of things begotten."[6]

And so, Arius maintained that there were three separate divine beings—which he calls by the technical name *hypostases* but which now, in this context, simply means something like "essential beings" or "persons." The Father alone has existed forever. The Son was begotten by God before the world was created. But this means that he "is neither eternal nor coeternal . . . with the Father." God is above, beyond, and greater than all things, including Christ.

Alexander of Alexandria

WE CONSIDER BRIEFLY THE alternative view affirmed, with some vehemence, by Arius's bishop Alexander, who was the head of the Alexandrian church during an eventful period, 313–328 CE. He is best known for spearheading the ouster of Arius and his followers, not only from his own church of Alexandria but from communion with the orthodox communities throughout the Christian world.

We know of Alexander's own Christological views from a letter he wrote to his namesake, Alexander the bishop of Constantinople, in which he complains, somewhat unfairly, of Arius and his colleagues because they allegedly "deny the divinity of our Savior and proclaim that he is equal to all humans" (*Letter of Alexander,* v. 4).[7] This claim is exaggerated and not at all accurate: Arius affirmed Christ's divinity and stated emphatically that Christ was superior to all humans. But when you're in the midst of a hot argument, you don't always present the other side fairly. For Alexander, if Christ came into existence at some point of time and was inferior to God the Father, then in both those respects he *was* like humans and not like God.

Later in the letter Alexander expresses Arius's view more precisely when he says that Arius had declared "that there was a time when the Son of God did not exist" (*Letter of Alexander,* v. 10). In response to this view, Alexander appeals to a passage in the New Testament, Hebrews 1:2, which says that it was through Christ that God "made the ages." Alexander reasons that if Christ made the ages, then there could not be a time before which he existed, since he was the one who created time and age: "for it is also idiotic and full of every kind of ignorance to claim that the cause of something's origin came to be after its beginning" (*Letter of Alexander,* v. 23).

Moreover, Alexander wants to insist that God cannot change—since he is God—and this means that God could not "become" the Father; he must *always* have been the Father. But this in turn means that he must always have had a Son (*Letter of Alexander,* v. 26). In addition, if Christ is God's "image," as scripture asserts (see Col. 1:15), then he must have always existed. For how could God exist if he didn't have an image? Since God obviously always had to have an image, and since he always existed, then the image itself—that is, Christ—must have always existed (*Letter of Alexander,* v. 27).

In sum, Alexander claims that Christ "is immutable and unchangeable like the Father, perfect Son lacking in nothing in resemblance to His Father, except for the fact that the Father is unbegotten. . . . We also believe that the Son has always existed out of the Father" (*Letter of Alexander,* v. 47).

The Arian Controversy and the Council of Nicea

IT MAY BE USEFUL to explore the controversy between those who sided with Arius and those who sided with his bishop Alexander by giving, first, in brief, a broader historical context.

The Role of Constantine

Since its inception, Christianity had periodically been persecuted by Roman authorities. For more than two hundred years, these persecutions were relatively infrequent and sporadic, and they were never promoted from the highest levels, the imperial government in Rome. That changed in 249 CE, when the Roman emperor Decius sponsored an empirewide persecution to isolate and root out the Christians.[8] Fortunately for the Christians, Decius died two years later, and the persecution by and large ceased, for a brief time.

Some of the following emperors were also hostile to Christians, whose numbers were growing and whose presence was seen as a kind of cancerous growth threatening the well-being of the empire, which had been established for so many centuries on solid pagan principles. The so-called Great Persecution came with the emperor Diocletian, starting in 303. There were several phases to this persecution, as imperial decrees were passed that were designed, in part, to force Christians to renounce their faith and worship pagan gods.

Constantine the Great became emperor in the year 306. He was born and raised a pagan, but in 312 he had a conversion experience and committed himself to the Christian God and the Christian religion. Scholars have argued long and hard over whether this conversion was "genuine" or not, but today most maintain that it was indeed an authentic commitment on Constantine's part to follow and promote the Christian God. The next year Constantine persuaded his co-emperor, Licinius, to issue a joint decree ending all persecution of Christians. From then on, things changed drastically for the Christian movement.

It is sometimes said—quite wrongly—that Constantine made Christianity the "official" religion of the empire. This is not at all the case. What Constantine did was to make Christianity a *favored* religion. He himself was a Christian, he promoted Christian causes, he gave money to build and finance Christian churches, and on the whole, it became a very good thing to be a Christian. The best scholarly estimates indicate that at about the time of Constantine's conversion, something like 5 percent of the empire's sixty million inhabitants called themselves Christian. When the church went from being a persecuted minority to being the hottest religious item in the empire, conversions increased dramatically. By the end of the century, something like 50 percent of the people in the empire were Christian.[9] Moreover, at that later point, under the emperor Theodosius I, Christianity did indeed become, for all intents and purposes, the "official" Roman religion. Pagan religious practices were outlawed. Conversions continued. All this led, ultimately, to Christianity being "the" religion of the West for centuries.

But back to Constantine. When I said that Constantine appears to have had a genuine conversion, I do not mean to say that he looked on the Christian faith from what we might call a purely "religious" perspective without a social or political element to it (I should stress that ancient people saw religion and politics so bound up together that they did not speak of them as different entities; there is actually no Greek word that corresponds to what we call "religion"). He was, above all else, the emperor of Rome, and no one at that time believed in what we today call the separation of church and state. Indeed, under all the preceding pagan emperors, there had very much been a sense of the unity of religious practice and state policy. During the reigns of all the earlier emperors it was believed that the pagan gods of Rome had made Rome great, and in response, the Roman rulers promoted the worship of the Roman gods. Constantine too saw the political value of religion. This does not mean that he did not really "believe" the Christian message, just that he also saw its social, cultural, and political utility. It was precisely this potential utility that upset Constantine when he learned that an enormous controversy was creating rifts in Christian communities. It all had to do with whether Christ was equal with God or was instead subordinate to him as a divine being who came into existence at some point in time.

Scholars have suggested several reasons why the emperor

would have even the slightest interest in getting involved in these internal Christian debates. There can be no disputing the fact that he did so. A biography written by Eusebius of Caesarea, *The Life of the Blessed Emperor Constantine,* reproduces a letter Constantine sent to Arius and Alexander in which he tried to get them to see eye-to-eye on the theological issue dividing them. The letter suggests that Constantine understood Christianity as a potentially unifying force in his socially and culturally disunified empire. Looked at even from a disinterested point of view, Christianity could be seen as a religion that stresses unity and oneness. There is one God (not lots of gods). God has one Son. There is one way of salvation. There is only one truth. There is "one Lord, one faith, and one baptism" (Eph. 4:5). The creation is united with God, its creator; God is united with his Son; his Son is united with his people; and the salvation he brings makes his people united with God. The religion is all about oneness, unity.

As such, it could be used to bring unity to a fractured empire. So Constantine acknowledges to the two recipients of his letter: "My first concern was that the attitude towards the Divinity of all the provinces should be united in one consistent view" (*Life* 2.65).[10] The problem was that there was no consistency in the church itself, because of the split over Arius's teachings. The split especially affected the churches of Africa, to Constantine's chagrin: "Indeed . . . an intolerable madness had seized the whole of Africa because of those who had dared with ill-considered frivolity to split the worship of the population into various factions, and . . . I personally desired to put right this disease" (*Life* 2.66). Constantine thus wanted to heal the theological division in the church in order to make the Christian faith more useful in bringing religious and cultural unity to the empire.

A second reason sometimes suggested for Constantine's concern relates more closely to his pagan inheritance. It had widely been believed for many centuries that the gods oversaw the best interests of Rome when they were properly acknowledged in cultic practices of the state. Worshiping the gods in the proper and prescribed way earned their good favor, and their good favor was manifest in their kind treatment of the state—for example, in winning its wars and in prospering during times of peace. Constantine inherited this perspective and may well have brought it with him into his Christian faith. Now he worshiped not the traditional gods of Rome, but the God of the Christians. But this God too must be worshiped properly. If there are serious divisions in the worshiping community, however, this could not be pleasing to God. Christianity was far more focused on "theological truth" than traditional Greek or Roman religions and placed greater emphasis on "sacrificial practice." It was important, in the Christian faith, to know and practice the truth. But widespread disagreements about the truth would lead to deep rifts in the Christian community, and God could not be pleased with that state of affairs. For the good of the state, which was overseen ultimately by God, it was necessary that these rifts be healed.

Constantine was not a trained theologian, and he found himself to be somewhat taken aback by the virulence of the debate between Arius and Alexander. To Constantine, the issues seemed petty. What does it really matter whether there was a time before which Christ existed? Is that really the most important thing? Not for Constantine. As he says in his letter: "I considered the origin and occasion for these things . . . as extremely trivial and quite unworthy of so much controversy" (*Life* 2.68). But contention there was. So he tried to encourage Arius and Alexander to resolve their theological differences so Christianity could move forward as a unified whole to confront the greater problems of the empire.

Constantine had the letter delivered by an important bishop of Cordova, Spain, named Ossius. After delivering the letter, Ossius returned from Alexandria by a land route that took him through Antioch of Syria, where a synod of bishops was being held to debate the theological questions raised by Arius. This synod devised a creedal statement (that is, a statement of faith) that contradicted Arius's views. Everyone at the synod signed this creed, with three exceptions—one of them being Eusebius of Caesarea. It was agreed, however, that these three could be given a further chance to defend themselves and their Christological views at another meeting. And this is how the Council of Nicea was born.

The Council of Nicea

Originally, the council was supposed to meet in Ancyra (in Turkey), but for practical reasons it was moved to Nicea (also in Turkey).[11] This was the first of the seven major councils of church bishops that historians have called *ecumenical councils*—which means something like "councils of the entire world." The term is not entirely apt in this case, since obviously the whole world did not participate in the council but only a group of bishops; moreover, these bishops were not widely representative of the entire world, or even of the world of Christendom. Hardly any bishops attended from the western part of the empire; most came from such eastern climes as Egypt, Palestine, Syria, Asia Minor, and Mesopotamia. Even the bishop of Rome, Sylvester, did not attend but sent two legates in his place. Historians differ on the number of bishops at the conference. Athanasius of Alexandria, who was a young man at the time (but who was eventually to become the powerful bishop of Alexandria), later indicated that 318 bishops were present. The council met in June 325 CE.

The key issue to be resolved by the council concerned the teachings of Arius and his supporters, including Eusebius of Caesarea. Eusebius began the proceedings by introducing his own creedal statement—that is, his theological exposition of what should be confessed as true and valid about God, about Christ, about the Spirit, and so on. Evidently, most participants at the council saw this creed to be basically acceptable; but it was ambiguous at key points, so most of the bishops were not satisfied because it did not directly refute the heretical claims of Arius. After hammering out their theological positions, the bishops finally agreed upon a creed. It consisted of terse theological statements: beginning with a very brief statement about God the Father (brief because no one was disputing the character or nature of God), followed in much longer order with statements about Christ (since that was the topic of concern), and concluding in almost unbelievably short order with a statement about the Spirit (since that too was not yet an issue). The creed ended with a set of anathemas, or curses, on people who made certain heretical declarations—these declarations all being claims connected with Arius and his followers. This creed eventually became the foundation of what is now called the Nicene Creed. Here it is, in full (readers who are familiar with the Nicene Creed as it is recited today will notice key differences—especially with the anathemas; the modern version represents a later revision):

> We believe in one God, the Father, almighty, maker of all things visible and invisible;
>
> And in one Lord Jesus Christ, the Son of God, begotten from the Father, only-begotten, that is, from the substance of the Father, God from God, light from light, true God from true God, begotten not made, of one substance with the Father, through whom all things came into being, things in heaven and things on earth, who because of us humans and because of our salvation came down and became incarnate, becoming human, suffered and rose on the third day, ascended to the heavens, will come to judge the living and the dead;
>
> And in the Holy Spirit.
>
> But as for those who say, "There was when he was not" and "Before being born he was not" and that "He came into existence out of nothing" or who assert that the Son of God is of a different hypostasis or substance or is subject to alteration and change—these the Catholic and Apostolic church anathematizes.[12]

Many people have written entire books on this council and its creed.[13] For our purposes, I emphasize just a couple of points. First, as I have already stressed, far more space is devoted in the creed to Christ than to the Father, and the Spirit is barely mentioned. It was important to get the teachings about Christ "right." To assure these teachings, and to avoid any ambiguities, the anathemas are added.

In the creed itself, Christ is said to be "from the substance of the Father." He is not a subordinate God. He is "of one substance with the Father." The Greek word used to indicate "one substance," which could also be translated as "same substance," is *homoousios*. It was destined to become an important term in later disputes over the nature of Christ. As it turns out, and as we will see in the epilogue, neither the council nor the creed resolved all the issues surrounding the nature of Christ. In fact, the issues lived on; Arianism continued to thrive; and even after the Arian issue was eventually resolved, a whole set of other issues, increasingly detailed, nuanced, and sophisticated, arose. If Constantine did not much like the controversy of his own day, he would have despised what was to come.

But it is important that the creed emphasizes that Christ is of the "same substance" as God the Father. This is a way of saying that God and Christ are absolutely equal. Christ is "true God," not a subordinate deity secondary to God the Father. And as the anathemas indicate, it is now a heresy to claim there ever was a time when Christ did not exist (or before which he did not exist), or to say he was created like everything else in the universe "out of nothing," or that he does not share God's very substance.

The Outcome of the Council

To make a long and complex story very short, there was widespread agreement among the bishops present about the details of the new creed, which was seen to be binding on all Christians. That is what the creed means when it states that it presents the view of the "Catholic and Apostolic church": it is the view of the church that descended in direct lineage from the apostles of Jesus and that is found scattered throughout the entire world ("catholic" in this context means "universal"). Sometimes you will hear that at Nicea it was "a close vote." It was not close. Only twenty of the 318 bishops disagreed with the creed when it was finally formulated. Constantine, who was actively involved with some of the proceedings, forced seventeen of those twenty to acquiesce. So only three did not eventually sign off on the creed: Arius himself and two bishops from his home country of Libya. These three were banished from Egypt. A couple of other bishops signed the creed but refused to agree to the anathemas at the end, which were directed specifically against Arius's teachings. These bishops too were exiled.

So the story of how Jesus became God appears to end. But as we will see in the epilogue, it did not really end. Quite the contrary. But for the time being, Alexander and his like-minded colleagues won the day, and Constantine believed he had attained a unified church. The issues were, for the moment, resolved. Christ was coeternal with God the Father. He had *always* existed. And he was "of the same substance" as God the Father, himself truly God, from back into eternity.

The Christ of Nicea is obviously a far cry from the historical Jesus of Nazareth, an itinerant apocalyptic preacher in the backwaters of rural Galilee who offended the authorities and was unceremoniously crucified for crimes against the state. Whatever he may have been in real life, Jesus had now become fully God.

Jesus as God: The Aftermath

As I HAVE BEEN writing this book I have come to realize that the history of my own personal theology is a mirror image of the history of the theology of the early church. To use the older terminology, in early Christianity the views of Christ got "higher and higher" with the passing of time, as he became increasingly identified as divine. Jesus went from being a potential (human) messiah to being the Son of God exalted to a divine status at his resurrection; to being a preexistent angelic being who came to earth incarnate as a man; to being the incarnation of the Word of God who existed before all time and through whom the world was created; to being God himself, equal with God the Father and always existent with him. My own personal beliefs about Jesus moved in precisely the opposite direction. I started out thinking of Jesus as God the Son, equal with the Father, a member of the Trinity; but over time, I began to see him in "lower and lower" terms, until finally I came to think of him as a human being who was not different in nature from any other human being. The

Christians exalted him to the divine realm in their theology, but in my opinion, he was, and always had been, a human.

As an agnostic, I now think of Jesus as a true religious genius with brilliant insights. But he was also very much a man of his time. And his time was an age of full-throated apocalyptic fervor. Jesus participated in this first-century Palestinian Jewish milieu. He was born and raised in it, and it was the context within which he conducted his public ministry. Jesus taught that the age he lived in was controlled by forces of evil but that God would soon intervene to destroy everything and everyone opposed to him. God would then bring in a good, utopian kingdom on earth, where there would be no more pain and suffering. Jesus himself would be the ruler of this kingdom, with his twelve disciples serving under him. And all this was to happen very soon—within his own generation.

This apocalyptic message does continue to resonate with me, but I certainly do not believe it literally. I do not think that there are supernatural powers of evil who are controlling our governments or demons who are making our lives miserable; I do not think there is going to be a divine intervention in the world in which all the forces of evil will be permanently destroyed; I do not think there will be a future utopian kingdom here on earth ruled by Jesus and his apostles. But I do think there is good and evil; I do think we should all be on the side of good; and I do think we should fight mightily against all that is evil.

I especially resonate with the ethical teachings of Jesus. He taught that much of the law of God could be summarized in the command to "love your neighbor as yourself." He taught that you should "do unto others as you would have them do unto you." He taught that our acts of love, generosity, mercy, and kindness should reach even to "the least of these, my brothers and sisters"—that is, to the lowly, the outcast, the impoverished, the homeless, the destitute. I agree wholeheartedly with these views and try my best to live according to them.

But as a historian I realize that Jesus's ethical teachings were delivered in a decidedly apocalyptic form to which I do not subscribe. Jesus is sometimes lauded as one of the great moral teachers of all time, and I sympathize with this characterization. But it is important to realize that the reasoning behind his moral teaching is not the reasoning most of us use today. People today think that we should live ethically for a wide variety of reasons—most of them irrelevant to Jesus—for example, so we can find the greatest self-fulfillment in life and so we can all thrive together as a society for the long haul. Jesus did not teach his ethics so that society could thrive for the long haul. For Jesus, there was not going to *be* a long haul. The end was coming soon, and people needed to prepare for it. Those who lived according to the standards he set forth, loving God with all their being and loving one another as themselves, would enter into the kingdom of God that was very soon to appear. Anyone who chose not to do so would be destroyed when the Son of Man arrived in judgment from heaven. Jesus's ethics were an "ethics of the kingdom" both because the kinds of lives his followers led when they followed these ethical principles would be the kinds of lives they would experience in the kingdom—where there would be no war, hatred, violence, oppression, or injustice—and because a person could enter into the kingdom only by living in this way.

This is not the worldview I myself have. I don't believe there is a God in heaven who is soon to send a cosmic judge of the earth to destroy the forces of evil. And yet I think that the ethical principles Jesus enunciated in that apocalyptic context are still applicable to me, living in a different context. To make sense of Jesus, I have recontextualized him—that is, made him and his message relevant in a new context—for a new day, the day in which I live.

I would argue that Jesus has always been recontextualized by people living in different times and places. The first followers of Jesus did this after they came to believe that he had been raised from the dead and exalted to heaven: they made him into something he had not been before and understood him in light of their new situation. So too did the later authors of the New Testament, who recontextualized and understood Jesus in light of their own, now even more different situations. So too did the Christians of the second and third centuries, who understood Jesus less as an apocalyptic prophet and more as a divine being become human. So too did the Christians of the fourth century, who maintained that he had always existed and had always been equal with God the Father in status, authority, and power. And so too do Christians today, who think that the divine Christ they believe in and confess is identical in every respect with the person who was walking the dusty lanes of Galilee preaching his apocalyptic message of the coming destruction. Most Christians today do not realize that they have recontextualized Jesus. But in fact they have. Everyone who either believes in him or subscribes to any of his teachings has done so—from the earliest believers who first came to believe in his resurrection until today. And so it will be, world without end.

This is certainly and most obviously true of the years we have examined in this book. It continued to be true in the years that followed, as we can now see as we consider what happened in the aftermath of the decision of the Council of Nicea that Christ was God in a particular sense, that he had been a preexistent divine being with God throughout all eternity, and that he was, in fact, the one through whom God had made all things.

Developments of the Fourth Century

IN THE POPULAR IMAGINATION it is widely thought that after the Council of Nicea there was a basic agreement among Christian leaders and thinkers concerning the nature of Christ and the character of the Trinity. In fact, nothing could be farther from the truth. Nicea and its creed were not the end of the story, but the beginning of a new chapter. For one thing, the defeat of the Arian side at Nicea did not stamp out the Arian view. Constantine backed the winning side—probably less because it was what he actually believed than because it became the consensus opinion and he was principally interested in having a consensus emerge to help unify the church. But the church was not unified and would not become unified. After Constantine other emperors came and went, and over the next several decades a number of these emperors leaned toward the Arian interpretation of Christ and acted out on their convictions. There were times—possibly most of the times—when there were more Arians than anti-Arians. That is why the church father Jerome, writing in 379 CE, could make his famous lament that "the world groaned and was astonished to find itself Arian" (*Dialogue Against Luciferians* 19).

As it turns out, the Arian controversy was not finally decided until the next major ecumenical council, held just two years after Jerome's lament, the Council of Constantinople in 381. At this council the decisions of Nicea were restated and reaffirmed, and Arianism came to be a marginalized minority view widely deemed heretical.

For those standing outside these theological controversies, the differences between the views of Arius and of Arius's opponents, such as his bishop Alexander and the young but brilliant Athanasius—himself soon to be bishop of Alexandria—are less striking than the commonalities. Even the "heretical" Arians agreed with Athanasius and others that Christ was God. He was a divine being who had existed with God before the beginning of all other things and was the one through whom God had created the universe. This was still a very "high" incarnational Christology. By the time of the debates between Arius and his opponents, and then, in after years, between the Arians and the followers of Athanasius, very few Christians doubted that Jesus was actually

God. Once again, the only question was "in what sense" he was God.

What is arguably most significant is that in the fourth century, when these disputes had come to a head, the Roman emperor Constantine had converted to the faith. That changed everything. Having a Christian emperor on the throne—one who believed and propagated the belief that Christ was God—had radical implications for the various interactions between orthodox Christians and others. In what remains of this epilogue I briefly consider the implications for three realms of dispute that Christians engaged in: disputes with pagans, disputes with Jews, and disputes with one another.

The God Christ and the Pagan World

SINCE THE DAYS OF Caesar Augustus, three hundred years earlier, inhabitants of the Roman world had understood and worshiped the emperor as a god. Moreover, from the time the earliest followers of Jesus came to believe that he was raised from the dead, Christians had understood and worshiped Christ as God. As we have seen, these two—the emperor and Jesus—were the only two figures that we know of from antiquity who were actually called "the Son of God." And in the Christian mind, at least, this meant that the two figures were in competition. In the early fourth century, one of the competitors caved in and lost the struggle. With Constantine, the emperor changed from being a rival god to Jesus to be being a servant of Jesus.

One of the most interesting works by the church historian Eusebius is his previously mentioned *Life of the Blessed Emperor Constantine,* a biographical account of the emperor that is, to say the least, effusive in its praise. Arguably the most valuable parts of the *Life* are those in which Eusebius quotes the actual words of the emperor. In a letter Constantine wrote to the Christians of

Palestine, it becomes clear that Constantine does not see himself as a competitor with Christ and God the Father, but rather stands in awe of God's power and recognizes his need to serve him as his servant on earth. At one point Constantine declares that the Christian God "alone really exists and holds power continuously through all time," and he says that God "examined my service and approved it as fit for his purposes" (*Life* 2.28). Or as he says later in the letter, "Indeed my whole soul and whatever breath I draw, and whatever goes on in the depths of the mind, that, I am firmly convinced, is owed by us wholly to the greatest God" (*Life* 2.24). Clearly there is no competition here!

As a result of Constantine's devotion, Eusebius writes, "by law he forbade images of himself to be set up in idol-shrines." Moreover, he "had his portrait so depicted on the gold coinage that he appeared to look upwards in the manner of one reaching out to God in prayer" (*Life* 4.15, 16). In other words, Constantine reversed the three-centuries-old procedures of his predecessors. Rather than allowing himself to be depicted as a god and worshiped as a god, he insisted that he be shown worshiping the true God.

Somewhat more striking, Constantine required the soldiers in his army not to worship him, but to worship the Christian God. This applied even to the soldiers who remained pagan. Eusebius indicates that Constantine required the non-Christian soldiers in the army to gather on a plain every Sunday and recite the following prayer to the Christian God:

> *You alone we know as God,*
> *You are the King we acknowledge,*
> *You are the Help we summon,*
> *By you we have won our victories,*
> *Through you we have overcome our enemies . . .*
> *To you we all come to supplicate for our Emperor Constantine and*
> *for his beloved Sons:*

That they may be kept safe and victorious for us in long life
  (Life 4.20)

Once the emperor became Christian, it is fair to say that everything changed with respect to Christian relationships with pagans and with the Roman government. Rather than being a persecuted minority who refused to worship the divine emperor, the Christians were on the path to becoming the persecuting majority, with the emperor as the servant of the true God who encouraged, directly or indirectly, the citizens of the state to join in his Christian worship. By the end of the fourth century something like half of the entire empire was converted to orthodox Christianity; the emperor enforced laws promoting the Christian religion and outlawing pagan sacrifice and worship; and Christianity triumphed once and for all over the pagan religions that had previously accepted the emperor as divine.

The God Christ and the Jewish World

THE CHRISTIAN BELIEF THAT Jesus was God had serious ramifications for Jewish–Christian relations in antiquity, because it was widely thought that the Jews were responsible for Jesus's death. If the Jews killed Jesus, and Jesus was God, does it not follow that the Jews had killed their own God?[1]

This was in fact a view held in orthodox circles long before the conversion of Constantine. Nowhere does it come in a more chilling rhetorical package than in a sermon preached by a bishop of the city of Sardis in Asia Minor near the end of the second Christian century, a man named Melito. This is the first instance we have on record of a Christian charging Jews with the crime of deicide—the murder of God. Melito delivers the charge in powerful and highly effective language. I quote here only a small portion of his long sermon. The occasion was the Jewish Passover, when Jews annually commemorated the great act of God when he delivered the children of Israel from their slavery in Egypt during the days of Moses. The Passover lamb that was slain on that occasion was, for Melito, an image of Christ himself, slain by the Jews. And rather than being an occasion for joyous celebration, the death of the true lamb was an occasion for hostile accusation. The Jews killed the one who had come to save them; they killed their own messiah; and since the messiah was himself divine, the Jews killed their own God:

> *This one was murdered*
> *And where was he murdered?*
> *In the very center of Jerusalem!*
> *Why?*
> *Because he had healed their lame,*
> *And had cleansed their lepers,*
> *And had guided their blind with light,*
> *And had raised up their dead.*
> *For this reason he suffered. . . .*
> *Why O Israel, did you do this strange injustice?*
> *You dishonored the one who had honored you.*
> *You held in contempt the one who held you in esteem.*
> *You denied the one who publicly acknowledged you.*
> *You renounced the one who proclaimed you his own.*
> *You killed the one who made you to live,*
> *Why did you do this, O Israel? . . .*
> *It was necessary for him to suffer, yes, but not by you;*
> *It was necessary for him to be dishonored, but not by you;*
> *It was necessary for him to be judged, but not by you;*
> *It was necessary for him to be crucified, but not by you, nor by your*
>   *right hand,*
> *O Israel!*

The rhetoric then moves to a climax as Melito delivers his ultimate charge against his enemies, the Jews:

> *Pay attention, all families of the nations, and observe!*
> *An extraordinary murder has taken place*
> *In the center of Jerusalem,*
> *In the city devoted to God's law,*
> *In the city of the Hebrews,*
> *In the city of the prophets,*
> *In the city thought of as just.*
> *And who has been murdered?*
> *And who is the murderer?*
> *I am ashamed to give the answer,*
> *But give it I must. . . .*
> *The one who hung the earth in space is himself hanged;*
> *The one who fixed the heavens in place, is himself impaled;*
> *The one who firmly fixed all things, is himself firmly fixed to the*
> *   tree.*
> *The Lord is insulted,*
> *God has been murdered,*
> *The King of Israel has been destroyed*
> *By the right hand of Israel.*[2]

It is, of course, one thing for a member of a relatively small persecuted minority that is politically powerless to attack others with such vitriolic rhetoric. But what happens when the persecuted minority comes to be a majority? What happens when it gains political power—in fact, supreme political power? What happens when the emperor of Rome himself comes to believe the Christian message? As you can imagine, what happens will not be good for the enemies who supposedly murdered the God the Christians worship.

In a book that has deservedly become a classic study of the

rise of anti-Judaism in the early church, called *Faith and Fratricide*, theologian Rosemary Ruether sets forth the social implications of Christian power in the fourth century for Jews of the empire.[3] The short story is that Jews came to be legally marginalized under Christian emperors and treated as second-class citizens with restricted legal rights and limited economic possibilities. Jewish beliefs and practices were not actually made illegal, in the way pagan sacrifices were at the end of the fourth century, but theologians and Christian bishops—who now were increasingly powerful not only as religious leaders, but also as civil authorities—railed against Jews and attacked them as the enemies of God. State legislation was passed to constrain the activities of Jews.

Constantine himself passed a law that forbade Jews from owning Christian slaves. This may seem like a humane measure in our day and age, when slavery of all kinds is viewed with disgust and contempt. But Constantine did not ban slavery and was not opposed to it. On the contrary, the Roman world continued to work as a slave economy. Without slaves one could not run any serious manufacturing or agricultural business. But if the population became increasingly Christian, and Jews could have only Jewish and pagan slaves, then any chance for Jews to compete economically with Christians was curtailed.

Eventually it became illegal for a Christian to convert to Judaism. Under the emperor Theodotius I, near the end of the fourth century, it became illegal for a Christian to marry a Jew. Doing so was considered an act of adultery. Jews came to be excluded from serving in public office. In 423 CE a law was passed that made it illegal for Jews to build or even repair a synagogue. Accompanying all these forms of legislation were acts of violence against Jews that, even if not sponsored by the emperor or other state authorities, were tacitly condoned. Synagogues were burned, lands were confiscated, Jews were persecuted and even murdered—and the authorities turned a blind eye. Why not? These were the people who had killed God.

A key example illustrates the situation. In 388 CE the bishop of a town called Callinicum incited his Christian parishioners to assault the local Jewish synagogue. They did so, leveling it to the ground. When the Jewish population in town protested to the emperor Theodosius, he ordered the bishop to have the synagogue rebuilt with church money. At that point, a powerful Christian leader interposed to try to reverse the emperor's judgment. One of the most influential bishops at the time was Ambrose, the bishop of Milan. When word of the emperor's intervention and demand for reparation reached Milan, Ambrose wrote a harsh letter in protest, arguing that the emperor was in danger of offending his own religious duty by this intervention and insisting that the bishop should by no means be required to restore the synagogue.

Here we have a remarkable situation. Less than a century earlier, Christian leaders were being hunted down and persecuted by the ruling authorities. Now Christian leaders were reprimanding the emperor in writing and expecting that they would be obeyed. How the tables have turned!

Theodosius decided to ignore Ambrose's protest, but as it happens, he made a trip to Milan and attended a worship service in the cathedral there. Ambrose claims, in his own account of the affair, that he preached a sermon directed to the emperor's "misbehavior" and afterward, in the middle of the service, walked down from the altar to confront the emperor face-to-face, publicly demanding that the emperor back down. In this very public arena, the emperor felt he had no choice. He acceded to the bishop's demand, the Christian mob in Callinicum went unpunished, and the synagogue remained in ruins (see Ambrose, *Letters* 40 and 41).[4]

Now, not only is Christ God, but his servants the bishops have real political power. And they are using that power in ugly

ways against their longtime enemies, the Jews, those who allegedly killed their own God.

The God Christ and the Christian World

WITH THE CONVERSION OF the emperor to the belief that Christ
was God and that the God of the Christians was supreme, the
discourse of Christians among themselves clearly changed. Earlier arguments of Christians with Christians were over issues that
came to be seen as basic and foundational. Was Christ God? Yes.
Was he a human? Yes. Was he, though, just one person, not two?
Yes. By the early fourth century, when Constantine converted,
the vast majority of Christians agreed with those affirmations.
You might think that this would put an end to the theological
debates and the search for heretics in the midst of the orthodox.
But the historical truth is that the debates were just starting to
warm up.

I have already mentioned the fact that the Arian controversy
did not die out with the Council of Nicea; it went on for another
half century or more. And new debates arose, over issues that
would have been unthinkable just a hundred years earlier. Theological views that developed in the wake of the conquest of orthodox understandings of Jesus as both divine and human became
increasingly sophisticated and nuanced. What earlier had been
acceptable positions among the orthodox came to be challenged
in their minutest details. The issues may seem picayune to outside
observers, but to insiders they were matters of real moment, with
eternal consequences. As a result, the vitriol did not lessen now
that the "major" issues had been resolved. If anything, the rhetoric was significantly ratcheted up, and error on even the smallest
point became a matter of enormous importance—the stuff of ex-
communication and exile.

I will not try to provide even a cursory treatment of the various theological controversies of the fourth, fifth, and later centuries, but instead will give the slightest taste, by briefly describing three views that came to be articulated, debated, and eventually denounced as heretical.[5] This quick overview will at least give an idea of the level of argumentation carried on between Christian and Christian.

Marcellus of Ancyra

One of the major proponents of the Athanasian, anti-Arian views adopted at the Council of Nicea was the bishop of Ancyra, named Marcellus (died 374 CE). He saw himself as hyperorthodox. But he realized that the decisions leading to the creed of Nicea left considerable room for development, especially on the question of how Christ—who was coeternal and equal with God—actually related to the Father. Were Christ and the Father two separate but equal beings, or hypostases (a term that now meant something like "person" or "individual entity")? Marcellus fully realized that a modalist view could no longer be accepted. But was there some way to preserve the oneness, the unity, of the godhead without falling into the trap of Sabellius and others like him, so that no one could charge the Christians of having more than one God?

Marcellus's solution was to say that there was only one hypostasis, who was Father, Son, and Holy Spirit. In his view, the Christ and the Spirit were eternal with God, but only because they were resident within him from back into eternity and came forth from the Father for the purposes of salvation. In fact, before Christ came forth from God—when he was resident within him—he was not yet the Son; he could be the Son only when he came forth at the incarnation. And so before that time he was the Word of God, within the Father. Moreover, on the basis of his interpretation of 1 Corinthians 15:24–28, which says that at "the end" of all things, Christ will "hand over the kingdom to God the Father," Marcellus maintained that Christ's kingdom was not eternal. Ultimately, God the Father is all sovereign; Christ will deliver his kingdom to the Father; and then he will return to be resident within him.

This view obviously toed the line on the major Christological issues of the second, third, and early fourth centuries. Christ was God, he became man, and he was only one person. And it was not a modalist view. But other church leaders thought it sounded too much like modalism and condemned it as a heresy. The matter was discussed and finally decided at the Council of Constantinople in 381. That is when the line was introduced into the Nicene Creed that is still said today, that "his [Christ's] kingdom shall have no end." This line was added to demonstrate the theological rejection of the views of Marcellus. Other church leaders disagreed with this rejection. And so the debates continued.

Apollinaris

Apollinaris (315–392 CE) was too young to have attended the Council of Nicea, but as an adult he became a friend of Athanasius and was appointed bishop of the city of Laodicea. Like Marcellus before him, he claimed to be a true supporter of the form of orthodoxy embraced by the anti-Arian creed of Nicea. But he was consumed with the question of how Christ could be God and human at one and the same time. If Jesus was a god-man, then was part of him God and another part of him a man?

We are a bit handicapped in knowing exactly how Apollinaris expressed his views, since very little of his writing survives. What he was later *accused* of teaching was that the incarnate Christ did not actually have a human soul. Like others at his time, Apollinaris appears to have understood that humans are made up of three parts: the body; the "lower soul," which is the root of our emotions and passions; and the "upper soul," which is our faculty of reason with which we understand the world. Apollinaris evidently maintained that in Jesus Christ, the preexistent divine

Logos replaced the upper soul, so his reason was completely
divine. And so, God and human are united and at one—there is
only one person, Christ—but they are united because in the man
Jesus, God had a part and a human had a part.

One result of this view was that Christ could not develop
morally, or in terms of his personality, since he did not have a
human soul but instead the divine Logos. This more than anything else is what led to the condemnation of the Apollinarian
view. If Christ was not fully human, in every respect, he could
not set an example for us to follow. We are not like him, so how
can we be like him? Moreover, if Christ was not fully human,
then it cannot be clear how he could redeem the entire human
being. In this understanding, Christ's salvation would extend to
the human body but not to the human soul, since he didn't have
a human soul.

Or so the opponents of Apollinaris argued. He and his views
were condemned at the Council of Constantinople in 381, and
even though in light of *earlier* controversies he seemed perfectly
orthodox, he was not allowed any longer even to worship in a
Christian church in public.

Nestorius

As a final example of a controversy that emerged from the conquest of orthodoxy, I turn to a later figure whose views came to
be attacked, even though he himself wanted nothing more than
to represent the orthodox views of the faith. Nestorius (381–451 CE)
was a leading Christian spokesperson of his day who was appointed to the prestigious position of bishop of Constantinople
in 428 CE. The controversy surrounding Nestorius and his views
relates to an issue I have not yet addressed. Once it came to be
affirmed that Christ was God by nature, from back into eternity,
theologians began to ask what it meant to say that Mary was his
mother. Mary herself, of course, came to be exalted as a person

of unique standing, and legends and traditions about her pro-
liferated. Theologians who considered her role in the salvation
brought by Christ began now to call her *Theotokos,* which means
"one who gives birth to God" but came to mean, more roughly,
"the mother of God."

This term was in wide use by the time of Nestorius in the
early fifth century, but he came to object to it, publicly. In Nestorius's view, to call Mary the mother of God sounded too much
like Apollinarianism—that Mary gave birth to a human being
who had the Logos of God within him instead of a human soul.
Nestorius believed that Christ was fully human, not partially so,
and also that Christ was fully God, not partially so. Moreover,
the divine and the human cannot intermingle, since they are different essences. Both the divine and the human were present in
Christ at the incarnation.

In stressing this view that Christ was both fully God and fully
human, Nestorius came to be seen as someone who wanted to
argue that Christ was two different persons, one divine and one
human—with his human element tightly embracing the divine
so that they stood in a unity (much like a "marriage of souls").
But by this time orthodox Christians had long maintained that
Christ was just one person. In the end, Nestorius's enemies attacked this "two-person" Christology by arguing that it divided
Christ and thereby made him a "mere man" rather than some
kind of "divine man." As a result, Nestorius and his views were
condemned by Pope Celestine in 430 and by the ecumenical
Council of Ephesus in 431.

My point in looking at these three later heresies is not to give
a full survey of Christological discussions of the fourth and fifth
centuries. It is rather to illustrate the fact that once Christ was
declared to be God from back into eternity who had become
a human, all the problems of interpretation and understanding
were not solved. Instead, new problems were introduced. And

once these were resolved, yet more theological issues came to the fore. Theology became more nuanced. Views became more sophisticated. Orthodox theology became even more paradoxical. Many of these issues were not finally resolved in any "official" way until the Council of Chalcedon in 451. But even that "resolution" did not end all disputes about God, Christ, the Trinity, and all related topics. Disputes would rage for many centuries to come and in fact continue in our own day.

Conclusion

IN NONE OF THE Christian controversies I have discussed in this epilogue was there any question of whether Jesus was God. Jesus was in fact God. All of the participants in these debates had a "Nicene" understanding of Christ: he was God from back into eternity; there never was a time when or before which he did not exist; he was the one through whom God had created all things in heaven and on earth; he was of the same substance as God the Father; he was in fact equal with God in status, authority, and power. These are all quite exalted things to say about an apocalyptic preacher from rural Galilee who was crucified for crimes against the state. We have come a long way over the three hundred years since Jesus's death.

But one could argue—and probably should argue—that in fact Christian thinking about Jesus had come an enormous way just twenty years after his death. It must have been no more than twenty years after Jesus died, possibly even fewer, that the Christ poem in Philippians was composed, in which Jesus was said to have been a preexistent being "in the form of God" who became human and then because of his obedient death was exalted to divine status and made equal with God, the Lord to whom all people on earth would bow in worship and confess loyalty. One German scholar of the New Testament, Martin Hengel, has famously claimed that "with regard to the development of *all* the early Church's Christology . . . more happened in the first twenty years than in the entire later, centuries-long development of dogma."[6]

There is a certain truth to this claim. Of course, a lot did indeed happen after the first twenty years—an enormous amount. But the major leap was made in those twenty years: from seeing Jesus as his own disciples did during his ministry, as a Jewish man with an apocalyptic message of coming destruction, to seeing him as something far greater, a preexistent divine being who became human only temporarily before being made the Lord of the universe. It was not long after that that Jesus was declared to be the very Word of God made flesh, who was with God at creation and through whom God made all things. Eventually Jesus came to be seen as God in every respect, coeternal with the Father, of the same substance as the Father, equal to the Father within the Trinity of three persons, but one God.

This God Christ may not have been the historical Jesus. But he was the Christ of orthodox Christian doctrine, the object of faith and veneration over the centuries. And he is still the God revered and worshiped by Christians throughout our world today.

NOTES

Chapter 1: Divine Humans in Ancient Greece and Rome

1. Those who have read my other books will recognize the story, as I have had occasion to tell it before. See my textbook, *The New Testament: A Historical Introduction to the Early Christian Writings,* 5th ed. (New York: Oxford Univ. Press, 2012), 32–34.
2. Translation of F. C. Conybeare, *Philostratus: The Life of Apollonius of Tyana,* Loeb Classical Library (Cambridge, MA: Harvard Univ. Press, 1950), vol. 2.
3. Since Philostratus was writing after the Gospels were in circulation, it is entirely possible—as many critics have pointed out—that he was influenced by their portrayal of Jesus and that, as a result, he himself created the similarities between his account of Apollonius and the Gospel stories. That may indeed be true, but my point is that his pagan readers would have had no difficulty accepting the idea that Apollonius was another "divine man," like others who were widely known.
4. Translation of A. D. Melville, *Ovid: Metamorphoses* (Oxford: Oxford Univ. Press, 1986). All quotations are drawn from Book VIII, 190–93.
5. My friend Michael Penn, professor of religious studies at Mount Holyoke, informs me that there are indeed cases of twins from different fathers—a phenomenon known as *heteropaternal superfecundation*—but the woman's two eggs need to be fertilized within a relatively short interval from one another. Amphytrion had been away at war presumably for several months.
6. According to the Greek biographer of philosophers, Diogenes Laertius, Plato was sometimes considered to have been a son of the God Apollo (*Lives of Eminent Philosophers* 3.1–2, 45).
7. Translation of B. O. Foster, *Livy: History of Rome Books I–II,* Loeb Classical Library (Cambridge, MA: Harvard Univ. Press, 1919).

8. For Suetonius, I am using the translation of Catharine Edwards, *Suetonius: Lives of the Caesars* (Oxford: Oxford Univ. Press, 2000).

9. For the information in this paragraph, see John Collins, in Adela Yarbro Collins and John J. Collins, *King and Messiah as Son of God: Divine, Human, and Angelic Messianic Figures in Biblical and Related Literature* (Grand Rapids, MI: Eerdmans, 2008), 53.

10. There are numerous valuable studies of the emperor cult. For one that has become something of a classic of modern scholarship, see S. R. F. Price, *Rituals and Power: The Roman Imperial Cult in Asia Minor* (Cambridge: Cambridge Univ. Press, 1984). More recently, see Jeffrey Brodd and Jonathan Reed, *Rome and Religion: A Cross-Disciplinary Dialogue on the Imperial Cult* (Atlanta: Society of Biblical Literature, 2011). Among studies of the imperial cult in relation to early Christianity, the following two are particularly noteworthy: Steven J. Friesen, *Imperial Cults and the Apocalypse of John: Reading Revelation in the Ruins* (New York: Oxford Univ. Press, 2001), and most recently, Michael Peppard, *The Son of God in the Roman World: Divine Sonship in Its Social and Political Context* (New York: Oxford Univ. Press, 2011).

11. Translation of H. E. Butler, *The Institutio Oratoria of Quintilian,* Loeb Classical Library (Cambridge, MA: Harvard Univ. Press, 1920).

12. For more on this point of view, see the older classic study by Lily Ross Taylor, *The Divinity of the Roman Emperor* (Middletown, CT: American Philological Association, 1931).

13. See the discussions in the books cited in note 10.

14. From Price, *Rituals and Power,* 31.

15. From Price, *Rituals and Power,* 54.

16. Translation of A. M. Harmon, *Lucian* V, Loeb Classical Library (Cambridge, MA: Harvard Univ. Press, 1936).

17. Price, *Rituals and Power,* 55.

18. For the idea of a divine pyramid, see Ramsay MacMullen, *Paganism in the Roman Empire* (New Haven, CT: Yale Univ. Press, 1983).

19. For a discussion of this view, and why it is a mistake to assume it when dealing with antiquity, see especially Peppard, *Son of God,* 9–49.

Chapter 2: Divine Humans in Ancient Judaism

1. For an authoritative account, see E. P. Sanders, *Judaism: Practice and Belief, 63 BCE–66 CE* (Philadelphia: Trinity Press International, 1992).

2. See the scholarly discussions of Loren T. Stuckenbruck, *Angel Veneration and Christology* (Tübingen: Mohr Siebeck, 1995), and Charles A. Gieschen, *Angelomorphic Christology: Antecedents and Early Evidence* (Leiden: E. J. Brill, 1998).

3. *The HarperCollins Study Bible,* ed. Harold W. Attridge (San Francisco: HarperOne, 2006), 88.

4. Gieschen, *Angelomorphic Christology,* 68.

5. It is important to note that the term *satan* in Job 1 and 2 is not a proper name but means *the accuser*. It refers to an angel in God's divine court who is in the role of "prosecutor."

6. Translation of J. Z. Smith in James H. Charlesworth, ed., *The Old Testament Pseudepigrapha*, vol. 1, *Apocalyptic Literature and Testaments* (Garden City, NY: Doubleday, 1983), slightly modified.

7. Translation of A. F. J. Klijn, "2 (Syriac Apocalypse of) Baruch," in Charlesworth, ed., *The Old Testament Pseudepigrapha*, vol. 1.

8. Translation of F. I. Andersen, in Charlesworth, ed., *Old Testament Pseudepigrapha*, vol. 1.

9. Larry W. Hurtado, *One God, One Lord: Early Christian Devotion and Ancient Jewish Monotheism* (London: SCM Press, 1988), 82.

10. Translation of E. Isaac, in Charlesworth, ed., *Old Testament Pseudepigrapha,* vol. 1.

11. See John J. Collins, "Pre-Christian Jewish Messianism: An Overview," in Magnus Zetterholm, ed., *The Messiah in Early Judaism and Christianity* (Minneapolis: Fortress, 2007), 16.

12. Michael A. Knibb, "Enoch, Similitudes of (1 Enoch 37–71)," in John C. Collins and Daniel C. Harlow, *The Eerdmans Dictionary of Early Judaism* (Grand Rapids, MI: Eerdmans, 2010), 587.

13. Knibb, "Enoch, Similitudes," 587.

14. Alan F. Segal, *Two Powers in Heaven: Early Rabbinic Reports About Christianity and Gnosticism* (Leiden: E. J. Brill, 1977).

15. For a slightly fuller treatment, with a bibliography for more complete accounts, see Thomas Tobin, "Logos," in David Noel Freedman, ed., *The Anchor Bible Dictionary,* vol. 4 (New York: Doubleday, 1992), 348–56.

16. All translations of Philo are from C. D. Yonge, *The Works of Philo* (reprint ed.: Peabody, MA: Hendrickson, 1993).

17. John J. Collins, "The King as Son of God," in Adela Yarbro Collins and John J. Collins, *King and Messiah as Son of God: Divine, Human, and Angelic Messianic Figures in Biblical and Related Literature* (Grand Rapids, MI: Eerdmans, 2008), 1–24.

Chapter 3: Did Jesus Think He Was God?

1. Dale Allison, *Jesus of Nazareth: Millenarian Prophet* (Minneapolis: Fortress, 1998); Bart D. Ehrman, *Jesus: Apocalyptic Prophet of the New Millennium* (New York: Oxford Univ. Press, 1999); Paula Fredriksen, *Jesus of Nazareth: King of the Jews* (New York: Vintage, 1999); John Meier, *A Marginal Jew: Rethinking the Historical Jesus,* 4 vols. (New York: Doubleday, 1991–); E. P. Sanders, *The Historical Figure of Jesus* (London: Allen Lane/Penguin Press, 1993); Geza Vermes, *Jesus the Jew: A Historian's Reading of the Gospels* (London: Collins, 1973).

2. I discuss these discrepancies, contradictions, and historical problems

at length in *Jesus, Interrupted* (San Francisco: HarperOne, 2009).

3. Among the classic studies are Alfred B. Lord, *The Singer of Tales* (Cambridge, MA: Harvard Univ. Press, 1960), and Walter Ong, *Orality and Literacy: The Technologizing of the Word* (London: Methuen, 1982). For a recent survey of all the important studies, see Stephen E. Young, *Jesus Tradition in the Apostolic Fathers* (Tübingen: Mohr Siebeck, 2011).

4. See my discussion in *Jesus: Apocalyptic Prophet,* or, for a thorough treatment, vol. 1 of Meier, *A Marginal Jew.*

5. See the discussion of the Pharisees in E. P. Sanders, *Judaism: Practice and Belief, 63 BCE–66 CE* (Philadelphia: Trinity Press International, 1992).

6. For a fuller account see my book *Jesus: Apocalyptic Prophet.*

7. I have seen this argument in various forms over the years, and I have to admit that I do not know who originally came up with it.

8. See my book *Jesus: Apocalyptic Prophet.*

9. See John J. Collins, *The Scepter and the Star: The Messiahs of the Dead Sea Scrolls and Other Ancient Literature* (New York: Doubleday, 1995).

10. See my book *The Lost Gospel of Judas Iscariot* (New York: Oxford Univ. Press, 2006), 153–70.

11. I do not think that the tradition of the "triumphal entry," where Jesus rides into Jerusalem to the acclaim of the crowd who acclaim him the messiah who is to come, can be historical. If such a scene had really happened, Jesus would have been arrested on the spot.

12. See the work cited in note 10.

Chapter 4: The Resurrection of Jesus: What We Cannot Know

1. Scholars are in wide agreement that the final twelve verses of Mark were added by a late scribe. The book almost certainly ended at 16:8. See my discussion in *Misquoting Jesus: The Story Behind Who Changed the Bible and Why* (San Francisco: HarperSanFrancisco, 2005), 65–68.

2. Raymond Brown, *The Death of the Messiah: From Gethsemane to the Grave* (New York: Doubleday, 1994), 106.

3. Scholars speak of the seven undisputed Pauline letters: Romans, 1 and 2 Corinthians, Galatians, Philippians, 1 Thessalonians, and Philemon. The other six do not appear to have been written by Paul. See my book *Forged: Writing in the Name of God—Why the Bible's Authors Are Not Who We Think They Are* (San Francisco: HarperOne, 2011), 92–114.

4. Historians have had numerous debates about the chronology of Paul's life, but it is reasonably clear that he became a follower of Jesus two or three years after Jesus's death, based on the chronological details he provides in some of his letters, especially in Gal. 1–2, where he writes such things as "three years later" and "after fourteen years." When

one crunches the numbers, it appears relatively certain that if Jesus died around the year 30, Paul became his follower around the year 32 or 33.

5. Daniel A. Smith, *Revisiting the Empty Tomb: The Early History of Easter* (Minneapolis: Fortress, 2010), 3.

6. For someone who wants to take the account as historical, the best solution is that Joseph was acting out of a sense of piety, wanting to provide a decent burial for someone—even an enemy—because that was the "right" thing to do. But nothing in Mark's account leads to this suggestion, so within the narrative itself, where the burial tradition comes on the heels of the trial tradition, it appears to create an anomaly.

7. Bruce Metzger, "Names for the Nameless in the New Testament: A Study in the Growth of Christian Tradition," in Patrick Granfield and Josef A. Jungmann, eds., *Kyriakon: Festschrift Johannes Quasten,* 2 vols. (Münster: Verlag Aschendorff, 1970), 1:79–99.

8. John Dominic Crossan, "The Dogs Beneath the Cross," chap. 6 in *Jesus: A Revolutionary Biography* (San Francisco: HarperOne, 1994).

9. Cited in Martin Hengel, *Crucifixion* (Philadelphia: Fortress, 1977), 76.

10. Translation from *The Works of Horace,* Project Guttenberg, http://www.gutenberg.org/files/14020/14020-h/14020-h.htm#THE_FIRST_BOOK_OF_THE_EPISTLES_OF_HORACE.

11. Cited in Hengel, *Crucifixion,* 54.

12. Translation from Robert J. White, *The Interpretation of Dreams: Oneirocritica by Artemidorus* (Torrance, CA: Original Books, 1975).

13. Hengel, *Crucifixion,* 87.

14. Quoted in Crossan, "Dogs," 159.

15. Translation of Charles Sherman, *Diodorus Siculus,* Loeb Classical Library (Cambridge, MA: Harvard Univ. Press, 1952).

16. Translation of J. W. Cohoon and H. Lamar Crosby, *Dio Chrysostom,* Loeb Classical Library (Cambridge, MA: Harvard Univ. Press, 1940).

17. Translation of Clifford H. Moore and John Jackson, *Tacitus Histories,* Loeb Classical Library (Cambridge, MA: Harvard Univ. Press, 1931).

18. Translation of William Whiston, *The Works of Flavius Josephus* (Grand Rapids, MI: Baker Book House, 1979).

19. Crossan, "Dogs," 158.

20. Translation of E. Mary Smallwood, *Legatio ad Gaium* (Leiden: E. J. Brill, 1961).

21. See, for example, Michael R. Licona, *The Resurrection of Jesus: A New Historiographical Approach* (Downers Grove, IL: Intervarsity Press, 2010), 349–54.

Chapter 5: The Resurrection of Jesus: What We Can Know

1. My thanks to Eric Meyers, scholar of ancient Judaism and archaeologist of Palestine, from crosstown rival Duke, for providing this information in a private correspondence.

2. It is important to note: I am not disputing that Paul and others thought that Jesus was raised on the third day. I'm saying that this view—important because it was a fulfillment of scripture (see pp. 140–41)—may not have arisen until weeks or months later.

3. For the ancient idea that spirit was still made of "stuff," see Dale B. Martin, *The Corinthian Body* (New Haven, CT: Yale Univ. Press, 1995).

4. For a relatively brief overview, see my book *Lost Christianities: The Battle for Scripture and the Faiths We Never Knew* (New York: Oxford Univ. Press, 2003), chap. 6. For the most up-to-date and authoritative treatment, see David Brakke, *The Gnostics: Myth, Ritual, and Diversity in Early Christianity* (Cambridge, MA: Harvard Univ. Press, 2010).

5. Translation of James Brashler in James M. Robinson, ed., *The Nag Hammadi Library in English,* 4th ed. (Leiden: E. J. Brill, 1996).

6. See my fuller discussion on pp. 305–7.

7. Dale C. Allison, *Resurrecting Jesus: The Earliest Christian Tradition and Its Interpreters* (New York: T & T Clark, 2005).

8. My friend Joel Marcus, New Testament scholar at Duke, has maintained that some apocalyptic Jews may have held an alternative view in which there would be a spiritual, not a physical, resurrection of the dead; he finds this alternative view in the book of *Jubilees.* If that is true, then this would have been very much the minority view among apocalypticists. And it is not in evidence in the teachings of Jesus, as is clear from his insistence that there will be "eating and drinking" in the kingdom and that people will be "cast out" of the kingdom, and so on. I scarcely need stress that if Jesus (like most apocalypticists) understood that the resurrection would be physical, this too would have been the view of his followers.

9. Richard P. Bentall, "Hallucinatory Experiences," in Etzel Cardeña, Steven J. Lynn, and Stanley Krippner, eds., *Varieties of Anomalous Experience: Examining the Scientific Evidence* (Washington, DC: American Psychological Association, 2000), 86.

10. Michael R. Licona, *The Resurrection of Jesus: A New Historiographical Approach* (Downers Grove, IL: Intervarsity Press, 2010); N. T. Wright, *The Resurrection of the Son of God* (Minneapolis: Fortress, 2003).

11. Gerd Lüdemann, *The Resurrection of Christ: A Historical Inquiry* (New York: Prometheus, 2004), 19.

12. Michael Goulder, "The Baseless Fabric of a Vision," in Gavin D'Costa, ed., *Resurrection Reconsidered* (Oxford: One World, 1996), 54–55.

13. Allison, *Resurrecting Jesus*, 298.
14. On visions of Mary, see pp. 198–199; on UFOs, see the fascinating study of Susan A. Clancy, *Abducted: How People Come to Believe They Were Kidnapped by Aliens* (Cambridge, MA: Harvard Univ. Press, 2005).
15. See Bentall, "Hallucinatory Experiences."
16. Bentall, "Hallucinatory Experiences," 102.
17. Allison, *Resurrecting Jesus,* pp. 269–82.
18. Bill Guggenheim and Judy Guggenheim, *Hello from Heaven!* (New York: Bantam, 1995).
19. See, for example, René Laurentin, *The Apparitions of the Blessed Virgin Mary Today* (Dublin: Veritas, 1990; French original, 1988). The examples that I give below are all drawn from this book.
20. I should stress that Wiebe is not a religious fanatic on a mission. He is chair of the philosophy department at Trinity Western University and is a serious scholar. Still, at the end of the day, he thinks that something "transcendent" has led to some of the modern visions of Jesus that he recounts. In other words, they—or some of them—are veridical.
21. I am not saying that Paul necessarily made up the story of the five hundred himself; he may well have inherited it from an oral tradition. Moreover, there is no telling how traditions such as this come to be made up—but it happens all the time, even in our day and age. It is not always the result of someone "lying" about it. Sometimes stories just get exaggerated or invented.
22. See John J. Collins, "Sibylline Oracles," in James H. Charlesworth, ed., *Old Testament Pseudepigrapha*, vol. 1, *Apocalyptic Literature and Testaments* (Garden City, NY: Doubleday, 1983), n. c2, 387.
23. In this case I am using the term *veridical* not only to mean that they saw "something" that was really there, but to mean that the something they saw really was Jesus.
24. Some manuscripts of the Gospel of Luke contain an account of Jesus's ascension in 24:51. As I argue in my book *The Orthodox Corruption of Scripture: The Effect of Early Christological Controversies on the Text of the New Testament*, 2nd ed. (New York: Oxford Univ. Press, 2011), that passage was probably added by scribes; it was not what Luke originally wrote.

Chapter 6: The Beginning of Christology: Christ as Exalted to Heaven

1. See my book *Forged: Writing in the Name of God—Why the Bible's Authors Are Not Who We Think They Are* (San Francisco: HarperOne, 2011), 92–114.
2. For a standard scholarly treatment, see James D. G. Dunn, *Christology*

in the Making: A New Testament Inquiry into the Origins of the Doctrine of the Incarnation, 2nd ed. (Grand Rapids, MI: Eerdmans, 1989), 33–36.

3. You can find discussions of all these issues in any good critical commentary. Two of the most authoritative and hefty are Robert Jewett, *Romans: A Commentary* (Minneapolis: Fortress, 2007), and Joseph Fitzmyer, *Romans: A New Translation with Introduction and Commentary* (New Haven, CT: Anchor Bible, 1997).

4. See pp. 76–80.

5. Michael Peppard, *The Son of God in the Roman World: Divine Sonship in Its Social and Political Context* (New York: Oxford Univ. Press, 2011).

6. Cited by Peppard, *Son of God,* 84.

7. Christiane Kunst, *Römische Adoption: Zur Strategie einer Familienorganisation* (Hennef: Marthe Clauss, 2005), 294; cited in translation by Peppard, *Son of God*, 54.

8. Larry W. Hurtado, *One God, One Lord: Early Christian Devotion and Ancient Jewish Monotheism* (London: SCM Press, 1988). A much fuller treatment can be found in his magnum opus, *Lord Jesus Christ: Devotion to Jesus in Earliest Christianity* (Grand Rapids, MI: Eerdmans, 2003).

9. See Raymond Brown, *The Birth of the Messiah: A Commentary on the Infancy Narratives in the Gospels of Matthew and Luke* (New York: Doubleday, 1993), 29–32.

10. See Dunn, *Christology in the Making.*

11. See Peppard, *Son of God*, 86–131.

12. See my brief discussion in *Misquoting Jesus: The Story Behind Who Changed the Bible and Why* (San Francisco: HarperSanFrancisco, 2005), 158–61; for a full discussion at a scholarly level, see my book *The Orthodox Corruption of Scripture: The Effect of Early Christological Controversies on the Text of the New Testament*, 2nd ed. (New York: Oxford Univ. Press, 2011), 73–79.

Chapter 7: Jesus as God on Earth: Early Incantation Christologies

1. See pp. 59–61.

2. Charles A. Gieschen, *Angelomorphic Christology: Antecedents and Early Evidence* (Leiden: E. J. Brill, 1998), 27.

3. I should say that this view of Christ as the chief angel has not always been a popular one among New Testament scholars. In no small measure this is because Christ is never explicitly called an "angel" the way he is called "Son of Man," "Lord," "Messiah," or "Son of God" in the New Testament. This is the view, for example, of D. G. Dunn, *Christology in the Making: A New Testament Inquiry into the Origins of the Doctrine of the Incarnation,* 2nd ed. (Grand Rapids, MI: Eerdmans, 1989), 158. But more recent research has shown that in part the rea-

son the view of Christ as a preexistent angelic being has not caught on more thoroughly is that researchers think that such a view is inadequately exalted for the early Christians. See, for example, Gieschen, *Angelomorphic Christology,* and Susan R. Garrett, *No Ordinary Angel: Celestial Spirits and Christian Claims About Jesus* (New Haven, CT: Yale Univ. Press, 2008).

4. See the preceding note.

5. Gieschen, *Angelomorphic Christology,* and Garrett, *No Ordinary Angel.*

6. Garrett, *No Ordinary Angel,* 11.

7. See the discussion of Romans 1:3–4 on pp. 218–25.

8. I should stress that even though I am calling this a "poem," literary scholars in ancient Greece would not have done the same because it does not scan. We do not know what the nonliterary elite (that is, the common people) would have accepted or understood to be poetry—or hymns—simply because we have no record of their views. But whatever we call this unit, it clearly is written in more exalted language than the surrounding parts of the letter, and in English usage we typically consider these kinds of exalted compositions to be poems, whether they scan or not.

9. The fullest and best known is Ralph P. Martin, *A Hymn of Christ: Philippians 2:5–11 in Recent Interpretation and in the Setting of Early Christian Worship* (Downers Grove, IL: Intervarsity Press, 1997).

10. See the discussion of James D. G. Dunn, "Christ, Adam, and Preexistence," in Ralph P. Martin and Brian J. Dodd, eds., *Where Christology Began: Essays on Philippians 2* (Louisville, KY: Westminster John Knox, 1998), 74–83.

11. For a discussion of Vollenweider's views, see the helpful article by Adela Yarbro Collins, "Psalms, Philippians 2:6–11, and the Origins of Christology," *Biblical Interpretation* 11 (2002): 361–72.

12. The Tetragrammaton in the Hebrew Bible, YHWH (= Yahweh), which serves as the personal name of God, was translated in the Greek version by the term *Kurios,* which comes into English as "Lord." And so, when the text indicates that every tongue will confess that "Jesus is Lord," it appears to mean that everyone will acknowledge that Jesus has the very name of Yahweh himself. It is important to note, however, that Jesus is still differentiated from God the Father, since all this is to happen to the Father's "glory."

13. See the fuller discussions in Robert Jewett, *Romans: A Commentary* (Minneapolis: Fortress, 2007), and Joseph Fitzmyer, *Romans: A New Translation with Introduction and Commentary* (New Haven, CT: Anchor Bible, 1997).

14. A famous instance occurs in John 3, in which different translators think Jesus's words end at 3:15 (before the famous line "For God so loved the world. . . ."), and others think they continue until 3:21. Je-

sus and the narrator sound so much alike that it is impossible to know for certain where one stops speaking and the other begins.

15. On the problems of using the term *poem,* see note 8 on p. 381. The same issues apply here as in the case of Phil. 2:6–11.

16. Among the many fine critical commentaries on the Gospel of John that deal with these issues, see especially the classic by Raymond Brown, *The Gospel According to John: Introduction, Translation, and Notes,* vol. 1 (Garden City, NY: Doubleday, 1996).

17. See note 15 on p. 375.

18. See my discussion in *Forged: Writing in the Name of God—Why the Bible's Authors Are Not Who We Think They Are* (San Francisco: HarperOne, 2011), 112–14; for an extensive scholarly treatment, see my book *Forgery and Counterforgery: The Use of Literary Deceit in Early Christian Polemics* (New York: Oxford Univ. Press, 2013), 171–82.

Chapter 8: After the New Testament: Christological Dead Ends of the Second and Third Centuries

1. See my discussion in *Lost Christianities: The Battle for Scripture and the Faiths We Never Knew* (New York: Oxford Univ. Press, 2003).

2. A number of these heresies persisted in marginal groups within Christianity, and some of them reemerged at different times and places over history; but the orthodox church deemed them false paths.

3. Translation of J. H. Macmahon in Alexander Roberts and James Donaldson, eds., *Ante Nicene Fathers,* vol. 5 (reprint ed.: Peabody, MA: Hendrickson, 1994).

4. Translation of G. A. Williamson, *Eusebius: The History of the Church from Christ to Constantine* (London: Penguin, 1965).

5. This is the thesis of my book *The Orthodox Corruption of Scripture: The Effect of Early Christological Controversies on the Text of the New Testament,* 2nd ed. (New York: Oxford Univ. Press, 2011).

6. All translations of Ignatius are from my edition in the Loeb Classical Library, *The Apostolic Fathers* (Cambridge, MA: Harvard Univ. Press, 2003), vol. 1.

7. The classic study of Marcion is Adolf von Harnack, *Marcion: The Gospel of the Alien God,* trans. John E. Steely and Lyle D. Bierma (Durham, NC: Labyrinth, 1990; German original of the 2nd ed., 1924). For a modern overview, see my *Lost Christianities,* 103–9.

8. See Karen King, *What Is Gnosticism?* (Cambridge, MA: Harvard Univ. Press, 2003); Michael A. Williams, *Rethinking Gnosticism: An Argument for Dismantling a Dubious Category* (Princeton, NJ: Princeton Univ. Press, 1996); and David Brakke, *The Gnostics: Myth, Ritual, and Diversity in Early Christianity* (Cambridge, MA: Harvard Univ. Press, 2010).

9. The traditional story of the discovery can be found in the Introduction by James M. Robinson, in James M. Robinson, ed., *The Nag Hammadi Library in English,* 4th ed. (Leiden: E. J. Brill, 1996).

10. Translation of Birger Pearson, *Nag Hammadi Codex VII* (Leiden: E. J. Brill, 1996).

11. I do not mean to say that the books that later became the New Testament which embraced such views—for example, Matthew and Mark—were considered heretical. But when exaltation Christologies were no longer acceptable, these sacred books were interpreted in such a way that they were no longer thought to *contain* exaltation Christologies.

12. Translation of Peter Holmes in Alexander Roberts and James Donaldson, eds., *Ante Nicene Fathers*, vol. 3 (reprint ed.: Peabody, MA: Hendrickson, 1994).

13. A view that the Father suffered was not only repugnant because it seemed illogical that the Creator of all would experience pain, but also because in ancient ways of thinking, suffering necessarily involves a personal change (one was not suffering; now one is). But God is unchangeable. And so it was unthinkable that God could suffer. My thanks to Maria Doerfler for this insight.

14. For an account of Origen's life and teachings, see Joseph W. Trigg, *Origen: The Bible and Philosophy in the Third-Century Church* (Atlanta: John Knox, 1983).

15. Translation of G. W. Butterworth, *Origen: On First Principles* (Gloucester, MA: Peter Smith, 1973).

16. If this notion of the preexistence of souls seems bizarre to some people today, it did not seem altogether odd for ancient thinkers, as it could be found in Greek philosophers such as Plato.

17. One of the reasons Origen's views came to be so heartily rejected by later orthodox theologians was that his view of the preexistence and "fall" of the souls was considered highly troubling. If these souls fell and were given the chance once again to be saved through the work of Christ, what guarantee could there be that once they were saved and returned to a place in which they contemplate the glories of God forever they would not fall yet again, starting the process over? For some Christian theologians, this view created enormous uncertainties concerning the finality of salvation and the assurance that a blessed eternal life waited for those who believed in Christ.

18. As Larry Hurtado has especially emphasized; see his *One God, One Lord: Early Christian Devotion and Ancient Jewish Monotheism* (London: SCM Press, 1988), and *Lord Jesus Christ: Devotion to Jesus in Earliest Christianity* (Grand Rapids, MI: Eerdmans, 2003).

Chapter 9: Ortho-Paradoxes on the Road to Nicea

1. Translation of Thomas B. Falls, *Saint Justin Martyr* (Washington, DC: Catholic Univ. of America Press, 1948).
2. Translation of Russell J. DeSimone, *Novatian* (Washington, DC: Catholic Univ. Press of America, 1974).
3. Translation of Henry Bettenson, *Documents of the Christian Church*, 2nd ed. (Oxford: Oxford Univ. Press, 1963).
4. See the discussion in Franz Dünzel, *A Brief History of the Doctrine of the Trinity in the Early Church*, trans. John Bowden (London: T & T Clark, 2007), 41–49.
5. Translation of Stuart Hall in J. Stevenson, ed., *A New Eusebius: Documents Illustrating the History of the Church to AD 337,* rev. ed. (London: SPCK, 1987).
6. Translation of Edward Rochie Hardy, *Christology of the Later Fathers* (Philadelphia: Westminster, 1954).
7. Translation of Andrew S. Jacobs in Bart D. Ehrman and Andrew S. Jacobs, *Christianity in Late Antiquity: 300–450 C.E.* (New York: Oxford Univ. Press, 2004).
8. Some scholars have questioned whether the persecution of Christians was actually the intention that lay behind Decius's edict. The edict required all inhabitants of the empire to perform a sacrifice to the traditional gods and to receive a certificate indicating that they had done so. Christians, of course, were not able to perform the sacrifices because of their religious commitments, and they were punished upon their refusal. The question is whether the point of the edict was to weed out Christians or instead to affirm the importance of pagan religious ritual. Either way, Christians who refused to follow the dictates of the edict suffered as a consequence.
9. On the growth rate of early Christianity, see Ramsay MacMullen, *Christianizing the Roman Empire* (New Haven, CT: Yale Univ. Press, 1984).
10. Translation of Averil Cameron and Stuart Hall, *The Life of Constantine* (New York: Oxford Univ. Press, 1999).
11. For a brief and precise discussion, see Dünzel, *Brief History,* 49–60; and Joseph F. Kelly, *The Ecumenical Councils of the Catholic Church: A History* (Collegeville, MN: Liturgical Press, 2009), 11–25. For a scholarly assessment of the theological issues, see Lewis Ayres, *Nicaea and Its Legacy: An Approach to Fourth-Century Trinitarian Theology* (Oxford: Oxford Univ. Press, 2004), 1–61.
12. Translation from J. N. D. Kelly, *Early Christian Creeds,* 3rd ed. (London: Longman, 1972).
13. See the books cited in note 11 above.

Epilogue

1. Among the classic studies of Jewish-Christian relations in antiquity and the rise of Christian anti-Judaism, still very much worth reading, are Marcel Simon, *Verus Israel: A Study of the Relations Between Christians and Jews in the Roman Empire (135–425)*, trans. H. McKeating (Oxford: Oxford Univ. Press, 1986; French original, 1964); Rosemary Ruether, *Faith and Fratricide: The Theological Roots of Anti-Semitism* (New York: Seabury, 1974); and John Gager, *The Origins of Anti-Semitism: Attitudes Toward Judaism in Pagan and Christian Antiquity* (New York: Oxford Univ. Press, 1983).

2. Translation of Gerald F. Hawthorn, "A New English Translation of Melito's Paschal Homily," in *Current Issues in Biblical and Patristic Interpretation* (Grand Rapids, MI: Eerdmans, 1975).

3. See Ruether, *Faith and Fratricide*. I rely on her account here.

4. Some scholars have questioned whether Ambrose actually played as significant a role in this controversy as he contends in these letters. However one decides the issue, it is quite clear that Christian leaders had assumed previously unheard-of power in their relationship to the state authorities by this time.

5. In addition to Lewis Ayres, *Nicaea and Its Legacy: An Approach to Fourth-Century Trinitarian Theology* (Oxford: Oxford Univ. Press, 2004), see the following two useful anthologies of texts from the period, with introductions: Richard A. Norris, *The Christological Controversy* (Philadelphia: Fortress, 1980), and William G. Rusch, *The Trinitarian Controversy* (Philadelphia: Fortress, 1980).

6. Martin Hengel, "Christological Titles in Early Christianity," in *Studies in Early Christology* (Edinburgh: T & T Clark, 1995), 383.

SCRIPTURE INDEX

SUBJECT AND AUTHOR INDEX